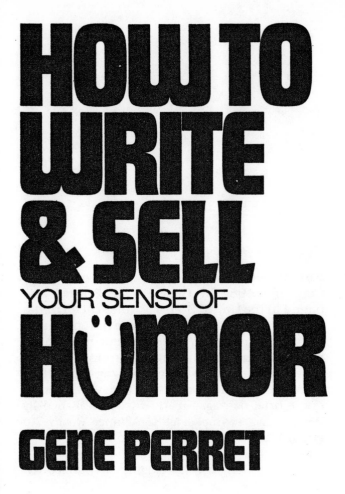

HOW TO WRITE & SELL
YOUR SENSE OF
HÜMOR

GENE PERRET

Writer's Digest Books

Cincinnati, Ohio

Library of Congress Cataloging in Publication
Data

Perret, Gene.
  How to write and sell your sense of humor.

  Includes index.
  1. Wit and humor—Authorship. I. Title.
PN6149.A88P47   1982   808.7   82-13606
ISBN 0-89879-092-1

Design by Charleen Catt

To my kids:
Joey, Terry, Carole, and Linda

Their life is exciting because it's all potential

This book is dedicated to potential—
that it will blossom into fulfillment and joy

PART ONE
DECIDING TO WRITE

9. THE VALUE OF MONOLOGUES 80

Showing off your material . . . enhancing individual jokes . . . the "peaks and valleys" principle . . . the steps to building and sustaining laughter . . . the most efficient way to set up jokes . . . how to prepare and write more material . . . diversifying your style . . . why monologues aid sales.

10. GETTING READY TO WRITE 89

The groundwork of comedy writing . . . why you should write out preparatory work . . . what productivity results from . . . the all-important choice: finding a topic . . . how to free-associate . . . organizing comedy ideas and channeling your thinking . . . the secret of subtopics.

11. GETTING THE JOKES FLOWING 98

The benefits of keeping a tally . . . the starting point: having something to say . . . prompting the punchline . . . how to ask the right questions . . . exaggeration and distortion: allowing your mind to play . . . exploiting clichés for fun and profit . . . getting 'em wholesale: formula jokes.

12. THE ART OF ROUTINING 108

How to determine a logical progression . . . a step-by-step guide to arranging gags and smoothing the edges . . . what the best transitions are . . . the importance of flow and the final polish . . . making the audience think—but not for too long . . . the most common weaknesses—and how to cure them.

. . . tips on overcoming writer's block . . . why you should save your work . . . how to reuse your material.

Every convenience that we enjoy around us—the automobile, the dishwasher, the toaster, the hot comb, and flip-top-lock baggies—began as an idea. Someone had to think that these things were possible and then work to make them a reality. Ideas keep the world progressing.

When someone has a funny idea and can put it on paper, that someone is a comedy writer. It's astounding to think that the wildly warped philosophy and insightful humor of James Thurber and the charmingly funny characterizations of Neil Simon were once blank sheets of paper.

Each morning in Hollywood a battalion of brilliant writers enter their offices, gulp down their coffee, and insert glaringly white sheets of paper into their IBM Selectrics. Then wheels start turning in their heads. Their fingers begin tippy-tapping at varying rates of speed, and humor magically appears on the page. Seemingly from nowhere, words, sentences, and scenes take shape.

It all begins with the words. They beget scenery, costumes, props, and most of all, glorious laughter.

We all depend on the writers. The first thing the performer asks when she shows up for work on Monday morning is, "Where's the script?" Without those pages there would be no reason for showing up at work.

Bob and Ray once did a routine in which they were supposedly performing in a summer theatre with a local, non-professional cast. One, as the interviewer, said, "Things seemed a bit ragged on stage tonight." His partner replied, "Oh. You're probably referring to that hour-and-a-half stretch when nobody said anything." That's where most of us would be without writers . . . we wouldn't say anything.

Outside of a relatively few classics, there aren't many "golden oldies" in humor. For comedy to work, it has to be unique. There will always be room for talented, imaginative new comedy minds.

If this book is your first endeavor in humor, hurry up and learn your craft. We need you.

—Carol Burnett
May, 1982

DECIDING TO WRITE

What I want to do is make people laugh so they'll see things seriously.

—William R. Zinnser

PART ONE

1 YOU CAN WRITE COMEDY

I've had a BALL writing comedy. I've written from my kitchen table back in Upper Darby, Pennsylvania, from a cocoon-sized office behind my house in California—even from a plane seat on the way to England to help write the command performance show for the twenty-fifth anniversary of Queen Elizabeth's coronation.

I've been on vacations with my family where we crammed in a tiring day of sightseeing—and then while the rest of them slept, I shut myself in the bathroom, curled up in the empty tub with pencil and notepad, and turned out my next day's quota of funnies.

I've written some good jokes in some bad places and some bad jokes in some good places, but I've been delighted with every minute of it. The one overriding message of this volume is that comedy writing is fun. It's a capitalized FUN . . . an underlined FUN. It's *fun* in italics, and fun in foreign languages: *C'est très amusant, es muy divertido, es macht mir Freude.*

Now, my wife is going to object when she buys a copy of this book and reads those opening paragraphs. She has to listen to my complaints each evening about recalcitrant associates, egomaniacal performers, moronic producers, and asinine executives. What she doesn't realize is that my complaining about the business is fun to me—*she's* the only one not having a good time.

My Comedy Ego and How It Developed

I've exulted in all the stages of my career—good and bad. When my career first showed signs of progress, I was so delirious that it wore a bit on my friends and family. I was proud of hobnobbing with celebrities and never stopped talking about my accomplishments. Every conversation was sprinkled with my latest witticisms.

In short, I was a bore. You'll notice as you read through the book that I've not been totally cured of this.

While I was in the most critical stage of the disease, I eagerly anticipated taking my checks from Phyllis Diller to the bank each Friday. I'd try to look my humblest—all the while waiting for the teller to notice the name on the check.

One lady saw the signature, chuckled a bit, and said, "Phyllis Diller, huh?" I modestly lowered my eyes and replied, "Yeah." Then she called another teller over and showed her the check. Pride swelled so much in me that it seriously threatened the buttons on my shirt.

"Is she anything like the *real* Phyllis Diller?" the teller asked.

"That *is* the real Phyllis Diller. She's a personal friend of mine." (I had talked to her on the phone.)

The lady calmly studied the check and signature with that air of expertise instinctive to bank tellers, began stamping the documents with whatever they stamp documents with and said firmly, "No, it's not."

I never did convince her it really was. In fact, she almost had me believing I was working for a fraud. This incident was not among the highlights of my career, or even of that particular day, but since then it has been good for laughs.

Another time my wife and I had a few laughs over an experience that is almost the flip side of the Phyllis Diller story. We had been vacationing (please don't think that all comedy writers do is vacation) at a California resort and were checking out when the cashier informed me that I had received a call from Bob Hope. He asked, "Is this the *real* Bob Hope?" We assured him that it was and he offered me a telephone a few feet down the counter.

While I was on the phone, another couple came to check in. The first thing the clerk said to them was, "Have you ever heard of Bob Hope?" They were a little confused as to what this had to do with checking in to a hotel, but said they had. The counter man motioned toward me with his thumb and said with feigned matter-of-factness, "He's talking to him."

I've even had some recognition that I didn't merit. Our writing staff was nominated for an Emmy one year, so the producer invited me to share his rented limousine for the evening—we wanted to arrive in style.

The festivities were being held very near my home, so my four youngsters rode there on their bikes and got right up front behind the police barricades. Our limousine pulled up to the front, we stepped out, and my kids and their friends immediately went wild with screams of delight. Being an incurable ham, I turned and waved to the adoring throng. Now everyone in the crowd started screaming. The fact that they didn't recognize me as a big star didn't deter them. They figured scream now and ask questions later.

One lady, though, turned to my most vocal daughter and said, "Who is that?" My daughter told her, "My Daddy."

There's a flip side to that tale, too. (Are you beginning to notice that all my stories have their own rejoinders?) Once we were at a rehearsal for a Bob Hope show originating from Palm Springs. Ex-President Gerald Ford was to attend the gala that evening, and some Secret Service men were combing the ballroom with dogs trained to locate bombs. Hope was on stage with a handful of script pages, saw me, and shouted, "Hey, Perret. They keep sniffing out your jokes."

You may be fearful now that you spent your hard-earned money on a book of Gene Perret anecdotes (I warned you that I'm not completely over my self-aggrandizement phase yet), but I'm just trying to illustrate and emphasize the laughs I've had with my career.

That's really the main reason for this book. I've had so much fun writing humor that I wanted to help other people share some of that. And you can.

A Universal Form

You may not believe it, but there is a fear of comedy writing. People feel that it's almost a sacred profession, that the finger of the Deity must reach down and anoint their heads before witticisms will germinate.

Nonsense. Comedy is the most universally practiced art form. As Jimmy Durante said so eloquently, "Everybody wants to get into de act."

Humor is universal. Every time your family gets together I'm sure friendly insult jokes pepper the room. Any time old friends gather, good humor is an invited guest, too. *Everybody* does jokes.

In my rookie year as a television staff writer, the producers asked the staff to come up with a new line for a guest performer. We were doing a tribute to Las Vegas, and needed a joke between verses of a song. Ten of us, newcomers and veterans, gathered in a room to write one joke. We threw ideas from 10 a.m. until 1 p.m., without one gag satisfying our collective judgment. When we broke for lunch, most of us stopped in the CBS men's room.

There was a nicely dressed youngster of about ten in there washing his hands. His hair was neatly combed, but one cowlick stood up in the back. I touched the recalcitrant locks and spoke to his image in the mirror.

"What's this?"

"Oh, that," he replied. "That's my personality."

And he walked out with the swagger of a performer who had just delivered a gem.

We professionals had just spent thirty man-hours with no results, and this kid came up with a great ad-lib in a split second. "Everybody wants to get into de act."

I was once the guest of honor at a dinner in my home town. In attendance was a remarkable former teacher of mine. Remarkable because she was a strong-willed woman of 93 who had never been married: she taught me in 5th grade and I must admit she looked 93 back then, too. (To her credit, she was the kind of person you could say that to.) A rumor was floating around the banquet hall that this lady had specified in her will she was to have no male pallbearers.

As the guest of honor, I dared to ask if it were true. She admitted it was. I asked why. "The bastards never took me out while I was alive," she declared. "I'll be damned if they'll do it when I'm dead."

You don't get lines funnier than that.

Of course, comedy isn't restricted to the cuteness of the very young or the very old. Once, when Don Rickles was heckled during his act—which takes not only a sense of humor, but foolhardy courage—Rickles couldn't resist a parting shot to his antagonist as he was leaving the stage.

"Lady," he said, "how much do you charge to haunt a house?"

She immediately shot back, "How many rooms?"

Yes, Mr. Durante, everybody *does* want to get into de act. Humor is universal.

A Matter of Discipline

Being witty upon occasion, though, or even every day, isn't the same as turning out enough humor to submit to a magazine or to a comic. The difference is not so much in the skill as in the discipline. The discipline can be learned and acquired. As a result of that training, your basic comedy skills can be refined.

When I first wrote for Phyllis Diller, I'd send her two routines a week, which amounted to about 60 jokes. The first time I met Phyllis after all the phone calls and correspondence, she said, "You don't write enough." I immediately set a quota of 90 jokes per week. It was difficult, and quite a strain for many weeks. Today, in contrast, I can come home from a full day of TV writing and production and, after a relaxed dinner, turn out 120 gags to be delivered to a freelance client the next morning.

Beginner's Fear

In dealing with beginning writers, the phrase I hear most often is, "Would you just read over my stuff and tell me whether it's any good or not?" Now when these people watch TV or go to a nightclub or read a book, no one has to tell them when to laugh. They know a good joke as well as anyone else. They know which material they're proud of and which they're not sure about. The statement—"Tell me if it's any good or not"—expresses fear of mixing with the professionals.

People sometimes label themselves as amateurs and the selling writers as professionals. That's technically correct, but amateurs don't have to *stay* amateurs. Good amateurs become good pros. Many of today's boxing champions are former Olympic medalists—good amateurs. Now they're knocking the blocks off of the professionals. We in the humor business know this— some amateur writers out there one day will knock our comedy blocks off.

One cause of the beginner's fear is comparing his or her writing to the best. But nightclub routines and television shows are the products of many minds. They've been rewritten and polished many times over. There's no way that you can sit at your kitchen table and duplicate that kind of communal expertise, but the important thing to remember is that *you don't have to.*

Young comics have come to me and other writers many times and asked for just one piece of material that will get them a spot on the Johnny Carson show, catapult them to national prominence, and allow them to set up residence on Easy Street for the rest of their professional lives. They promise to send the writer a few bucks after they've made it.

If I could write the piece of comedy that would accomplish that, I'd deliver it myself and build my own abode on Easy Street. But I can't do that. My friends can't do that. Neil Simon can't do that. Nobody can sit in front of a typewriter and create that piece of material. Why should a beginner expect to?

Playing the Percentages

To be a good writer, *everything* you write doesn't have to be good—just a fair percentage of it. A baseball player doesn't hand in his spikes and burn his bat if he doesn't hit a home run each time he steps to the plate. If he gets a hit just a third of the time, he can ask for a hefty raise next season. Pretty much the same percentages apply to comedy writers.

One comic I worked for, along with eight or nine other writers, had each of us doing 20 to 30 jokes on a given topic. That meant he'd have available anywhere from 200 to 300 jokes *on one topic.* And only 15 of those jokes at the most would be included in his finished monologue.

Occasionally I deliver some of my own material at after-dinner speeches. (The checks aren't as large as for writing, but it's nice once in a while to hear the laughter.) For each topic I speak on, I write 25 to 30 gags. Rewriting, I cut this down to 12 or 15 of the best. Composing the final speech, I slice even more of the funnies. After I deliver the talk once or twice, it will be obvious that certain lines aren't working. From the original 30, six to eight solid jokes might result. And that's my *own* brilliant stuff I'm cutting.

TV shows are rewritten endlessly. If some producers and writers had their way, they'd make changes even as the show was being broadcast coast-to-coast.

One incident stands out in my mind. My partner and I had written a script for "All in the Family." The producer of the show continually called us to come back and submit new ideas so we could write a second script. When our episode aired, only one line in the entire half-hour script was one we had written! Our script had been completely rewritten, yet they wanted us to come back and do more.

Another friend of mine scripted a "Dick Van Dyke Show" and then went to Arizona to see it taped. His script was rewritten so completely that when the producer came to him after the taping and asked that he do another, the writer replied, "I don't have to. Just use the one I gave you in the first place."

Don't defeat yourself before you get started. If you can write funny and are willing to learn and apply some of the skills, you can be a humorist. Every line you write doesn't have to be a gem. There just have to be enough gems there to be worth mining.

Folks who don't write professionally are sure they never will. I was in this class—I wrote funny fillers for magazine, but I convinced myself that I was really just collecting rejection notices as a hobby. Then something happened: I got a check for one of my jokes. My life changed. But before that I was among those who have what I call the "I'm not a joke writer" syndrome. Such people envision themselves as homemakers, or electricians, or salespeople. Someone *else* is always the humorist.

That's baloney. Phyllis Diller buys material from folks in every geographical location, and though I haven't seen them all, I'd hazard a guess that they come in all shapes, sizes, and every persuasion imaginable.

Early in my career, after selling regularly to Phyllis Diller and still gleefully wallowing in my own image of myself as a writer, I went to see Phyllis appear on the "Mike Douglas Show." While I was waiting outside the studio with everyone else in the audience, a gentleman came up to me and said, "Are you Gene Perret?" I told him I was and he said, "Phyllis wants to see you before the show goes on."

After a brief meeting with Phyllis, I talked with the man. I was curious: We had never met before, yet in that mass of people he came right up to me and asked if I were Perret. I wanted to know how he managed that. A bit reluctantly, he told me that Phyllis asked him to bring me backstage. He asked, "How will I know who he is?" Phyllis said, "Just walk along the line, find the guy that looks least like a comedy writer, and bring him up here." He did.

If you have a sense of humor, if things appear funny to you, if you think you can write—you *can*.

2 YES, IT CAN BE LEARNED

Some of my comedy writing colleagues will chastise me for authoring this book. They'll argue that you can't *teach* anyone to write comedy.

That reminds me of an assignment I had before turning to humor for a livelihood. Working in the electrical engineering department of a large corporation, I was slated to computerize the engineering logic we used. My job was to assemble all our engineering reasoning, organize it, and reduce it to a form that could be fed into a computer.

The first phase of this investigation was to interview the engineers. The engineers objected.

"You can't do that," they insisted. "Too many variables exist to ever compile what we know for a non-thinking machine."

"But don't you go through a series of steps to compile your information?" I asked.

"Certainly," they conceded, "but it's too complex for a computer to understand."

"But if you could," I persisted, "how would you go about it?"

"The first thing we'd do," they replied, "would be to . . . " and then they furnished me all sorts of information. Each engineer defined for me in detail what he had said was impossible.

We have the same phenomenon here. Professional comedy writers insist that no one can write professional comedy except professional comedy writers. Yet their existence contradicts their precept. They weren't *born* comedy writers, so they must have learned it somehow. Why do they maintain that no one else can learn it? Well, they know that because they've been writing comedy now for twenty or twenty-five years. Yet when they boast of their longevity, they're implying that during those years, they've learned about comedy. If comedy can't be learned, how did *they* accomplish it?

This "can't teach" bromide is particularly insidious because it prevents many talents from developing: "What's the point in trying to become a writer," some fledglings say, "if it simply can't be done?"

Young writers occasionally have asked me to review and critique their work. Often my first inclination is to say, "This is terrible." Then I'll review my own writings from twenty-five years ago and find it was just as bad as the sample I'm reviewing. The moral is that there is potential there. The writing isn't bad; it's just inexperienced. That writer can improve as he or she learns or is taught.

An Ongoing Process

The truth is, all of us—beginners and veterans—can improve. We improve by eliminating errors. We *learn* not to make those mistakes any more. In this sense, the beginner can learn much more than the old pro simply because the beginner has more mistakes to remove.

Over the years, I've learned a few things about humor writing. Perhaps I've read about it, or learned from listening to more experienced writers, or discovered through trial and error some of those things I should or shouldn't do. Why can't I tell a less experienced writer what I've learned? Isn't that teaching? If she listens, isn't she learning?

You may argue that you can't "teach" the basic something that makes a person funny. And while that argument may technically be true, in practice it just doesn't wash. You can't teach that innate something that makes an athlete a baseball player, a football player, or a tennis star, yet every professional team has high-paid coaches who teach players how to field ground balls, or how to block, or how to hit an overhead smash. Once you concede that a person has a certain amount of coordination, you can teach that person to use that talent more efficiently and more intelligently. You can't teach a person to be fast or agile, but a wily old pro can instruct a novice in how to use the speed and agility he has to get where he wants on the court. The veteran has taught; the youngster has learned. We may play with semantics all we want, but certain aspects of humor can be taught, they can be learned, and *each of us can improve.*

Another harmful response to this "can't be taught" cliché is that if you can't teach everyone to become another Woody Allen, why bother with instructions at all? The reason is because hobbyists, part-timers, and those with a professional career in mind are all entitled to learn as much about the business as they want.

Here's another example. I've always been a frustrated musician, and annoyed many a comedy-writing partner with my constant humming or whistling because there's always a melody rolling around in my head. Over the years I've attempted to learn the harmonica, the ukulele, the banjo, and the guitar. My family has been extremely patient throughout this ordeal. (They've been thankful I never tried to master the drums.) I did manage to acquire some self-taught proficiency with the guitar, but it was limited. Finally, I decided that if I were going to *play* the instrument, I should learn about it. I enrolled in a class on music theory, and another in playing skills. Music began to lose its mystery as I learned the logic and the mathematics behind it, and my fingers took on dexterity as I was faithful to my practice assignments.

The storybook end to this anecdote would be that I now play with a jazz group on weekends for some inordinate amount of money. I don't. In fact, I still have trouble getting the family to listen. The important thing is this: I can play reasonably well and I get hours of relaxation and enjoyment from my guitar strumming. No one can tell me I shouldn't have invested time and money into those lessons simply because I would never become another Segovia or George Benson.

If the only people who took piano lessons were those who were assured of becoming virtuosos, the world would be deprived of a lot of music.

Teaching Yourself

There *is* one sense in which we cannot teach a skill: each person must teach him or herself. Let's go back again to our tennis player and her instructor. The veteran may expound all sorts of wisdom and knowledge about tennis, but unless the instructee converts this through practice and application, she will not improve.

There are two types of knowledge: intellectual and practical. As an example, let's suppose there was a very intelligent college professor who decided to learn all he could about swimming. He studied textbook after textbook on the different strokes. He even studied anatomy to learn which muscles should be developed for swimming proficiency. However, in the course of this extensive research, our professor never went near water.

Now, let's create another fictitious character—a young man who took a job as a lifeguard. He went through the Red Cross lifeguard certification course, and each day had to swim two miles for training. During the course of his job, he was involved in many life-saving ventures under varying conditions.

Now assume that you fell out of a boat and yelled for help. Which of our two characters would you prefer volunteered to save you? The professor or the swimmer?

Certainly, the professor had all the intellectual knowledge he needed about swimming, but he never tested it. He never learned firsthand about currents and lifesaving techniques. The second man knew little about the anatomical mechanics of swimming. He just knew how to do it.

I once heard this referred to as water knowledge and wine knowledge. Book information is water knowledge, which is practically useless until converted through application and practice into wine knowledge.

This is where it becomes obvious that only you can teach yourself. Only you can feel a crawl stroke that you have been told about. Only your body can repeat it over and over again until your muscles learn that movement and make it your own.

The writing faculty is like a muscle. In the practical sense, only *you* can teach yourself to write. The only way you can do this is by writing, writing, and more writing.

Taken individually, practical knowledge is much more beneficial than book knowledge. Book knowledge is almost useless until it's backed up with practical knowledge. Practical knowledge, though, even if it's somewhat inaccurate, is always valuable. If you give a person who wants to learn a racquet and a can of tennis balls and have him play tennis for two hours every single day for two years, at the end of that time he's going to be a fairly representative tennis player. He may hit the ball incorrectly, but he will have learned how to hit it effectively. He will certainly play a better game than a gentleman who *read* about tennis for two hours each day for two years.

Obviously, the ideal is a combination of both: some water knowledge backed up with wine knowledge. Learn what to do and how to do it—and then go out and do it.

3 THE SKILLS YOU'LL NEED

When I was teaching a course in comedy writing, a student told me analyzing comedy was like dissecting a frog: "You may learn a little bit about it, but the poor creature dies in the process." That may be the way some readers are feeling at this point. . . . "Enough *about* comedy. When are we going to *write* some?"

I honestly sympathize with you because I know the feeling well. The tendency when given a comedy assignment is to just sit down and crank out the funnies: that's what we're paid for, that's what's fun.

Prepare! Prepare!

Having been faced with many difficult assignments with distressingly pressing deadlines, I've learned one thing: get them done quickly so that I can get back to relaxing. Naturally, I want to do them well so that I still have a job next week to pay for my relaxing.

I've also learned through experience that the quickest and easiest way to complete an assignment well is not to rush headlong into it, but to spend some time preparing. It makes the job easier and the end results better.

That's why we're taking a chapter to discuss the skills necessary for comedy writing, so you'll be aware of them and can practice and develop them.

Let me use music again as an example. I've already told you how I took some courses to learn about music in general and the guitar in specific. Undeniably, it was tedious learning scales, then chord formations. At first, none of it seemed to have any relationship; it wasn't helping me play the guitar.

But with patience, study, and diligent practice, it all came together. I found I could play more and varied pieces. I could ad-lib or improvise with my instrument. I was playing music. Somehow the frog had lived.

You will find the same as you study and practice your comedy skills. No one thought or idea will hit you and change your work in a single instant, but gradually, almost unwittingly, you will absorb what you learn and it will become part of your writing arsenal.

Fortunately, one important difference in practicing writing skills and practicing musical or athletic dexterity is that the writing exercises are fun along the way. There are no scales to master in comedy.

Let's discuss some of the skills that you will need for your writing. When we get to Part Two we'll actually write—I promise.

A Sense of Humor

Perhaps it's a little silly to list this as one of the skills. It's like all of us sitting in a guitar class that we paid $120 to take, each with a $600 guitar on his knee, and the teacher starting out by saying, "How many of you like to play the guitar?"

Obviously, you have a sense of humor or you wouldn't have been attracted to this book. However, we might learn a bit about comedy, and about ourselves, by studying the sense of humor for a page or two.

I define a sense of humor as the following three abilities:

    a) to *see* things as they are
    b) to *recognize* things as they are
    c) to *accept* things as they are

Let me use a rather grim example—one totally separated from the world of humor—to explain this concept further.

Last year, I discovered I had cardiovascular problems and had

heart by-pass surgery. The operation was completely successful, the problem has been solved, and I'm hitting the tennis ball
as badly as ever. Nevertheless, the chain of events serves to illustrate the difference between seeing, recognizing, and accepting
reality.

My first symptoms were grouchiness and fatigue. I never noticed them until close friends pointed them out to me. I didn't
see things as they were.

After being told the facts, and finally admitting that they were
true, I tried to explain them away. I was tired because I was
working too hard, or I was a bit out of shape. I was grouchy simply because other people were obnoxious. I didn't *recognize*
things as they were.

Finally, I had tests that confirmed there was a problem requiring surgery. At this point I did *accept* things as they were. It
wasn't easy though. The inclination was to say, "I'll eat better,
I'll exercise more, I'll behave myself and the problem will go
away."

That helps to explain the difference between seeing, recognizing, and accepting, but what does that have to do with a sense of
humor? Just as I would never have been cured if I hadn't ful-
filled all three steps, so we all fail to see humor in any topic if we
don't satisfy all three.

Let me use myself again as an example. Along with thickening
arterial walls, I'm also afflicted with thinning hair. Can I be kidded about this? I hope so because my children are relentless in
their attack. Let me tell you a story that combines the two mala-
dies, and which shows the value of comedy.

I've confessed that I was already a grouch, but on finding out
about the necessary surgery I was also depressed and expert at
feeling sorry for myself—not a lot of laughs to be around. To
compound my suffering, I was given medication that had to be
taped to my body. I complained to my family that it was a terrible
inconvenience because my body is fairly covered with hair and
there was no place I could affix the medicine. My daughter said,
"Why don't you put it on top of your head?

That may sound like a cruel line, but it was a loving quip that
snapped us all out of our melancholy and got us laughing again.
It restored my sense of humor because I could see, recognize,

and finally accept the reality of my illness.

To get back to illustrating the sense of humor, when would I not be able to accept jokes about balding? First of all if I weren't aware of it. Many people begin thinning at the back of the crown and don't even know it's happening. If you joke about losing their hair to these folks, they look at you as if you're crazy.

Second, if they fail to recognize they are losing their hair. I was convinced for years that by combing my hair a different way, no one would notice a few strands had departed. If anyone had joked about it during those years, I would have been offended rather than amused because it would have been proof that my ploy wasn't working.

Third, some of us fail to accept it, and jokes about our balding pates are not well received at all.

It's especially important to be aware of these three abilities in speaking to audiences, because not all audiences have a sense of humor about all topics. You must know what they see, recognize, and accept before kidding them.

Humor and Well-being

Completely aside from comedy writing, developing a sense of humor will help your well-being. How do you develop a sense of humor? Just by being aware of the three abilities it comprises. Many times you will be in situations that test your patience: if you can learn to see, recognize, and accept reality, it will be much easier on your nervous system.

Here in Los Angeles we are sometimes trapped on the world's longest parking lots, the freeways. Once you're caught in slow- or non-moving traffic, it's hard not to see it. However, it's sometimes hard to recognize it. We say to ourselves, "Maybe it's just an accident and will clear up in a few more blocks." The real optimist says to himself, "Maybe the lane I'm in will start moving faster." There's the other guy we all know and love who figures, "If I just blow my horn, the whole problem will be settled."

Then we tend not to accept it. We torture ourselves by saying things like, "I was going to go the other route, but thought this would be faster," or "I should have left work a bit earlier."

The reality is that you didn't do either. You see, recognize and accept that you are in a traffic jam, you set your radio to a pleasant station, and you relax until traffic progresses again. (Or do what I do . . . blow your horn.)

The Ability to Analyze and Prepare

There are two general thought processes involved in writing a joke. The first is rapid, and almost unnoticeable. It consists of rolling different ideas through your brain and instantaneously analyzing them for any relevant connection with another thought.

In general, a joke comprises two distinct ideas that come together to form one. Think of a few of your favorite one-liners and you'll discover that there are two thoughts there. Sometimes these thoughts are strikingly similar; other times they are intriguingly opposite. Sometimes they are totally nonsensical and other times simply ironic. But 99 percent of jokes are two ideas tied together in a funny way.

In forming the joke, your mind begins with one idea, then with computer-like speed generates and appraises other ideas for a humorous connection with the original. When it strikes that deliciously witty combination, the joke pops out of your head.

Since our minds are so active, that combination can happen by accident. That's why anyone can write a joke.

However, writers can't depend on accidents or coincidences. That's why the second thought process is so important. It is slow and methodical. It is simply a method of preparing the mind to go through the first process.

All jokes are generated by the first process, the rapid assessment of ideas rolling through your brain. However, it stands to reason that the more thoughts you can get rolling the better selection you will have, consequently the more jokes you'll generate and the better they will be.

These two thought processes are similar to the way your mind functions in playing a game of Scrabble. You have seven letters arranged in no particular order in front of you. You struggle to get the word with the highest point value. You mentally rearrange the letters and pass judgment on the arrangements. Your mind rejects W-E-L-B as a non-word, but BLEW pops into your mind as acceptable. The more ways you can rearrange those letters, the better selection of possible words you have. When that high-scoring word finally pops into your mind, it feels as though it literally came from nowhere.

As a humorist, you will want to be able to thoroughly dissect a topic and prepare a list of relationships before getting around to the actual joke creation.

The Ability to Correlate Ideas

As part of analyzing and preparing, the writer will want to find words, phrases, events, people, facts, things and symbolisms that are either similar or opposite to the main topic.

It's not unlike the faculty you use in doing crossword puzzles. When given one word, you mentally search for all other words that have a relationship to the clue until your mind presents you with the right one.

The Ability to See Non-Standard Meanings

A good humorist must learn to go beyond the obvious. When you see a picture, a word, or a phrase, you are aware that it has a standard meaning. With a little bit of effort, however, you can create another meaning for it. Often, that other meaning will lead to the joke you are looking for.

For instance, a man in a tuxedo is a man in a tuxedo, but he can also be a penguin. A man in a white dinner jacket can also be a Good Humor man, or a doctor.

I did a joke for Bob Hope about how much tape professional football players wear. He said,

> "My wife watched the game on television and said, 'These players can't be too old. Some of them haven't been unwrapped yet.'"

This device works equally well for words as for visualizations. Groucho Marx was a master at finding an alternate meaning in a word or phrase. In one movie he said,

*"Last evening I shot a lion in my pajamas. How he ev-
er got in my pajamas, I'll never know."*

Another old joke also illustrates this point: "Can you tell me
how long cows should be milked?" You expect an answer relating to time: five or ten minutes. The comic reply is, "The same as
short ones." A different meaning was found for the question.

The Ability to Scan Ideas

You probably have noticed that most of these skills run together. The comedy writer must utilize all of them at the same time
when he sits to compose his jokes.

The ability to scan ideas is one of the most important, though,
because it basically is the gag-writing process. The writer ana-
lyzes and lists all her correlations to a given topic, but to write
she has to roll all these ideas through her head one by one until
she hits a joke. Generally, she starts with what she wants to say,
then scans her brain searching for that perfect second idea to
form a funny line.

Eventually, a writer learns to do this mentally, but I recommend that the newcomer actually write out these lists to help
stimulate the funny bone.

The Ability to Visualize

This is a mental skill that will produce many jokes. If you analyze some of your favorite gags, you'll notice that many are funny
because they conjure up a ridiculous image. I once did a joke for
Phyllis Diller's mother-in-law routine that fell into the "she's so
fat that . . . ." category. It read:

*"My mother-in-law is so large, one day she wore a
gray dress and an admiral boarded her."*

The imagery here is that the woman looked like a battleship.
The joke evolved as I let my mind wander into exaggerated vi-
sions of her size. I pictured a whale, a building, a truck, a tank, a
battleship, and hundreds of other weird things.

As a comedy composer you take the realistic image in your
mind and distort or exaggerate it out of all proportion to see

what funny images you can visualize. Then you find the right words for the new image.

A Facility with Words

All of our comedy is expressed in words, so naturally it behooves the writer to be proficient with them. Some of our gags even depend *entirely* on the words. I once did a gag for a woman who worked with a starlet known for being well endowed. The comedienne looked at the bosomy lady and said, "I feel sorry for her. She's a hunch front."

The writer has to develop an ear for words and phrases, even compiling a list of some of the trendier ones so that they can be used in joke writing.

On one Christmas show, someone asked Bob Hope how he stayed so young-looking. He replied, "I use industrial-strength Oil of Olay." That combined two popular commercial phrases of the day into a good joke.

The Ability to Pick up Comedy Rhythm

This skill is largely inbred. You hear rules like the comedy rule of three, and putting the punchline close to the end of the joke, and that words with "K" in them are funny. All these rules apply, but the rhythm and timing of a joke are mostly individual, and we're not going to make any attempts to teach it in this book.

I have seen five comedy writers argue for hours over the precise wording of a particular joke. No one was right and no one was wrong: it's an individual judgment.

Don't be frightened away by all these seemingly complicated skills that are required for comedy writing. Most of them are inherent in anyone with a sense of humor. Chapter 8 contains exercises that work on different aspects of gag writing, and we'll go through each aspect in detail. You'll find that all these techniques come easily. (At least more easily than I've explained them.)

They are listed here mostly for your information. We're dissecting that poor frog again.

4 COMEDY AS A HOBBY

I once attended a writer's workshop where the main speaker was Charles Schultz, creator of the comic strip PEANUTS. During his talk, Mr. Schultz mentioned that Snoopy, the precocious beagle in the strip, was a frustrated author. Though he worked at his craft seriously and with foolhardy optimism, Snoopy, Mr. Schultz conceded, had not and would never sell any of his writings.

A questioner from the audience then stated that many of us attending were like the pen-and-ink beagle. We might never make a literary sale either. Did Mr. Schultz, she asked, have any words of encouragement for these people?

I recall feeling some sympathy for Schultz when the question was asked because he and the audience had been referring to Snoopy and frustrated authors in a spirit of fun; now this query turned it all into a heavy and rather depressing topic.

But Schultz never faltered. "I certainly do," he said. "The reward is in the doing."

The Rewards of an Avocation

I've always believed that we need an escape from the stressful, results-oriented world where we make our living. Now there's nothing wrong with results, and there's certainly nothing harmful about earning our daily bread: the problem is that the two of them are so dependent on each other. It's refreshing to struggle with some challenge and never really be worried about the results, since it's not a matter of economic survival.

As you've probably guessed by now, one of my hobbies is tennis. I take it seriously. I've had my share of lessons and on the court I play hard to win. But if I'm beaten (and occasionally I *am* beaten even though I cheat as much as I can) it's not catastrophic. Having lost a close match takes no food from my table, nor does it hurt my career. Naturally, I dislike losing, but the after-effects are mild; I've lost nothing but a tennis game.

The other side of this coin is that it's nice once in awhile to earn a little bread that you didn't expect. A hobby can do that for you, too.

I don't play tennis for money—if I did, I wouldn't make any—but I did make money with my hobby of writing comedy. In fact, when people ask how I got started in the business, I tell them that it was a hobby that got out of hand. People embark upon a career in comedy writing the same way a person enters into a life of sin. First you try it for the fun of it, then you begin entertaining a few close friends, then you say, "What the hell, I might as well make a buck at it."

That may be an irreverent way of stating it, but it serves as notice that your hobby could very well lead to a part-time business or perhaps a full-time career. We'll discuss those in the following chapters.

I found, though, that when my hobby became a profession, I still needed some diversion, and tennis and the guitar came to my rescue. . . .

We all need some activity where the reward is in the doing. We need some pleasurable pastime where we can charge full speed ahead and "damn the results."

Humor writing can fill that need. It's certainly convenient. You don't have to buy a kit. You need no expensive equipment. In fact, all you need is a pen and a blank sheet of paper. It fits into anyone's schedule because there's no time-consuming preparation necessary, nor any clean-up afterwards. You can write on a bus, during your lunch break, while shaving—almost any time you have a free moment or two.

My children once cajoled me into taking them across town to

see a Marx Brothers movie. They had been enthused about it for some time, but just as we were leaving, I got a call from one of my clients to do some monologue material. Unfortunately, the material had to be ready in an hour. When the youngsters heard the news, they went into a tantrum and berated me for reneging on a promise. I *did* feel guilty—but some ingenuity saved the day and my parental reputation.

The theatre was a good 45-minute drive from our house, so I issued each of my four children a notepad and pencil. The oldest one was to copy down the first joke I recited, the next in age was to jot down my second witticism, and so on. As I drove I dictated my gags and they recorded them. We arrived at the movie house, bought our popcorn, settled in our seats—then *they* watched the film while *I* collected the notebooks and called the routine in to my unsuspecting client. A fair percentage of the gags worked, the Marx Brothers were hilarious, the children were delighted, and I was a good Daddy.

I classify this incident in the hobby area because by the time I paid for the theatre tickets, the gas, and then treated everyone to dinner afterwards, I made no profit on the deal. It does show, though, that comedy can be created under any conditions. You can't top that for convenience. Imagine the confusion if I had tried to complete a crossword puzzle or knit a sweater while navigating the Los Angeles freeway.

Humor writing is a provocative, entertaining and exciting hobby because it employs many different skills. As we saw in Chapter 2, it requires a facility with words, visualization, memory recall, and a touch of psychology. It's demanding and challenging.

Humor is also a *fun* hobby. You know how entertaining it is to listen to a smart comic. It's that much more invigorating to create the humor yourself.

It can be fun on a shared basis too. When I worked in an engineering office, a group of us used to devise humor projects. One that I recall was a variation of "the Great Carsoni" that Johnny Carson does. Steve Allen did a similar routine as the "Answer Man." Each of us submitted a few standard phrases, quotations, or sayings that had been in the news. These were something like, "a hole in one," or "have a Coke and smile."

Then each of us would spend the rest of the week, working during lunch hour, during our free time at home—or perhaps when we should have been doing engineering—creating funny questions that might have generated those replies, like:

> *"When Robert Ford met the James Brothers,*
> *what did he leave?"* (. . . *a hole in one.)*

> *"What will two dollars get you today*
> *at the local bordello?"* (*a Coke and*
> *a smile.)*

You can see that a bit of competitive enjoyment is thus added to the hobby. You not only have the fun of making humor but delighting in what other people have created too. In Chapter 8 we'll discuss writing exercises, some of which can be converted to group projects.

Humor can also be of actual practical use. People love comedy, especially when it's personalized. Years ago, Don Rickles used to display his unique comedy style in a Los Angeles nightclub: He attacked ringsiders with the same comic viciousness that he does today. Celebrities who came to catch his act were not exempt from his tirades—in fact, for them his assaults took on added fervor. Consequently, more and more celebrities showed up at ringside: they wanted to hear what the irreverent Rickles would say about them.

I discovered firsthand how much people love to be kidded when I first began in comedy. My writing got me a bit of a reputation and I was asked to be master of ceremonies at banquets. I always wrote comedy material specifically about the guest of honor. After the ceremonies, he or she usually asked for a copy of the monologue as a memento. Eventually, I began putting a nicely typed copy into a binder as my gift to the honoree.

Your humorous writing can create many treasured gifts. Your own ingenuity will provide an endless supply of innovative ideas, but here are a few that I've enjoyed.

I've written monologues for and about family and friends, and put together bound collections of humor, cartoons, and original one-liners for special occasions like showers, birthdays, or anniversaries, composing personalized captions for family photo albums or collections of old movie photos or monster pictures to be made into a friend's life story. I've made funny, personalized greeting cards and individualized cartoons that are drawn large enough for framing.

There's no end to the ideas that can be conceived for using comedy. As we said in the beginning of this chapter, though—or as Charles Schultz said—the reward is in the doing. And that reward is much multiplied when you share it with others.

A writing associate of mine always championed this cause. He told his children not to spend money for expensive gifts for him. He preferred that they put a little bit of themselves into their gifts and present him things that they made . . . things like we've discussed here. One evening his children threw a birthday party and presented him with a large gift-wrapped package. As he opened it, he noticed that it was a bit warm. His kids had given him his dinner, still in the pot it was cooked in. True to his request, they gave him a gift they had "made."

5 COMEDY AS A SECOND INCOME

With all due respect to the "reward is in the doing" quote, Charles Schultz is living proof that there's nothing wrong with getting a bit of remuneration for your efforts. Creating humor is fun—but so is going shopping with the checks you receive in return.

The value of money doesn't have to be touted by this author, but I can tell you that there's a fringe benefit in being compensated for your writing: a check is one of the greatest inspirations to team up with your typewriter again. It's a driving force that keeps you writing. Friends and acquaintances may say you're funny and laugh hysterically at your creations, but when you get something you can take to the supermarket, you *know* you're a writer.

Comedy writing can be an excellent second income. You can work at home, at your own convenience, and you can pretty much be your own boss.

I began writing in 1959 and it took me almost ten years to break into television and the "big time." During that decade of apprenticeship, I made enough money to justify the time and effort I put into my writing: my income from writing ranged from $1,500 to $10,000 per year. Today those figures could probably be doubled.

The important thing is that I maintained a steady job during all this time, and didn't overtax my leisure. My moonlight income was almost all profit, too, because comedy-writing over-head is minimal. A typewriter, some blank pages (not blank for long, we hope), a bit for postage, maybe an extra phone call now and then, and that's about it.

The marketing possibilities for comedy skills on a part-time basis are practically limitless. It's largely dependent on your own ingenuity and enterprise. Here are two stories I take great delight in to this day.

During my apprenticeship, I wrote several humor columns for newspapers. These consisted of 12 jokes on a local topic. I wrote them in the morning—notepad on the countertop—as I shaved before going to work. I'm still proud of the fact that each morning I made ten bucks while I shaved. (Today I have a full beard so you know I either can't land another newspaper column or I'm independently wealthy.)

In time, though, I became frustrated that my career wasn't proceeding as quickly as I would have liked. I wanted to take a correspondence course in comedy writing, but the cost was prohibitive. So I contacted a local comic, told him my plans, and sold him the rights to all my homework from the writing course. He got material rather cheaply—and I got to learn a little bit more about comedy.

Humor is in demand in every community. You'll be able to find the need and fill it where you live right now. Following are just a few suggestions that might stimulate your thinking.

Magazines

Many magazines solicit fillers and short humor pieces of vary-ing descriptions. *Changing Times* runs a page of topical jokes and *Reader's Digest* runs short jokes on more general topics.

My first check came from a Sunday supplement magazine and paid me $5, but there was an added bonus: on the cover of this particular issue was a photo of my idol, Bob Hope, along with a story about his greatest golf jokes. (So I bend the truth a little bit and say that the first time I appeared in print, I shared the billing with Bob Hope.)

A handy reference guide for filler writing—in fact, for most writing—is *Writer's Market*, published annually by Writer's Digest Books. In it you'll get a complete list of publications that need short humor, what style they prefer, and what price they pay.

Making a concerted effort to sell to this market requires a little extra time because some bookkeeping is necessary. You want to know just who you sent your material to and if it has been returned or not. That way you can resubmit some of the gags to other magazines.

Writer's magazines, like *Writer's Digest* and *The Writer*, also publish books on writing. Here, you can find how-to books on writing short humor pieces and fillers for magazines. They'll go into much more detail than we can in this volume.

Over and above filler and short humor, most magazines publish humorous essays or features, either in every issue or whenever a funny piece comes in. Editors love genuinely funny pieces, but rarely can get enough of them. Again, check *Writer's Market*.

Humor Services

Comedy newsletters offer jokes, one-liners, and quips to people who need a steady supply of humor. These publications carry 4 to 8 pages of gags, a good number of which are purchased from freelancers. The newsletters may pay a little less than most magazines, but they buy more material, so your sales may increase.

The best-known newsletter is probably *Bob Orben's Current Comedy*, 1200 N. Nash Street, #1122, Arlington VA 22209. There are others, though, like Marty Ragaway's "Funny, Funny World." You can find these newsletters in a good market list.

Enterprising writers who've got some experience and aren't afraid of writing a lot of material can even begin their own comedy newsletters. Many people need an inexpensive source of comedy material. If you can write enough, and can find subscribers, go to it.

Greeting Cards

No doubt you've noticed over the years the trend has been away from sentimental and toward impertinent greeting cards. Consequently, there is a demand for inventive witticisms from all such card manufacturers.

Here again, I suggest a good book to learn the basics of this sort of writing and marketing. Check the backlists of publishers who specialize in books about writing. Also, *Writer's Market* is again invaluable for up-to-date marketing information.

Cartoonists

Being blessed with artistic skills doesn't always mean someone is also blessed with comedic talent. Most cartoonists are looking for a supply of comedy to illustrate.

The same two principles apply: a good book on fundamentals found through writers' magazines, and a comprehensive market list.

Newspaper Columns

You have an advantage over such talents as Erma Bombeck and Art Buchwald in that you can localize your humor. Some local newspapers are willing to pay for comedy dealing with the specifics of their community.

Here you may do a little speculative work writing a few columns that deal with local headlines, and presenting them to editors.

I have done several columns of this type and have always found them to be very popular, for two reasons. First of all, people love comedy, especially in the midst of all the negative news on the front page. Second, they enjoy a few clever comments about their home town—things no national columnist could be aware of.

Try the suburban weeklies and other small papers, which are much easier to crack than the metropolitan dailies. You can always work up.

Radio and TV Personalities

Disc jockeys and local television personalities have a lot of air space to fill. They're desperately in need of comedy material. Most of them subscribe to one or more of the comedy services, but again, you have an advantage: you can write on national topics, but you can also do material that only locals will know and appreciate.

Here the best approach is a letter of introduction with a sample of the sort of material you can write. If the personalities are impressed with your skill, they'll get in touch, and both of you can take it from there.

Many of these personalities do as much work off the air as they do on. Their marquee value gets them many local speaking engagements. They'll need material for most of these appearances, too. (See how easy it is!)

Professional Speakers

A whole subculture exists that many of us know nothing about: the professional speaking circuit. These are people who deliver lectures on technical subjects, motivation, salesmanship or are simply humorists who entertain at banquets. Almost all of them are searching for a good supply of wit because even the technical and the motivational speakers find that some humor is required to keep an audience awake and listening.

Many of these people belong to the National Speakers Association, P.O. Box 6296, Phoenix, AZ 85005.

Dottie Walters, a fine professional speaker, publishes a newsletter entitled *Sharing Ideas among Professional Speakers.* It keeps us all informed on the latest activities and projects of most professional speakers. For information on her publication, write to Royal CBS Publishing, 600 W. Foothill Boulevard, Glendora, CA 91740.

To bring writers and speakers together, I recently began my own educational newsletter, which includes how-to articles, interviews with top humorists and writers, and a showcase of writers' material. It's called *Gene Perret's Round Table,* P.O. Box 13, King of Prussia, PA 19406.

Executives

Management is discovering that a dash of wit in a presentation helps listeners not only to listen but to retain what they've heard. Consequently, business executives are searching for consultants to add a bit of flair to their speeches.

It's difficult to solicit work in this area, but oftentimes the execs will find you. Your local reputation will precede you, and they'll come for help.

While I was serving my comedy apprenticeship and holding down a full-time job at the same time, the executives at our plant often asked for help writing some business presentation. This might be a difficult area to crack, but it's worth noting and possibly exploring.

Your Own Speaking

People hunger for the lighter touch—especially people who are constantly subjected to heavy, technical dissertations. The program chairman of every organization forages each year for one or two speakers who can introduce fun into the proceedings.

This is actually how my career as a writer began—as a speaker. People who had heard about my "custom-tailored" comedy hired me as an after-dinner speaker for business meetings. That led to other people hearing about my comedy and offering to buy it. Eventually, writing became more lucrative than speaking and I devoted full time to the typewriter.

Now I've begun doing some speaking again and have discovered an interesting phenomenon: people who *won't* pay for speakers *will* pay for humorists. The reason many organizations don't normally pay for speakers is because they can get their fill. Local service clubs usually don't have to reimburse lecturers for their weekly or monthly meetings, because businesses will gladly provide spokesmen as a community service or for the promotional return. However, if the organization can find a good humorist who'll lighten up their meetings occasionally, they'll offer a fee.

There are other avenues for a writer who can also function as a humorist or an emcee. Every bowling, softball, and bridge league has an awards banquet sometime during the year. Leagues avoid hiring professional comics for these things because they generally don't have the funds, but you can step in there for a smaller fee, one they *can* afford.

Speaking, as I've said before and will probably say many more times before the final pages of this book, is excellent training for a comedy writer. Writing for others, you're tempted to just do adequate material and let the comic suffer through it. When you're up there on your own, though, you learn what good and bad material can do for or against you. You appreciate the need for quality material. You learn what the speaker has to endure when the material is only "good enough."

Local Comics

Almost every area has its own "Mr. (or Ms.) Comedy." Larger cities may have several comics vying for the title. These people need material as much as David Brenner or Joan Rivers does—maybe more.

Selling to them is beneficial for two reasons. First of all, you get a check. Second, you get a chance to learn by studying audience reaction. That's almost as good as being up there delivering the lines yourself.

With local comics, you can travel to their appearances with them and study the audience as they perform. With national comics you can't always afford that luxury; you get your feedback secondhand.

Some of my writing in the early years was for local comics and people who worked at their trade on weekends only. With one gentleman I drew up a contract to receive a weekly stipend in exchange for a set amount of gags. With another comedian, I wrote a set amount of material, but received a percentage of his fee for each performance.

National Comics

It is quite possible to sell to many big name performers without ever leaving your home town. I wrote for Phyllis Diller for many months before I ever met her. Most of our dealings were by mail and phone.

Most of the national comics buy from freelance writers. Phyllis Diller is famous for buying material from housewives across the nation; she selects the jokes she wants to keep and pays a set fee for each gag. Joan Rivers has purchased routines this way.

Rodney Dangerfield also looks at freelance material.

None of these people are listed in a writer's market list: you have to discover them on your own. The weekly *Variety* lists the appearances of many well-known comics. If you keep track of them through the pages of *Variety*, you may be able to contact them by mail or phone at the club where they're appearing. You'll be surprised to find that most comedians will at least look at material. They need it so badly they're not likely to pass up a potential source of comedy.

Television

I list this here as a caution only. It's very difficult for a part-time writer who doesn't live in New York or Hollywood to sell material to network television.

Television material changes almost hourly. You may sell a story idea in the morning and be called to a meeting in the afternoon to get notes on the "new" story line. Then you'll write it and present it to the producers, and it will be changed as you sit there. After the final draft is written, it will be changed again, and will constantly undergo modifications even until—and while—they're taping it.

It's difficult to do this sort of work by mail. It's almost impossible to do it with five or six writers in the room—but through the postal services, forget it.

Even story ideas or series ideas are not easily sold from a distance. Television executives buy names rather than stories or ideas. Ninety-nine percent of these ideas are purchased from established writers: the reputation is being bought in the hope that a workable idea will follow.

So until your reputation is more firmly established, I suggest you forget network television and concentrate on more accessible markets.

Local Television and Cable

Not all television today originates with the networks. Everything that's a drawback for a local writer who wants to work for network television becomes an asset in writing for locally produced shows, especially for local cable franchises.

You can tailor your own market list of local TV shows. Watch them, note those you feel you can write for, and contact the producers or the stars through the station.

Your Hobby Expertise

In the last chapter we discussed gift ideas based on humor writing. Other people may enjoy these items and want them for friends. You might pick up a few second income dollars doing photo albums or writing personalized monologues about people you don't even know.

These are only some of the ways you can enjoy your comedy writing habit and generate a supplemental income at the same time. Probably you've already got several variations on these or entirely new schemes running through your head. Explore them.

How Much Is It Worth?

We may be getting a little ahead of ourselves here, but you may be wondering how much to charge for all these services. In many cases—such as for magazine fillers, humor services, greeting cards, and cartoonists—the fee is predetermined. In other instances, the fee structure is personal. Charge enough to make it worth your while to do it.

A danger here is that beginning writers may read about how much money an established writer makes, then try to set their fees comparably. You must realize that we all lie about the money we make and the rates we charge. (I would be a happy and comfortable man today if I made as much as I told my friends I did.) Besides, those writers have built their way to that fee.

It's better to charge less than you think is fair, to gain experience and collect another credit. Each time you sell comedy you establish more credibility—which means your services will be worth more in the future. Should you begin too high, you may not *have* a comedy-writing future.

Be fair to yourself, but not unreasonable. Eventually you will get so much work that you will have to be selective, and then you can accept only those assignments that pay the highest return.

For an Emmy-cast tribute to writers, I was asked to write a pithy phrase that explained what a good joke was. I submitted this:

"A good joke is a series of words that ends in a check."

6 COMEDY AS A CAREER

Ed Simmons, a Hollywood producer and writer, used to be a baby photographer. As he tells it, "I spent my days eliciting laughter from toddlers. After a few years, I became power-crazed. Getting one baby to laugh wasn't enough. I started to concentrate on twins, then graduated to triplets, and by the time I was exclusively into quadruplets, the short supply sent me into bankruptcy. Then television came into being and I luckily rode in on the first wave."

That's a whimsical bit of underplay. Mr. Simmons was indeed a baby photographer, but—along with a partner—he worked evenings writing song parodies. Success in this endeavor lead to writing for some well-known nightclub comics. When the young TV industry was looking for writers who weren't jaded by years of radio writing, one producer turned to Ed and his partner. This led to a string of credits dating from those early years to the present, credits that included Dean Martin and Jerry Lewis, Danny Thomas, Eddie Cantor, Martha Raye, George Gobel, Red Skelton, and the show where Ed was my boss for five years, "The Carol Burnett Show."

The progression from baby photographer to head writer and producer of major television shows sounds bizarre, but it really isn't. Each writer in Hollywood has his or her own strange tale of transition to comedy writing. I was an electrical engineer before being invited into television. I've met doctors and lawyers who abandoned their practices to make it in show business. There is no one road that leads to professional comedy writing, but there is also no place from which you can't get there.

I opened this chapter with Ed Simmons's story, though, because many readers question the practicality of beginning a career as a professional humor writer. Is it possible? Is it easy? How long will it take? Mr. Simmons recently consented to doing an interview for *Round Table*, our comedy-writing newsletter. He was asked this question: "Can you give our readers some idea of how accessible TV is to new writers? Is the door open? Are new writers needed or wanted?" He replied, "On the down side, TV is not accessible to new writers, the door is closed and new writers are neither needed or wanted. On the up side, every year dozens of new writers break through."

A comedy writing career is always possible; whether it is easy or not requires a qualified answer. It cannot be accomplished without a great deal of effort, perseverance, and diligent study. In that sense, it isn't easy. But if you're willing to put in the necessary apprenticeship and keep at it, it's almost impossible to fail. In that sense, it's easy.

I equate it to learning a musical instrument. When I see a person playing a piano, my mind tells me that it's impossible, all at the same time, to see musical notes scribbled on paper, make sense of them, translate them into physical movements, and then have ten digits make those varied moves simultaneously—all of this, oftentimes, while singing. It's so complicated that it would seem to be an unattainable skill. Yet anyone with professional lessons and devoted practice can learn to play a piano. It's not a gift given to a select few: *anyone* can play a piano. How well you play it depends on how much time you're willing to put into your education and your practice.

Working on variety shows, I meet many of the top musicians in the country. I've asked them how much time they devote to practicing. Even after they are accomplished professional musicians, they sometimes practice up to six to eight hours a day to become better musicians.

I don't tell you this to scare any fledgling writers away from a career, because musicianship is much more difficult than writing; it's a much more exact skill. You have to hit the right notes at the right time . . . if you can't, you can't play with a group.

Writing doesn't require that sort of precision. Also, writing doesn't demand physical dexterity as music does. But writing does illustrate the different meanings of "easy." If you are willing to work, learn, and stick with it a writing career can be easy. If you are not, a writing career may be almost impossible.

The Luck Factor

Many talented people—not only writers—are tempted to use "luck" as an excuse for not embarking on a new career.

"Oh, I couldn't make it as a comedy writer. You have to be lucky to do that."

"Oh sure, she made it, but that's because she got lucky."

Let's look at two professional comedy writers who are both temporarily out of work. Writer A keeps calling his agent to find him some kind of work because he has to pay the bills. Writer B pesters her agent, too, but while she's on a forced hiatus, she creates and outlines twenty-six ideas for situation comedies.

Finally A does get a job and commands a nice salary. B sells one of her pilot ideas, it's a hit, and she becomes a millionaire. Now Writer A sits in his office and moans, "Oh sure, Writer B is on Easy Street now because she got lucky."

Luck is something that happens after the fact. It didn't cause Writer B's success. If none of these shows had sold, chances are B would have created more shows, then more, until one of them sold—and then that moment would have been termed "lucky."

One of the great rags-to-riches stories of our time is Sylvester Stallone's quick rise to fame with his screenplay *Rocky*. How lucky can you get? But Stallone tells us that he wrote nine or ten screenplays on speculation before he sold *Rocky*. That's not luck. That's dedication.

We create our own good fortune. Don't use luck as an excuse to avoid the challenge, and don't depend on it for your success. Substitute confidence and diligence instead—and then let Writer A complain about how "lucky" you got.

Why New Writers Break In

The popular conception is that comedy writing is a "closed"

profession: no newcomers are needed or welcome. That just isn't true. The door to a writing career is not standing wide open, but it *is* ajar.

Even if those of us already in the field wanted to make writing an exclusive fraternity, we couldn't do it for the following reasons.

Comedy Is Popular

Humor is a commodity in constant demand because it is tremendously popular. If you study most fields of entertainment, you'll discover that comedy is the big money-maker. Good comedy is what's wanted most in the movie industry, in television, in books, and in nightclubs (even singers are doing comedy lines). The public's appetite for comedy is so voracious that no fixed group of writers could ever satisfy it. We will always need more and more suppliers to meet the demand.

Comedy Changes Constantly

At one time, most comedians were the stand-up variety like Jack Benny. Then Lenny Bruce introduced a new and unique style. Bill Cosby does yet a different kind of comedy routine, and now Steve Martin has created a new craze.

Not all of us can write varying forms of comedy. I remember that when we were doing "The Carol Burnett Show," the writers of "Saturday Night Live" were quoted as saying that we were tired old writers who couldn't deliver fresh comedy any more (even though three of our staff were in their twenties). It was an interesting competition, because during my five years on the Burnett show, our staff collected three Emmies and the "Saturday Night Live" staff collected two. Their premise is valid, though. Every new style of comedy demands new writers who specialize in it.

Music, again, is a perfect analogy for comedy. It changes constantly—drastically in recent times. When hard rock was introduced, established musicians didn't convert: the new form brought with it an entire new generation of musicians.

The same happens with humor. Modern alterations in style open the door for a new breed of comedy writer.

Comedy Is Not Recyclable

Start telling a joke and people will hold up their hands and say, "I heard it." No one enjoys a comic story they've already heard. But no one does that to a singer. When Sinatra starts crooning, "I get no kick from champagne," no one in the audience says, "Don't sing that song. We've already heard it."

Comedy material is used up at an alarming rate. Once it's on the airwaves, it's gone. In fact, not only specific jokes and premises are lost, but other jokes that are too similar. Once I was writing a sitcom segment that had to do with a minstrel show. We had to change our storyline because Archie Bunker was doing an "All in the Family" episode in which he appeared in blackface.

With the enormous demand that all entertainment forms create, and since humor can't be re-used too soon or even copied too closely, fertile new comedy minds are always wanted to fill the bill.

A Constant Supply of Comedy Is Needed

Because you can't recycle comedy, people who buy it always need a fresh source. Comics, television hosts, and other comedy consumers work constantly yet can't use the same material, so they need someone who can always bring them fresh ideas. This creates a tremendous need for comedy minds.

Humor is the lifeblood that keeps careers alive. Entertainers can never be satisfied with what they have because in a short time it will be gone. They can only relax when they know there is an inexhaustible supply of neatly typed gags sliding under the office door. That's why we always need a steady influx of new comedy minds into the field.

Good Writers Move On

One of the most difficult problems of staffing a television show is finding good writers. This is not to say that competent writers aren't in Hollywood; they are. However, they progress so rapidly that when you want them, they've already been assigned somewhere else.

Writers advance to script consultants and story editors. Eventually they become producers and executive producers. This movement upward creates a vacuum that has to be filled with new talent.

New Writers Are Desirable

For comedy to be anything at all, it has to be fresh, enthusiastic, and exciting. Those are the qualities that new writers are infused with. Veteran writers are eminently competent, but (much as I hate to admit it) sometimes competence isn't enough. It has to be combined with flair—something unique, something different, something daring.

In all fairness, you sometimes pay a price for the individuality of eager young writers; sometimes their friskiness has to be tempered with the wisdom of the veterans. The National Football League would be a shambles if we allowed the players to run things. The coaches' know-how and discipline are necessary— yet what a sad team you would field if it comprised only 40- and 50-year-old coaches.

There's room in comedy for both dependable pros and zealous newcomers.

Begin Where You Are

We mentioned earlier that each successful writer has tried his or her own peculiar road to professionalism. Your story will be as distinctive and remarkable as each one of these. They all have one common feature, though: each began small.

Having writing heroes like Erma Bombeck or Woody Allen is commendable, but the beginner has to be careful not to try to parallel their success from the start. Today's name writers began with unlimited potential and no successes. Gradually, they converted their potential to fulfillment.

You must begin your career right where you are. I've often heard people say that they were going to try to come to Hollywood to "make it." That's fine, because that's probably where most television writers *do* make it. But they begin "making it" in their own home town.

Hollywood or New York is the ultimate goal for most writers, but you should establish a solid foundation in your craft before attacking either town. Arriving there too soon can be hazardous. It is much safer to have an extensive background and then extend it further to Hollywood or New York, rather than come to the big city as a raw beginner and risk being rejected completely. Many would-be successes never recover from that first rejection.

I had written for Phyllis Diller for several months, via telephone and mail, before I met her when she was appearing at the Latin Casino in Cherry Hill, New Jersey. I visited with her backstage between shows and the first thing she said to me was, "You're my best writer." I was thrilled and flattered and tried to capitalize on it: I said, "Then how come I'm not in Hollywood?" She answered, "Because you're not ready yet."

I never appreciated Phyllis's wisdom until I arrived in Hollywood. Naturally, my rookie year coincided with the first year of many other writers, and I could see the difference: those of us who had served an apprenticeship adapted more readily to the rigors of the weekly television deadline. We may not have been great writers, but we could alter our styles as we learned what TV needed. Many of those first-year writers with less background than I had haven't survived in television.

In an interview in the pages of *Round Table*, we asked Phyllis Diller what the biggest piece of advice she could give to young writers would be. She said, "Start right where you are. You offer to do it for nothing at first; you get paid a little if you can. But you have to prove yourself right where you are. Work banquets, send lines or monologues to local TV hosts, try to send out material regularly. Some say you have to go to Hollywood or New York to get into the business; I say, a trip around the world starts with the frst step, and the first step can only be taken in one spot—where you're standing right now."

In constructing your comedy writing career, you must build on small successes and transform them into larger ones. As Phyllis Diller advised, do free assignments for awhile. If you do well at these, you'll eventually be able to charge for them. That's taking one success and building it into a bigger one. I've already told you how I began doing master of ceremony chores where I worked. This was great training, though I received no salary for it. But it also provided excellent exposure, because people in the audience organized different functions outside the company. They had seen my work, and hired me—at a small fee—to entertain outside, too.

Almost every assignment, performed well, can multiply into other assignments. You'll also discover that the marquee value increases as you go along. That is to say, you might write for a local comic, then a not-too-well-known national comic, then a well-known comic, then perhaps television or the movies. The name value of the people you work for will increase the assignments you get—and the price you can command.

In beginning a professional comedy career, all the markets we mentioned in the previous chapter on part-time writing apply. The difference between a second-income career and a full-fledged pro career is simply a matter of degree. Some people decide that they are putting enough time and effort into their writing and are satisfied with the returns. But a would-be professional has to continue to grow.

In Part Three of this book we will discuss how to market your skills to build a professional career. The first step, though, is to know that it can be accomplished. Your efforts would be fruitless—and practically impossible to undertake—if you didn't think you could make it. The second step is to get to work and do it.

Again I offer a word of caution. Developing your skills may take much energy and certainly some time. A successful career requires, along with determination and toil, a bit of patience and understanding. Patience because you must allow time for your apprenticeship, and understanding because you must realize that even after you perfect your craft and become supremely accomplished, it will take time for buyers to realize that. You must not only become proficient, but you must prove to others that you are. Both take time.

The Way I Did It

It took me nine years from the time I committed to a writing career until I became a full-time professional. Simply to serve as an example, I'll list my progress here. My path is longer or shorter or otherwise different from that of other writers. Besides, there is no guarantee that the routes I took were most correct or most efficient. My narrative isn't included as your unalterable roadmap to success, but simply so you can see what someone else experienced—and perhaps know what you might encounter on your journey.

I thought I had the skills necessary for comedy and wanted to try it. I had no contacts or education in the field, but determined to give it a try anyway. My thinking was that it would be better to try and fail than to spend my later years saying, "I wish I had tried that when I was younger."

I began by taping all of Bob Hope's television monologues, then typing them out, studying them, and trying to duplicate the joke forms and styles with different topics. (Years later, when I got a call from Bob Hope to do some material for his Academy Awards performance, I wrote about 300 jokes; he used 10 of them on the telecast. When we talked later he said, "Your material looked like you'd been writing for me all your life." I said, "Bob, I have, only you didn't know about it.")

Magazines seemed an easy way to make a bit of money, so I began sending short filler jokes to several of them. With a lot of bookkeeping effort and some postage I could sell about $20 of comedy a month.

Simply as a comedy writing exercise, I captioned a book of baby pictures about the office where I worked. This led to my being invited to emcee several twenty-fifth anniversary and retirement parties. This was both speaking and writing training, but it had another fringe benefit: it was great exposure.

Someone who knew a local comedian mentioned to him that I was funny. He called and asked me to write some material for him. The material never sold, but he recommended me to a local television host who wanted a writer for his daytime show and a ghost writer for a humorous newspaper column. I did both, but again, never sold them. However, a visiting comic saw my material and my letterhead on the TV host's desk and called me to write for him. That led to a fairly lucrative contract that ran for six years.

During this time I was also visiting every nightclub in the Philadelphia area, calling on comics with copies of my most recent and brilliant gags. I made a few sales but mostly learned to cope with rejection. (The list of comedians who've turned me down is much longer than the ones who've hired me, but the ones who hired me paid more.)

Finally, I connected with and impressed Phyllis Diller. She prompted me to write more and better material. Eventually, she starred in a network TV show and hired me to do the monologues. This introduced me into television—and then one job led to the next.

It started small. It started in my home town. It progressed gradually. It was fun all along the way, and it was an education that served me well when I reached Hollywood.

Your journey is ahead of you, but the groundwork must be laid now. I envy you because it should be exciting and it should be fun.

Part One of this book was to help you overcome that first great obstacle . . . that little something inside you that whispers "I can't write." Yes you can. You know you have a sense of humor. and perseverance if you have managed to listen to me for this long.

Move on with me to Part Two where we'll convert your potential to product. As we say in the profession, "We'll put it on paper."

BUILDING YOUR SKILLS

If the desire to write is not accompanied by actual writing, then the desire is not to write.
—Hugh Prather

PART TWO

7 WRITE, READ, AND LISTEN

In Part Two of this book, you will take over as author. You will do much of the writing. It's guaranteed to be more fun than listening to me.

However, I can't let you rush to your typewriters and dismiss me that easily—yet. Allow me one more chapter to yap at you before unleashing all that pent-up creativity.

Before going any further, we should both understand our roles in this volume. This is definitely a "how-to" book, but it's not the complete, definitive, solitary bible on comedy. It has suggestions for beginning your comedy writing and some hints for sharpening your comedy skills, but the genius must come from you.

Comedy is such a subjective art that no one can or should have all the answers. If anyone ever did, comedy would no longer exist. To be anything at all, humor must be fresh and ever-changing, innovative and inventive. For your comedy to be bright it has to have a touch of *you* in there—certainly not all me.

A sign in the "Carol Burnett Show" producer's office read, "There are few good judges of comedy. And they don't agree." One day we had a serious discussion about that sign: some of the writers wanted to change it to read, "And *we* don't agree." That's how subjective comedy is.

And Now a Word from the Author

I hope the material in this book will help each reader. However, don't permit anything in here to stifle your creativity or your particular brand of zaniness. This volume doesn't have all the answers, simply a few of the things I've learned, from doing comedy and from listening to others do comedy. But the tips are available to help you get started and learn on your own.

This book is like the faint outlines on needlework patterns: it's there as a guide to get you started. The real artistry appears when you provide the stitchery.

Or better yet . . . the book is like a blasting cap. It will provide a spark; the explosion will come when you start generating your own comedy.

The lessons and the exercises in these pages are very fundamental. I wanted the book to be a step-by-step progression so that any reader, whether acquainted with comedy writing or not, could pick it up, follow it through, and be turning out humor with professional potential by the back cover.

At the same time, for the more experienced humorist, it can serve as a refresher course and reminder of the fundamentals of good comedy technique. Professional golfers sometimes have to remind themselves to keep their heads down or their wrists firm. Writers may also get a bit lax on good basic technique occasionally.

A good percentage of these pages is devoted to joke or gag writing and monologues. That's because I feel that comedy is based on jokes, the basic building blocks of humor. If you compiled a list of television's most successful comedy writers you'd find that most of them served an apprenticeship as gag writers. Norman Lear began by doing song parodies for nightclub comics, then wrote nightclub material for Martin and Lewis, Martha Raye, and others. Larry Gelbart did one-liners for Bob Hope. Ed Weinberger, who did the "Mary Tyler Moore Show" and now "Taxi," was a writer for Johnny Carson and Hope. Woody Allen's delightfully bizarre movies evolved from his experience as a gag writer for newspaper columnists—and, of course, later the material for his own stand-up comedy.

I don't mean to imply that stand-up, one-line routines are the only or even the best form of comedy. However, they do serve as a superb apprenticeship for all other varieties of comedy.

Picture yourself buying a racket, a can of tennis balls, a cute little dress, and walking out to a tennis pro and saying, "I want to be an attacking player. I'd like to hit the ball crosscourt most of the time, then close in to the net for the putaway shot." He'd say, "Fine, we'll work a few weeks on the backhand, then a couple weeks on the forehand, practice your volleys, your overhead, then work on your serve." You can't formulate any strategy until you get the basic strokes down. Then you'll discover your strengths and your faults—and your preferences. From that you'll be able to design your strategic game plan.

The same principles apply in music, dancing—almost any learning process. That's why we'll be devoting most of our time to the simpler humor forms, although we will discuss other writing after learning the "strokes."

This book can only be your third best teacher of comedy. The first two will always be your own writing, and reading and listening to other humorists.

The Best Way to Learn

Lillian Hellman once made a statement that may apply to much of this book. She said, "If I had to give young writers advice, I'd say don't listen to writers talking about writing."

On "The Carol Burnett Show" we once had a takeoff sketch on the popular show, "Kung Fu," in which Harvey Korman played the wise priest. He would expound long, complicated, almost unintelligible philosophical gibberish to his students and then always follow with, "Of course, that's only a theory." That's what you ought to remember when you listen to writers talking about writing: it's only a theory. The only real education you get is the practical one of writing and listening for audience response.

Some readers may be shy about sitting before a blank sheet of paper and turning out humor. They ask, "Should I write if I don't feel I'm ready?" Certainly. That's *how* you get ready.

How many people would be playing golf today if they refused to pick up a club until they knew they could shoot in the low 80s? If no one were willing to be a clumsy beginner, tennis courts would be deserted. No one would ever learn to play a musical instrument. You learn by doing—in fact, it's the *only* way to learn.

In working with newcomers, the best advice I can give (and the advice that is least followed) is to set a rigid quota and then stick to it. There's no need to make the quota unreasonably demanding; that sort of bravado only makes it easier to abandon. Make it simple on yourself. Start with three jokes a day or ten jokes a week, but *be faithful to it.*

Doing your own writing consistently and religiously will help in the following ways.

Improvement by Repetition

Remember our novice tennis player who played tennis for an hour every day? At the end of the year he won't be Bjorn Borg, or a tournament player, or even a real good club player, but he will be hitting the ball well. Even if he hits the ball wrong, he will be hitting it wrong consistently and with some confidence. I've played against unorthodox tennis players who do everything wrong except win. Repetition has to beget improvement.

Obviously, the optimum course is the combination of study with practice. With that mixture you improve correctly. However, study or training with no practical application is virtually worthless.

Gaining Confidence

"Having written" is the greatest proof that you can write again. Each time you do an exercise or assignment, you'll do one or two little things that delight you. You may not be entirely happy with the results but there will be a few gems in there to thrill you.

Going back to my favorite game, tennis, will help explain this point. I've played with folks who were having particularly bad days, but when they hit a rare good shot they'd say, "Ah, that shot made it worth getting up early." It's those brilliant moments that convince you you can do it.

As you work on your writing, you'll be faced with exercises or assignments that initially seem impossible. Yet you'll persevere and complete them, and the next time you face an "impossible" assignment it won't seem nearly as threatening, because you know you've completed similar ones before.

Many times I'm assigned to write jokes on topics that simply aren't funny, or I'm faced with deadlines that are unmeetable. But because I've faced those seemingly insurmountable odds before—and conquered them—I set my schedule, turn on my typewriter, and complete the chore.

Learning Strengths and Weaknesses

Hanging in my office is a cartoon from the Sunday papers that I had framed. It tells a beautiful story about writers. The cartoon strip is MacNelly's "Shoe." The first four blocks of the strip picture an owl (the Professor) seated at a typewriter, struggling to come up with an idea. The balloon above his head, though, is blank each time. Then, in the fifth frame, he strikes a great thought. In the balloon over his head is a glorious, ornate letter "A." Inspired with this stroke of genius, he taps his typewriter, looks at what he has just written—and it's just a simple, type-written letter "A." In the final frame he crumples up the paper and goes back to his empty thinking.

I keep this in my office to remind me that sometimes there's a tremendous gap between what we conceive and what we execute. It's easy to say, "I want to write the greatest love song of all time." It's difficult to deliver.

All writers discover their inadequacies sooner or later. William Saroyan said, "You write a hit play the same way you write a flop." Perhaps Robert Benchley best expressed this realization when he said, "It took me fifteen years to discover that I had no talent for writing, but I couldn't give it up because by that time I was too famous."

There will be certain types of writing you do very well, and some you have to struggle to complete. Some of your work will be excellent, some adequate. Only by writing and trying different types of composition can you learn which is for you and which isn't.

You'll also learn which you prefer and which you'd rather not be bothered with. You'll learn which skills you'll have to practice more to improve.

Developing New Skills

As you write faithfully, you will discover and experiment with new talents. Ralph Waldo Emerson said, "Good writing is a kind of skating which carries off the performer where he would not go."

For all these reasons, as a form of training and discipline I once determined to write a full screenplay. Good, bad, or indifferent, I vowed to complete a full story and 120 pages of dialogue. I was prepared for extremely tedious work.

But I discovered a fascinating phenomenon: I got into my work and was enthralled by the characters. I couldn't wait to get to the typewriter each morning to find out what they'd do and say. I found out that I loved dialogue writing.

Other writers detest doing dialogue. But only by trying it do you discover whether you like it or not.

The Second Best Way

Listening and reading is the second best practice for a comedy writer because it is almost effortless learning. I've already mentioned how I taped and typed out Bob Hope's monologues, studying them for form and style. But I listened to a lot of other comics too, and I read as much comedy and about comedy as I could. You absorb something from all this contact.

We absorb more than we're aware of from contact with the greats. Don Rickles is a very dynamic and very funny performer. I'm amazed at how much I see of him in so many other performers. If you ask if they're copying Rickles they deny it, and they're being truthful: they don't even realize they've adopted his style.

Listening to other humorists and reading comedy will help you learn in the following ways.

Learn What Does and Doesn't Work

There is only one good judge of comedy and that is the audience. All the rest of us are merely guessing.

I have written jokes that I've absolutely loved. I'd sit in the audience hardly able to contain my anticipation until the comic got to my treasured joke. Then when he'd deliver it, it would get nothing. I'd convince him to try it again—again nothing. I'd work with the comic on the delivery. He'd incorporate my suggestions—and be greeted with stony silence again. We'd give it one more shot for good measure, and then I'd have to admit that it was a great joke, but nobody loved it but me.

Other times the audience responds to a simple joke with big laughs. Neither the comic nor I can explain it, but we enjoy it.

Watching other performers work and noting what sort of response they get will clue you in to the pitfalls of certain types of humor. The audience will always be the master of the comedy, but you'll learn to become one of the good guessers.

Joke Forms

Not too long ago Bob Hope called me to do some material about Ronald Reagan once being a liberal Democrat. He said, "There should be something funny about that, you know . . . Ronald Reagan as a liberal Democrat. That's like (fill in the blanks)." That's a joke form.

Joke forms come in handy when you're trying to turn out a lot of material because the form itself stimulates the mind. It goads you into filling in the blanks.

Each comedian has his own collection of these. Johnny Carson has "It was so cold today that . . . " With Bob Hope we do definitions: "You all know what the trickle-down theory is, that's (fill in the blanks)." We do new meanings for initials. "With the new season going the way it is, NBC stands for (fill in the blanks)."

You'll absorb many of these simply by hearing other comedians, and they will serve you well in the future.

New Topics and Slants

A writer for Johnny Carson's "Tonight Show" told me that one of the most difficult parts of the assignment isn't the actual writing, but getting new topics each day. The work is relentless because it's five days a week, fifty-two weeks a year. Writing isn't always tough—but finding out what to write about can be.

Listening and reading will give you a whole new catalog of topics. You'll discover what humorists are talking about and what audiences are responding to.

You will also learn from other comics how to give a standard topic a fresh slant. By a slant, I mean the way you approach the humor in a given topic. For instance, while President Reagan was recovering from the assassination attempt, we were asked to do some comedy material about it. Now that's a very touchy subject; you don't want to say anything that might be considered in bad taste. So the first question is, how do you address such a topic? What slant do you use? Some writers spoke about how physically uncomfortable it must be for a President to be in the hospital.

> *"Ronald Reagan doesn't like it in the*
> *hospital. It's hard to take jelly beans*
> *intravenously."*

Other writers kidded about the jokes the President cracked while he was hospitalized.

> *"Ronald Reagan has been doing nothing*
> *but telling jokes. The theory is that*
> *the bullet passed through Henny Youngman."*

There is any number of slants or approaches you can take to a given topic, so it pays to learn as many as you can. It will not only help you on the particular topic, but can help you find an approach for topics that you may have to work on later.

Different Styles

The one thing that sets good comics apart from bad or mediocre ones is that good comics have a definite style—a definable character. Bill Cosby has some hilarious lines in his act. Alan King can't use them. Bill Cosby can't use any of King's material. I just selected these names randomly, but the same principle applies to almost any top-notch comics. Their material isn't interchangeable because their styles and characters are unique.

Style and characterization are a larger part of comedy than most people realize. When I write for various comedians, I automatically adopt their speech patterns. When I worked for Jim Nabors I threw a lot of "gollies" around the dinner table. I spent a year with Bill Cosby and walked around the house doing his particular rhythms of speech. I worked for Carol Burnett for five years and started dressing like her. (That's all been worked out, and thankfully, I'm down to doing it only on weekends now.)

It will serve you well to become acquainted with as many different styles as you can.

How to Blend Styles

By exposing yourself to varied styles, you will begin subconsciously—or consciously—to adopt some of them. You'll start with a bit of George Carlin, a sprinkling of Rodney Dangerfield, a dash of Joannie Rivers, with some Steve Martin for flavor. You'll begin to fashion a new style—your own.

There's nothing wrong with borrowing from the greats. Every comic you see has a touch of some great comic in him. Johnny Carson admits that Jack Benny influenced his style. Woody Allen did a movie for the Film Society that shows how much his movie characterization was influenced by Bob Hope.

My wife, my mother-in-law, and my wife's grandmother all make spaghetti sauce from the same recipe. All of them are delicious and all of them are different. Why? Because each one puts a bit of her own personality into the recipe.

By being aware of different styles, you'll learn all the ingredients you can use in your own unique comedic recipe.

Inspiration

Listening to other humorists can be a stimulus to get you to your typewriter. When I was a youngster, I'd watch my brother play high school football on Sunday afternoons. The first thing I wanted to do when I got home was get a bunch of guys and play two-hand touch. Watching that much football made me want to get out and play. So, when you see or read some excellent comedy, it might inspire you to try the same.

The big-time comics can add something intangible to your work, too. They instill something in you that makes you work better and harder. One of the Hope writers told me that when he hits a writer's block and can't think of anything funny, he puts on a tape of an earlier Bob Hope monologue, listens for a while, and goes back to the typewriter with renewed vigor.

Now, as I promised at the beginning of this chapter, we're going to get you writing. Find some blank paper, a pencil, and turn the page.

8 COMEDY WRITING EXERCISES

In Chapter 3 we discussed several comedy-writing skills. Many of these, though, involved preparatory work. When it comes to the actual writing of comedy, three skills become paramount. They are:

Recognizing relationships and ironies
Visualization and imagery
Facility with words

It's easy to categorize these skills and list them separately, but in practice they are intertwined; in the creative process you employ them all as one.

We're back to dissecting our beleaguered frog again. You can study his cardiovascular system to see how it operates and what functions it performs; you can investigate the workings of his nervous system for its particular purpose. But if they're to work properly they cannot be detached. The heart cannot beat without the signals from the nervous system; the nerves cannot operate without blood supplied through the circulatory system.

We will consider these skills separately, but be careful—you might find it cumbersome and fruitless to try to create comedy by using them apart from one another. Be inventive, using all of them, and let your meanderings lead you where they may.

Relationships and Ironies

Most comedy, as I've stated before, is a combination of two or more ideas: it's the relationship of these ideas that generates the humor. Some ideas are very similar; some are quite different. Some appear to be different, but are really the same, and vice versa. The skillful humorist will discover these relationships.

> *"Any time you see a man open a car door*
> *for his wife, either the car is new*
> *or the wife is."*

That's a simple little statement, but what a delightful observation. Obviously, the joke stands on its own. Any joke that needs an explanation has something lacking. But for our discussion, we might look deeper into it.

The comedy basically comes from the fact that the statement is for the most part true. Married men get lax about the nicety of opening car doors for their spouses. But a new car brings out the macho in a man. It fills him with masculine pride and can unconsciously goad him into opening the door for his "bride." It's a beautiful little joke because the observation is recognizable, but is expressed unusually tightly. It took a creative humorist to do that.

> *"Have you ever noticed how those Jehovah's*
> *Witnesses are always at your door? Hey,*
> *I got a great idea. Why don't we let*
> *them deliver the mail?"*

Again, here is a delightful observation that no one quite ever made before. A comedian named Gallagher included this in his act. It's a concise little gag, but it says much because the relationship and the irony not only are recognized, but beautifully expressed.

Visualization and Imagery

Most jokes are pictures. That is to say, with words we create an image in the listener's mind. The distortion or the ridiculousness of that image generates the humor. That's why puns have the reputation as the lowest form of humor. I have worked with clients who refuse to buy any gag that depends on pure word-play. Words are powerful tools of the humorist—as we'll see in the following section—but comedy that depends on word-play alone often does not create a graphic image in the mind of the listener; therefore it's usually not as funny—clever, maybe, but not funny.

This is also why humor is so subjective. Some people love a particular joke or story; others won't appreciate it at all, because the image is different in each person's mind. The joke is not the collection of words; it's the scene that appears in the listener's mind as a result of those words. Skillful use of words will create a stronger image, but it is usually the image that produces the humor.

Television writers often discuss TV vs. radio. Popular radio shows used to run for lifetimes compared to the five-or six-year spans of successful television shows. One theory is that radio had a greater longevity because it was constantly changing to suit each listener's taste. Not that the shows themselves changed, but the listener did. There were no sets, there were no faces. Everything existed only in the minds of the listeners. Each person painted his own image of Ellery Queen in his mind. If that listener changed his preferences, he could change Ellery Queen also. Television doesn't permit that.

The mind can be extremely elastic, which is an aid to humorists. Our minds easily accept distortions and impossibilities. Think back to some of the dreams you've had: in them you wander from place to place with no trouble. People change before your very eyes. The situations become so bizarre that you can't even relate them coherently, yet during the dream your intellect accepts every outlandish occurrence without questioning it.

Many times, in writing sketches for television, other writers or I describe funny moves the performers are to carry out. But when we get to rehearsal, we discover the moves are physically impossible—for example, a one-armed man is to hold his adversary against the wall and draw his sword. With what? Yet in the writer's mind these moves are perfectly feasible.

Humorists can often use the mind's flexibility to advantage.

Below are some random lines I have written about Phyllis Diller's (fictitious) mother-in-law. In her act, Phyllis calls her Moby Dick.

> *"Talk about fat people, you ought to*
> *see my mother-in-law. She's so big,*
> *she has two ZIP codes.*

> *"The first time I met her Fang said,*
> *'Who does Mom remind you of?' I said,*
> *'North Dakota.'*

> *"I don't know what her measurements*
> *are. We haven't had her surveyed yet.*

> *"She's a nice woman, though. Nicest*
> *three acres of flesh I've ever met.*

> *"She gave me one of her old dresses.*
> *I plan to have it starched and made*
> *into a summer home.*

> *"Once she was coming to visit us, but*
> *I didn't want her staying with us. I*
> *made reservations for her at a motel.*
> *She stayed in Cabins 13, 14, and 15.*

> *"When you get on an elevator with her,*
> *you better be going down.*

> *"Once she got on a bus and six men got*
> *up and offered her their seat. If two*
> *more had done it, she could have accepted."*

Disregarding the comic value of these lines, notice the liberties I took with imagery. First the lady is the size of two ZIP codes, then she becomes as large as a state. I define her as three acres and the mind accepts that. In another line she is no longer the size of North Dakota, only the size of a small house. She requires three motel rooms, but can get on an elevator and a bus.

My descriptions of Moby Dick would hardly be acceptable evidence in court, but the adaptability of our minds allows me to have some fun—create some comedy—with exaggerated and distorted images of this lady.

Yet another mental phenomenon can be used advantageously by comedy writers: audiences tend to fill in any gaps. Our minds continue an image on to its natural conclusion and supply anything that might be missing. It's this peculiarity that makes stage magic work. Magicians show an audience only so much— the audience assumes the rest. The key to the trick is generally where that assumption is made. People say, "I know he put the coin in his right hand. I saw it there." They really didn't; they just assumed it should be there and so their minds told them they "saw" it there.

Humorists manipulate this tendency by leading an audience's thinking in one direction and then suddenly changing that direction. Comedy depends on the unexpected. (Remember, no one enjoys hearing a joke they've already heard.) I've even seen a joke diagrammed like this:

That indicates a thought continuing along in a certain direction and abruptly changing direction. The author explained that that was what evoked laughter in the classic example of a man slipping on a banana peel: he's walking contentedly on his way. All of us assume he will continue to walk merrily along that same way. Suddenly, he is abruptly upended. It may be a tremendous over-simplification, but the principle applies.

W.C. Fields said that real comedy was when you expected something to break and it only bent.

As humorists, we can take advantage of people's thinking patterns. The following story illustrates this very well:

> "Once I was in a hotel and the walls
> were kind of thin. The couple in the
> next room came home very late and were
> talking kind of loud. So I quickly rushed
> and got a glass and held it to the wall.
> I heard her say to him, 'Take off my
> dress.' Then she said, 'Take off
> my slip.' Then she said, 'Take off my

> *bra.' Then she said, 'If I ever catch*
> *you wearing them again, I'll divorce you.' "*

Notice how your thoughts were led in one direction, then abruptly changed. The rug was pulled out from under your mind.

This doesn't apply only in longish stories either. One Bob Hope joke uses this same strategy. He told it on a day when the United States had just launched another in a series of unsuccessful attempts to get our space program operable.

> *"I guess you've heard the good news*
> *from Cape Canaveral. The United States*
> *just launched another submarine."*

Your mind is going in one direction right up until the last word of the joke.

Facility with Words

For the most part, words are the medium we use to convey our witty creations. There are funny pantomimists, of course, and some jokes are enhanced by facial expression or inventive stage business. Nonetheless, most humor is conveyed by words.

Words have a playfulness all their own. Norm Crosby has built a hilarious act out of malapropisms; he has found incredibly clever ways to misuse words. He might say, "An ounce of perversion is worth a pound of cure." And Archie Bunker over the years has found ways to change words just enough so that they almost excuse his bigotry.

Some folks can misuse phrases so that their meaning is conveyed—just about. Sam Goldwyn had so many that they became known as "Goldwynisms." I think we all know what he meant when he said, "Oral contracts aren't worth the paper they're written on." And what could be more definitive than to say about someone, "I never liked him and I probably always will."

One of my favorite misusages was uttered by my tennis partner while we were being badly beaten in a match. "Okay," he said to me, "we've got them right where they want us."

Word jokes have fallen into disrepute with the axiom about puns being the lowest form of humor. But it simply isn't true;

puns can be really inspired at times. Samuel Johnson once boasted to his drinking companions that he could instantaneously compose a pun on any subject. "The King," someone volunteered. Johnson replied, "The King, sir, is not a subject."

I know I said earlier that puns weren't funny; you don't have to start paging backwards now. That was when we talked about visualization and imagery. The point I was making then and still maintain is that puns that depend *totally* on word-play generally aren't funny. However, some puns can create a funny image and produce a good joke. Bob Hope's monologue featured one like that on a recent Christmas show. President Reagan was annoyed by some statements that his economic advisor David Stockman had made. The line went:

> "Ronald Reagan is ready for Christmas.
> His Stockman is hung by the chimney
> with care."

The word-play of substituting "Stockman" for "stocking" also produces an image of the poor gentleman hanging forlornly by the President's fireplace.

Woody Allen is also a clever punster; here's one that's a classic—it not only got many laughs, it also got him sued. A news story had broken about his ex-wife being molested. Allen said, "She claims she was violated. Knowing my ex-wife, it wasn't a moving violation."

There is hardly any word you can think of that doesn't have at least one other meaning—most have several. Once I was trying to disprove this statement and a word I came up with that could have no possible other meaning was "butterfly": it can only mean an insect. But as soon as I said that, the obvious other meaning popped into my head. Literally, it can denote a dairy product that flies.

Try it yourself. Think of a word or two and almost immediately you'll discover another meaning for each word. Take an ordinary word like "house." As you read it, you instantly visualize what I mean by that word—but do you? Which of the following meanings of "house" was I trying to convey:

a dwelling

> a brothel
> a legislature
> an audience
> the management of a gambling casino
> a business

A good humor writer, with effort and practice, can learn to use the idiosyncrasies of the language to good advantage.

Following are eight comedy writing exercises that will help you develop your writing skills. Some favor language skills, others visualization, but, for the reasons we discussed earlier, no attempt is made to differentiate them. You do yourself no favor by separating the skills. If an exercise features language, the best jokes will be those that not only use words cleverly, but that also conjure up a humorous image and present an ironic observation.

Have fun with these exercises. They're not homework assignments or chores. They're fun, provocative excursions into the creation of comedy.

(If you choose, you can attack these assignments with a purpose. As we discussed in Chapter 4, comedy writing can be practical. With a bit of ingenuity on your part, many of these exercises can become keepsakes.)

Work at them. The tendency among comedy writers is to quit too soon. You can just treat these exercises lightly and skim the surface, or you can put in a little more effort and surprise yourself with the results. If you apply yourself to these, it will be good training for the discipline you'll need to write good comedy material later on.

Exercise One:

Step 1. Collect 50 jokes from any source. They can all come from a single joke book, they can be fillers from a magazine, or just some favorite jokes that you remember other comedians delivering on records or television. The only criterion is that these should be gags you particularly like. Don't just go to a joke book and jot down numbers 1 to 50.

Step 2. Type or print these jokes on a piece of paper and analyze them. List next to them what you think makes them funny and what form they take. Are they word jokes, or do you laugh because they create a funny image in your mind? Or both? You don't have to be too technical, just jot down the reason you like each gag.

This exercise serves several purposes. You'll familiarize yourself with the style and the form of some great jokes, and you'll begin to understand your own likes and dislikes and generate your own style of writing.

You'll see the different forms that gags can take. You'll learn what your own tastes are in comedy, and consequently the type of comedy that you probably can write best.

Another important aspect of collecting a series of jokes you particularly like is that they will be an inspiration to you. Seeing expert craftsmanship can motivate you to simulate it.

This collection will also serve as a nice reference. As we discuss different types and forms of jokes later in the book, you can refer to your own compilation for examples.

Exercise Two:

Step 1. Make a list of ten adjectives that you might use in comedy writing. These should be very simple, ordinary words.

Step 2. For each word on your list, compile a grouping of other words or symbols that can represent the original.

As an example, suppose we select the adjective "white." Some symbols or other words that convey the same meaning might be:

> movie screen
> Good Humor man
> wedding dress
> purity
> snowman
> nurse

blank pages
paleness
ghost
bedsheets

This exercise is practice in discovering the relationship between words or facts. It will help you to become skilled at finding a word or phrase that might substitute for the most obvious word in your joke.

Many jokes are too obvious or too direct. These gags can be improved by substituting a word or a phrase that implies the meaning rather than stating it directly.

It might be a good idea right now to refer back to your joke collection from Exercise One to see how many of your jokes employ this device.

Remember Phyllis Diller's joke about her mother-in-law, Moby Dick? "This woman is so huge that when she wears a white dress, we show movies on her."

That's a case where the related idea created a joke, but the wording implied the meaning rather than stating it. A weaker joke would have been, "When she wears a white dress, she looks like a movie screen."

Many times you can use the symbolism to completely replace the meaning. In the last joke, we used the word "white" and a symbolic meaning along with it. Suppose, though, you meet a gentleman who is dressed in a white suit. You might say, "If I stick a carrot on your nose and a broomstick under your arm, will you stand on the front lawn for my kids?"

In this case, you're implying that he is wearing so much white that he looks like a snowman, but you never actually say it.

Exercise Three:

Step 1. Collect a series of at least 30 unusual photos. They can be interesting baby photos, old movie stills, strange photos like those featured sometimes in photography magazines, or any other source you might discover.

The photos should be unusual in some way, so I wouldn't recommend family snapshots. (Unless you come from a stranger family than I do.)

Step 2. Write humorous captions for the photographs.

In writing the captions, try to create new meanings for your photos, rather than just commenting on the action depicted in them.

We sometimes write jokes that are too direct or too obvious: the same fault creeps into captioning. We tend to comment on the obvious—the photograph itself. It will be worth the effort to find a different meaning in your captioning.

For example, suppose your baby photo shows an infant with baby food all around his mouth. One caption might read, "Boy, do I hate spinach," or "That's the last time I ever let that lady feed me." Both of these still depict a child with food all over his mouth.

However, a caption like, "That's the last time I let my wife buy me spinach-flavored shaving cream," changes the action in the photo. It's no longer a baby, but a man whose wife bought him some exotic shaving paraphernalia.

If the photo lends itself to this, it might even be captioned with, "Tell me the truth, Myrtle. Do I look like Clark Gable in a moustache?"

Undeniably, some hilarious captions can be written directly about the activity in the photograph, but since avoiding the obvious is so important in comedy writing, I urge you to try to generate a new meaning for each picture you caption.

And remember, you can put this exercise to practical use by captioning the pictures for the gang at the office, the family, a friend, or whomever.

Exercise Four:

Step 1. Collect at least 25 cartoons that you especially like. You can find these in newspapers or magazines.

Step 2. Recaption the cartoons with lines of your own. You don't have to limit yourself to one caption for each cartoon. Do a few.

This exercise is similar to Exercise Three, except in this case, you can't deny the activity in the drawing. It exists as the straight line, and you'll learn to use it as a springboard to other jokes. No matter how great the cartoon is, there's no guarantee that the caption already on it is the only one that can be written, or even the best one.

You might paraphrase the original caption, improving the wording, or you might go for a whole new angle on the joke. The caption you write may even have nothing to do with the original. Don't limit yourself.

A valuable lesson of this exercise is that you'll learn not to quit on a joke too soon. The cartoon has been well executed, purchased, and printed by a newspaper or magazine. The tendency is to feel that it cannot be improved. However, keep trying. You might surprise yourself. The important thing is to resist the temptation to surrender on it.

Many times you will be faced with a topic that seems to have nothing inherently funny in it. By perseverance, you'll find it.

Exercise Five:

Step 1. Create at least 25 cartoons of your own, using common items as your "characters." These items can be simple geometric shapes, household items, objects that exist where you work, fruits and nuts, or whatever. (I know this sounds bizarre now, but I'll explain it more in the example.)

Step 2. Caption your creations.

The scenes that you create should be set up in your mind in such a way that they could actually be photographed or drawn. You needn't go to the trouble or expense, but the perspective should be real enough to translate to an actual photograph.

The following examples—using food as "characters"—should make this exercise clearer.

Picture: Two soft pretzels. One without mustard, and one covered with it. *Caption:* You're a nice girl, Mabel. It's just that you use too much make-up.

Picture: A peach next to a plum. *Caption:* I don't care how late we are. You're not leaving this house until you've shaved.

In another exercise that we labeled "Nicotine Nifties," we used only tobacco and smoking accessories.

Picture: Seven cigarettes standing in a line. One of them is a burned-out and crushed cigarette butt. *Caption:* All right, which of you men was off limits last night?

Doing a series of gags using geometric figures prompted the following:

Picture:

Caption: All right, Orville, the guests have gone. You can take off that silly lampshade now.

This is similar to Exercise Three, except here you have the thrill of beginning from scratch. You literally have the entire universe to choose from.

The following is an exercise that at first glance seems like a real toughie, but if you get into it and work at it—and allow others to work with you on it—you'll find that pretty soon you'll be bombarded with terrific jokes from people who never thought they could write a funny line before.

I guarantee you'll have fun with it.

Exercise Six:

Step 1. Write 101 "Tom Swifties." A "Tom Swiftie" is a joke that uses a slightly different double meaning for an adverb. The Tom Swift series of children's books used this sentence structure liberally, and now we're going to turn this sentence structure into gags.

Example: "I dove into the pool and knocked all my teeth out," he explained shallowly. Obviously here we have the double meaning of the word "shallow."

You can get even more bizarre and give whole new meanings to the words you feature.

Example: "What this team needs is a good home run hitter,"

the manager said ruthlessly.

In that one, "ruthlessly" means without Babe Ruth. But you can become even more exotic and creative in playing with words.

Example: "Your dog tore the back out of my trousers," the man said deceitfully. Here "deceitfully" means "de-seat-fully."

The only rule is that the adverbs end in "-ly". Other than that, just be creative, crazy, and have some fun.

Obviously, this exercise will develop your skill with words.

Should you think that 101 is too many and a totally impossible quota, I've listed my 101. (Please don't judge my gag-writing abilities by this sampling. They were done in one evening, purely to exercise my word-making mechanism, and to serve as an example and inspiration for the readers of this book. Notice, also, how a good joke writer protects himself.) I advise that you try your own and keep going until you're convinced that you can't create any more. Only then should you turn to the examples on the following pages, to convince yourself that it can be done.

101 Tom Swifties

1. "Do you think this print is too dark?" the printer asked boldly.

2. "I suppose this means you've won the sword fight," he said pointedly.

3. "What kind of cheese is this?" he asked sharply.

4. "They have a funny name for streets in France," he said ruefully.

5. "My favorite singers are Ray Charles and Stevie Wonder," he proclaimed blindly.

6. "My brother and I were Siamese twins at one time," he shouted half-heartedly.

7. "I have a bigger piano than this," he exclaimed grandly.

8. "I've finally won the Academy Award," said Henry fondly.

9. "The smog is really bad today," he cried breathlessly.

10. "I'm not staying in this scary house overnight," he said hauntingly.

11. "I'm simply not a nice girl," she whispered tartly.

12. "I'll fix that blown fuse with this penny," he said glowingly.

13. "I'm sorry, Rocky, but the Governor refused to pardon you," he said shockingly.

14. "I've gained over fifty pounds," he explained roundly.

15. "You have diabetes," the doctor said sweetly.

16. "We're going to have to operate," the medic said cuttingly.

17. "I'll let my company pick up the check," the salesman offered firmly.

18. "I can't march any more," the soldier said haltingly.

19. "Then you'll spend the weekend on the base," his sergeant said impassively.

20. "Camping out in the woods is fun," the family said intensely.

21. "I've been asked to sing carols with the school choir," the girl said gleefully.

22. "Can you read music?" the choirmaster asked notably.

23. "I play music every Sunday for my church," she replied organically.

24. "Big deal," the choirmaster responded shufflingly.

25. "Why, you've shot me," Jesse James said holily.

26. "I'd like the printing in this book to be a little bigger," the author stated boldly.

27. "This chicken is burned again," the husband bellowed heatedly.

28. "I forgot to mail the check to the electric company," the man said delightedly.

29. "All right, who stole my thermal underwear?" the hunter shouted coldly.

30. "It wasn't me," his hunting partner lied warmly.

31. "But I assure you my intentions are honorable," her boyfriend pleaded gropingly.

32. "You other six dwarfs can stay up if you want to, but I'm going to bed," he pronounced sleepily.

33. "Don't ever sneeze when you've got nails in your mouth," the carpenter's assistant said tactfully.

34. "I'll connect this doo-hickey to the thing-a-mabob and that'll stop the clanging in the watchamacallit and that'll cost you $200," the workman pronounced mechanically.

35. "Some day my face will be on Mount Rushmore, too," the man exclaimed stonily.

36. "I did not do that to your lawn," the gentleman said doggedly.

37. "The robbers took my wallet and my trousers," the victim said briefly.

38. "There are too many logs and ashes in your fireplace," the woman said gratefully.

39. "I'm too tired to put icing on one more cake," the baker said glazedly.

40. "I am not a crook," Mr. Nixon said resignedly.

41. "How many times do I have to tell you—no starch!" the customer said stiffly.

42. "I never have liked Thanksgiving Day," the turkey said stuffily.

43. "But Doctor, you promised the Pill would work," the woman complained expectantly.

44. "But I thought you were on the Pill," the man said kiddingly.

45. "If you live here, you'll never be bothered by earthquakes," the agent explained faultlessly.

46. "I dance at a topless club," the girl said barely.

47. "I dance at a bottomless club," another said cheekily.

48. "And I work for the vice squad," the officer said arrestingly.

49. "I'm going to kill Able," his brother said cannily.

50. "When Cain swings at me, I'll duck," said his brother ably.

51. "And I'm going to tempt Adam," said the woman evilly.

52. "I wish I had left my wife home," Lot stated saltily.

53. "There's a short in my electric toothbrush," the woman screamed frothily.

54. "I can't decide whether to become a Moose, an Elk, or a Lion," the man said gamely.

55. "I've just devoured the Princess of Monaco," the dragon exclaimed gracefully.

56. "I don't know what those silly bushes out there in the desert are called," the cowboy stated sagely.

57. "I'm sorry, soldiers, but our Christmas Show has been cancelled," the General announced hopelessly.

58. "I couldn't help but overhear your conversation," the man pronounced eerily.

59. "I've just swallowed an entire window," the woman shouted painfully.

60. "Oh, I can't kick," the man answered lamely.

61. "But I can't perform a transplant now," Dr. Christian Barnard answered heartlessly.

62. "The shark tore off one half of my body," the man said decidedly.

63. "Don't kiss me again until after you've shaved," she scolded abrasively.

64. "You should never try to force-feed a lion," the trainer said off-handedly.

65. "I'll bring your coffee right away, sir," the secretary said perkily.

66. "I'm going to put some sugar topping on that cake," Betty Crocker said icily.

67. "Oh no, I'm standing in quicksand," the woman shouted defeatedly.

68. "Doctor, I keep thinking I'm a gun," the patient declared repeatedly.

69. "Someone stole my ept," the child screamed ineptly.

70. "Help, I'm trapped in the hall of mirrors," the youngster yelled reflectively.

71. "I should never have worn my golf shoes in a rubber raft," the man moaned deflatingly.

72. "I'm not a member of any organized political party," the man declared democratically.

73. "There, I've given the baby her bottle," the husband stated decryingly.

74. "There must be some meaning to this story," Aesop exclaimed morally.

75. "Help, I can't swim," the man shouted deeply.

76. "I'll help you," Mark Spitz replied swimmingly.

77. "Not if I get there first," the shark countered bitingly.

78. "Have a nice hunting trip and I hope you bag something," the wife said dearly.

79. "I'm afraid you've flunked the test," the professor said degradingly.

80. "It appears this road doesn't lead out of the forest after all," the troop leader said densely.

81. "This bunion will have to be removed," the doctor stated callously.

82. "I'm sorry the plastic surgery was a failure," the doctor said defacingly.

83. "I'll take this bra," the customer said upliftingly.

84. "I think I'd like to wear a robe in all my movies," Charlton Heston said prophetically.

85. "Why, that chicken has no beak," the man pronounced impeccably.

86. "Mr. Geppetto, how come the other kids keep carving their initials in my thigh?" Pinocchio queried woodenly.

87. "I was not born; I was baked in an oven," the strange man declared gingerly.

88. "I'd like a pair of shoes that I never have to shine," the customer said patently.

89. "Yes, I'm a hooker, but you're my one millionth customer," the woman said freely.

90. "I think I'll date every sailor I see tonight," the woman said fleetingly.

91. "Are you going to Scarborough Fair? Parsley, sage, rosemary, and thyme," the vocalist sang spicily.

92. "Maybe I should wear those stockings that also give your legs support," the woman said supp-hosedly.

93. "I don't like this offer the company made to me," the union leader said strikingly.

94. "I'm only a cartoon character and I can always be erased," Mickey Mouse said self-effacingly.

95. "Hey, bartender, this beer has no foam," the patron yelled light-headedly.

96. "I try to entertain a different dwarf each evening," Snow White said weekly.

97. "All right, I'll dress in a tuxedo, but I'm still going to wear my tennis shoes," Woody Allen said sneakily.

98. "I'll watch the football game when I'm finished spreading this fertilizer," the man said posthumously.

99. "I play a 14-foot-tall clown in the circus," the performer said stiltedly.

100. "Welcome to the annual teetotalers awards banquet," the emcee began drily.

101. "I've read all 101 of these Tom Swifties," the reader said (check one) ☐ humorlessly, ☐ laughingly.

Exercise Seven:

Step 1. Select a topic that you would like to write jokes about. It can be either a general subject or a topical subject chosen from the headlines of the day.

Step 2. Research your selected topic and write a series of 20 factual statements about it. The sentences should not be comic in any way, nor should you attempt to make them humorous. Simply list truthful statements about your subject. If you choose a statement from the newspapers, read through the article and list several of the sentences. "The price of stamps rose to 20 cents today." "The Postmaster General announced the additional cost was necessary to improve the efficiency of the mails." Should your topic be of a general nature, you can still find factual sentences. "My husband sleeps on the couch every night after dinner." "He snores through my favorite TV programs."

Step 3. Treat each of your factual statements as the set-up for your punchline, or as the "picture" that you are going to caption the same way you captioned the photographs earlier. When you're finished, you'll have 20 or more jokes. (You don't have to limit yourself to one caption per set-up.)

Examples: "The price of stamps rose to 20 cents today. That settles it. I'm sending my Christmas cards out in the form of a chain letter this year."

"The Postmaster General announced the additional cost was necessary to improve the efficiency of the mails. Baloney. The best way to speed up the mails is to mail the postal workers their paychecks."

This exercise helps you learn how to analyze a topic in order to generate ideas for jokes. It also helps you to see how jokes are formed. In many cases a good gag is simply a caption for a factual statement.

Exercise Eight:

Step 1. Make a list of 50 nouns. You can get a little bizarre here because these words are going to be used for graphic jokes. You may want to pick the funniest nouns you can think of.

Step 2. Divide the list into two groups. The first should contain 20 nouns and the second 30.

Step 3. Go down the first list and make each word the subject of your joke—combining it, however, with one of the words from the second list to make the punchline of your joke.

Example:

1. Fruitcake	21. Goat
2. Garbage truck	22. Peanut butter
3. Water buffalo	23. Floor wax
4. Shortstop	24. Jockey shorts
5. Odor eaters	25. Cross-your-heart bra
etc.	etc.

Example: "My grandmother made a fruitcake out of floor wax. When my grandfather ate it, it killed him, but he did have a fine finish."

This is a tough exercise that will teach you that writing jokes is not always easy. More importantly, it will show you that a joke is made up of two separate ideas; it's the combination of these ideas that often leads to bizarre comedy.

This exercise is good practice in looking for the attributes of each topic and rolling them through your head until you find that comic combination. In combining these two unconnected items you're forced to search for several characteristics of each item. You must ask yourself what does floor wax do? What is it good for? What are its bad qualities? When do people use it? And similar questions. Eventually you will find a characteristic of each noun that will blend together in some way to form the joke.

Later we'll find that this skill will be especially useful in finding blend lines for a comedy monologue. When you want to switch from subtopic A to subtopic B, it's nice to find a joke that combines one element of each.

THE VALUE OF MONOLOGUES

In Chapter 7 we discussed the joke as the basic building block of humor, just as the brick is the basic building block in construction. However utilitarian it is, though, no one can live in a brick. It has to be bonded together with other bricks in some sort of predesigned form to create a useful structure. The same is true of comedy.

Jokes have to be coupled together with continuity and structure to fashion a practical humorous piece. This is a monologue.

Don't think that this minimizes the joke. Bricks or stones do not a cathedral make—but just try to build one without them. Even well-manufactured bricks are not particularly attractive piled helter-skelter on an empty lot, but those same bricks rearranged into an elegantly designed structure take on a new beauty.

In the same way, well-written gags, blended masterfully into a well-conceived routine, take on more mirth.

Certainly single jokes have their place. Magazines looking for fillers, cartoonists, and greeting card companies all buy single gags. And beginning with the next chapter, you're going to write some jokes. However, I recommend that you write a full routine rather than isolated jokes. Let's investigate some of the more important reasons why it's advantageous for you to write in the monologue form.

Good Showcase

The beginning writer should be building up a showcase portfolio of his material. Opportunity can knock at any time and when you open the door, you'd darn well better have some material to display.

I have worked with many novice writers. As I've mentioned before, my first advice is to set a quota each week, and meet it. Since the advice is rarely followed, when I receive calls from producers looking for new one-liner writers for various television shows, there is no way that I can recommend these novices—I haven't seen enough to prove their talent and they have nothing to show producers anyway.

That's why a portfolio is so important: you have to have something tangible to show a producer. When you compile that portfolio, though, completed monologues are much more valuable than a collection of isolated jokes, regardless of how good the jokes are.

Disconnected gags are difficult to read. All the jokes in Erma Bombeck's bestselling books, for instance, are organized into essays. How many people do you think would read a book of collected jokes from cover to cover? I bet that hardly anyone ever has. It's almost impossible because reading single gags is tiring. Reading a collection of Art Buchwald's or Erma Bombeck's essays is exhilarating; struggling through an assortment of disjointed one-liners is exhausting. If you're presenting your work to a prospective buyer, which would you prefer he have?

Jokes also suffer in comparison to each other when they are simply listed in catalog form. There is no way all your gags can be of equal value; consequently, the good ones stand out and make the others look worse than they really are. They're just standing there for inspection like people in a police line-up. All their flaws are exposed to the reader's critical eye, which gets more critical as he gets more and more tired of reading them.

Let's go back to our building block analogy. No one looks at a completed structure and criticizes individual bricks or stones. The eye takes on the finished form and judges the separate components in relationship to the whole.

Jokes Are Enhanced

A well-organized routine not only hides the weaknesses of some jokes, it can actually make jokes funnier. Comedian Slappy White used to tell this story in his nightclub act:

> *"There was this man who died and went*
> *to heaven. When he got there, he discovered*
> *there were only two people there—the*
> *Lord and George Washington. The man*
> *said, 'I don't understand it. Where*
> *are all the people?' The Lord said,*
> *'They're down below. Come here and I'll*
> *show you.' Sure enough the Lord opened*
> *up a hole in the sky and the man looked*
> *down below. There were people singing*
> *and dancing. A big band was playing*
> *and they were having a great time. The*
> *man said, 'How come they're singing*
> *and dancing down there? They got a big*
> *band playing and everything, and there's*
> *nothing going on up here?' The Lord*
> *said, 'You don't think I'm gonna book*
> *a big band for two people, do you?' "*

Slappy told this story exquisitely and it always got a big laugh. While the laughter was continuing, he would add the line:

"And George can't dance." The laughter would erupt again.

"George can't dance" isn't a classic comedy line. You couldn't sell it to *Reader's Digest*. No cartoonist would purchase it. It would look silly in a greeting card. In that particular place, though, in that specific routine, it worked. It got a big response from the audience and that's what jokes are supposed to do.

A good monologue works on a "peaks and valleys" principle. Not all jokes can have the same relative humor content. Even if they could, it wouldn't be any good anyway because it would be monotonous and comedy has to be modulated. The laughs should build to a crescendo and then taper off, build up again and gradually descend.

When you see a comic that you don't particularly like, it's not usually because he isn't funny: it's because his material doesn't build properly. All comics, even the great ones, have moments that are not hilarious. They can't all be. During those moments, they are leading you somewhere—they are building. When they get you where they want you, they hit you with the payoff, the big laugh. Then, as a listener, you feel justified in having invested the time listening to the softer material. A poor comic doesn't deliver that payoff. Consequently, you feel disappointed. Your time was wasted. You were used. The poor comic didn't need a whole lot of new material, simply a few strong jokes strategically placed.

Let me give an example of what I mean by the "peaks and valleys" principle. This is a story I've heard on the public speaking circuit that illustrates the principle well. I've numbered the different parts of the routine so we can discuss them later.

1. I love working in comedy because it's one of the few things I do better than my wife.

2. It's true. It's terrible to be married to someone who is skilled and intelligent and creative, although she does have her faults. Like one time my wife went to the hospital to have our fourth child, and I stayed home and took care of the other three. She knew she would be gone about six days and she only left enough clean dishes to last five.

3. The house was a shambles by the time she was scheduled to come home and I knew she would be upset, so I devised a little scheme to cheer her up. I had the other kids paint a sign that said, "Welcome home, Mommy," and we hung it where the dining room *used to be*.

4. But my wife rubs it in that I'm so helpless. Like sometimes we'll be getting ready to go out and I'll offer to help with the kids. She'll say, "No, I'm in too much of a hurry to have you help."

5. I took this as a challenge. I told my little daughter that I was going to get her washed and dressed faster than she ever got washed and dressed before. I took her into the bath-room and told her this was going to be like a game. When I gave her the signal, she would raise her arms, I'd get her undressed and put her in the tub. I got the water ready, tested it, and said, "Okay." She put her arms up, I whipped off her dress, her slip, her little pant-ies, picked her up and sat her in the tub. I said, "Now, Honey, did Mommy ever do it any faster than that?" She said, "No, but Mommy always takes off my shoes and socks first."

6. I not only made a fool of myself, I had to buy a new pair of shoes.

Item 1 is a weak joke that simply serves the purpose of getting into the routine. People know it is not the big joke, so they lis-ten, expecting more to follow.

Item 2 is a stronger joke that illustrates the helplessness of the husband.

Item 3 is a strong line, but again, it has that feel that it's not the ending. It does, however, build up anticipation for what's coming. The audience might subconsciously be thinking, "Here are two funny lines and he hasn't gotten to the main point yet. It's probably going to be very funny when he gets to it."

Item 5 is the payoff line that delivers very well. It gets a big laugh and justifies the audience's anticipation. It's the peak of the routine.

Item 6 is a weak line that only capitalizes on the laugh that preceded. It will regenerate laughter. A few more of these might have been used to milk more audience response while getting back to one of the comedy valleys.

That's another advantage of clever routining: it allows you to sustain the laughter from good material. It's a delicious mo-ment when a sure-fire story or joke gets that explosive audience response; it's a pity to just allow it to dissolve. Some very soft jokes placed at the right spot can intensify that laughter and keep it rolling for much longer than the story actually deserves.

In the example above, Item 5 could have stood on its own as a story, but it works much better when you build audience antici-pation. Let them know something special is coming—and then deliver it.

Some Good Jokes Need Set-ups

Frequently, even powerful jokes need a bit of explanation or set-up to make them understandable, perhaps because the gag is based on a premise that's not easily recognizable. In other words, you've written a joke you're proud of, but it can't stand on its own. A monologue enables you to use that gag without any clumsy preamble. The jokes that go before it set it up or explain it.

For example, suppose you've created a fantastic gag about people who always cough at piano recitals. You might have to do a few simple gags that state the premise very directly, then deliver the line in its pure form.

Earlier I used an example of a joke about football players being so heavily taped. The joke was:

> "My wife watched a game the other day
> and said, 'This game can't have started
> too long ago. Some of the players haven't
> been unwrapped yet.' "

In using it as an example, I had to explain what the set-up was. On its own, the joke makes no sense.

The following football joke needs no preamble or explanation. It stands on its own:

> "Football is pretty complicated today.
> They have Z-outs, curl-ins, double flare-
> outs . . . and those are all just different
> ways of spiking the ball."

Do we just throw away the first joke because it needs an explanation? No. We explain it in the monologue by doing some simpler jokes that set up our premise. Put these following jokes ahead of it, then you can do the gag as written.

> "There's a lot of money in professional
> football today. I'd like to have what
> they spend on tape alone.

> "I haven't seen that much tape on the
> human body since the last time Phyllis
> Diller changed at my house.

> *"Have you looked closely at some of*
> *those players? They're just an Ace*
> *bandage with cleats."*

With a few simple laugh lines, you've set the premise for your joke, which can now be told concisely.

Years ago I did a banquet for a friend of mine who was retiring. This gentleman used to take off his glasses after one or two drinks at every party we had. As a standing joke, we greatly exaggerated his drinking feats. I wrote a line that's still one of my favorites, although I list it here as an example of a flawed line.

Not everyone at the banquet knew about the glasses being removed after a few drinks, so that premise had to be set up. I delivered the joke as follows:

> *"You all know Jimmy likes to have a*
> *few drinks at these parties, and he*
> *always takes his glasses off after one*
> *too many. I was talking to his wife*
> *of twenty-eight years before dinner tonight and*
> *I said, 'I guess you can always tell*
> *when Jimmy's had one too many any time*
> *he comes home from work without his*
> *glasses.' She looked at me and said,*
> *'What glasses?' "*

The line worked fine with the audience and, as I say, it's still one of my personal favorites, but isn't it awkward? The facts that he removed his glasses and that he had been married a long time should have been set up with simpler jokes. Then the big line would have been much simpler and more concise.

Monologues Require Preparatory Work

I consider a monologue to be a routine of 25 to 35 jokes. That's not a strict rule of comedy, it's simply a convenient measure that I use. In Chapter 10, we'll discuss the reasons for this number. For now, though, it's enough to say that it's a formidable task to begin with a blank sheet of paper, knowing you're going to have to create two to three dozen comedic gems. Consequently, you have to do your homework. You can't "wing it" for that much material. You have to get organized and do some research and planning—you'll find that your material will be more creative as a result.

Later chapters will discuss preparatory work.

Monologues Force You to Write More

A tendency among comedy writers is to quit too soon, both on each joke and on each topic. I used to note that my strongest lines in a routine were the first one and about the eighth one. The reason was that the first gag I wrote was the inspired one, the one that popped into my head and motivated me to write the routine. Then I did the standard, the obvious, the lines that everyone would think of. When those were exhausted (about the seventh joke) I would be forced into being more creative.

Naturally, it's not exactly mathematical, but we all tend to hit that point when we say, "There is nothing funny left in this topic." It's when you struggle beyond that stopping point that your work becomes more inventive.

Monologue Writing Diversifies Your Style

A monologue is designed to be read or listened to as a complete piece. It has to be interesting enough to keep an audience captivated. Therefore you have to incorporate a fair amount of variety into each piece. Even though the one-line joke form is essentially the same, you must invent ways of varying the form.

For example, take the standard joke form, "My brother-in-law is so lazy that . . . " You might be able to write 15 variations on this joke, but you can't do a routine in which every gag begins with "my brother-in-law is so lazy that . . . "

You might come up with openings like the following:

"My brother-in-law is so lazy that . . . (joke)"
"I mean he really is lazy . . . (joke)"
"I won't say he hates work, but . . . (joke)"
"Let me give you an idea how bad he is . . . (joke)"

The very same joke form can be used with each of those opening handles.

You'll also learn to look for other variations to relieve the monotony.

By forcing yourself to write complete, structured monologues, you'll improve your writing style.

Monologues Do the Work for the Buyer

You'll have a better chance of selling anything if you make the sale easier on the buyer. Structured monologues do that.

If you present a comic with a collection of one-liners in no particular order, he'll find it hard to read—as we discussed before. Even if he likes some of the jokes, he still has to incorporate them into a routine. If they're already in a workable routine, his work is done for him.

Plus, the sheer volume of a routine makes a sale more likely. In a monologue of 25 to 35 jokes, the comic can edit out those gags he's not sure of and still have enough left for a respectable piece of material. Even if your monologue is edited down to 8 gags from the original 35, that's still enough to be included in an act. However, if you turn in only 5 to 6 jokes and the comic edits the same percentage, he's left with only 1 or 2 jokes. What good are they to him?

The joke remains the basic building block. We'll get started on that now.

10 GETTING READY TO WRITE

I've read that nightmares of frustration are fairly common. Pilots have told me that they frequently dream of taking off and immediately confronting obstacles like overhead wires or bridges. When I committed to comedy as a profession, I had a recurring dream. I'd be attending some gala festivity and would be called up from the audience to dazzle the crowd with a few insightful witticisms. I would march up to the microphone to much applause, feeling a warm glow of excitement within. Then I'd get to center stage and have absolutely nothing to say. I couldn't think of a joke, a rhyme, a riddle . . . not even a simple song to sing. All I could do was stand there silently and wish that I could disappear.

Comedy requires preparation. Some comics are masters of the ad lib and spontaneous humor brightens any presentation, but professionals never depend on spontaneity totally. They always have their standard sure-fire material to fall back on.

As the source of that humor, you need ample groundwork, too; the writer, after all, begins with blank pages.

I'd like to travel through the joke-writing process with you from beginning to end. Obviously, a description of a thought takes longer than the thought itself, so this may seem a bit sluggish and unwieldy. Be patient. It's like reading the instructions to a new game: they sound complicated and take forever to get through, but once you begin playing the game they are logical and become second nature to you. The same will happen with your writing. Journey through this deliberately with me a few times and you'll soon be able to fly through it on your own much more quickly.

I remind you also that there are two thought processes involved in writing gags. One is the almost instantaneous, computer-like procedure of rolling thoughts through your mind. The other is the more systematic and tedious research system. Admittedly, it is slow and routine, and some beginners may be tempted to bypass it and get right to the writing.

We've said a few times already and will repeat many more times: one failing of novices is quitting too soon—on preparation, on topics, and on jokes. I recommend that you be diligent with your preparation in the beginning. Write things out rather than skip over them. Eventually, you'll be able to shorthand many of these procedures, doing them mentally. You'll learn to work much more quickly—perform some of the routines mentally and rapidly—and you'll get to the jokes sooner. But at the beginning, this is not advisable. Even today, if my deadline permits, I still prepare all my monologue work before getting around to writing any jokes: the quantity and the quality are always improved by it.

Vic Braden, the famed tennis authority, told me that as a youngster he used to fantasize about playing on the Davis Cup team and having those great coaches whisper words of tennis wisdom to him between games. He used to watch big matches and wondered just what secrets the coaches whispered to their players. Eventually, he earned a spot on the Davis Cup team, and between games the coaches would whisper to him, "Bend your knees" or "Keep your head down." Their only secret was, "Be well schooled in the fundamentals."

Enough sermonizing. You're ready to go to work. You've got a sharpened pencil or a trusty typewriter nearby, along with some blank paper. (Why does it always have to be blank?) What's your first step?

Let's go back for a moment to my horrible nightmare: it was a nightmare because I had nothing to say. Your first job in writing is to find something to say.

Select a Topic

You have to select a topic. What are you going to be brilliantly witty about? It can be anything: current events, family life, social ironies, fantasy . . . anything at all. You simply need something to "unblank" that paper.

Where do you get that topic? Anywhere. You might read something ironic in today's paper. Look through magazines for something that intrigues your funny bone. Things are happening around your house that could be satirized. Listen to what other people are talking about—the "topic du jour."

If you have a paying client, she will dictate the topics—but that's all right because she will also sign your check. If you're free to select your own topic, be nice to yourself and try to make writing easier.

I'm sure you have some topic that inspires you. I generally find that I write best about some item that irritates me. Once I was driving along daydreaming about topics and the driver behind me became justifiably annoyed. He honked and nearly sent me through the windshield, it startled me that much. So I wrote an angry monologue about idiotic drivers who honk their horns for no reason. (Comedy writing can also be therapeutic as revenge, too.)

From this point on we will be proceeding in a step-by-step outline for writing a full monologue. Why don't you select a topic here and work through the next several chapters until you have a completed monologue of your own. For this first journey don't be too ambitious. Select a topic you're reasonably certain you can be funny about.

Free Association

Now that you've selected your topic, allow your mind to consider anything and everything related to that topic. Don't attempt to be funny here. You're simply providing fodder for when you later start composing your jokes. You're not trying to be particularly selective, either. You don't have to pass judgment on the items that pop into your mind; simply write them down. Some may be useful in your writing, others may not; you won't be required to use each and every thing you jot down.

Let your mind roam freely and keep your pencil moving or your typewriter clattering.

As an example, suppose I had selected "owning a dog" as my topic. My list of free associations might read something like this:

> **Dogs:** wet noses, cold noses, wetting on the rugs, chewing things, "Fetch," "Sit," "Heel," bringing pipe and slippers, bringing the evening paper, teaching tricks, biting the mailman, watchdog, scaring burglars, "Beware of the Dog" signs, "His bark is worse than his bite," chasing cats, shedding, begging for food, cleaning up after, cost a fortune to feed, chasing cars, burying bones, veterinarian visits, shots, in heat, spayed, human years and dog years.

That's all there is to this step. Another admonition—or rather, the same admonition offered once again: don't quit too soon. Push yourself at this step and get a few more relationships than you think you can get. Creativity comes with that little bit of extra effort.

This may seem to be a waste of time, paper, and typewriter ribbon, but there are benefits. A joke is a combination of two or more ideas blended into one. Generally you have a point of view and a related idea. This list can often provide both, but let's assume you have one or the other. The joke writing process is to find the one you don't have. The list may provide it, or it may provide the springboard for finding it.

To illustrate, imagine that I want to say about my subject that I don't like dogs because they wet on the rugs. How can I say that in a funny way? Well, I might quickly run down my list of topics searching for some relationship. Let's try "wet noses."

> *"I have a lot in common with this dog.*
> *He always has a wet nose, and I always*
> *have a wet rug."*

Maybe "bringing pipe and slippers."

> *"This dog wets on the rug so much that instead*
> *of bringing my slippers when I get home,*
> *he brings me my galoshes."*

How about "scaring burglars."

> *"We can always tell if there's a burglar*
> *walking around the house. You can hear*
> *the rug go squish, squish, squish."*

Without the list to refer to, these gags probably would have taken much longer to write, if indeed they ever would have popped into my mind at all.

The list can trigger a point of view, or a related idea. After you've worked with it a few times you'll see the benefits much more graphically than I can ever describe them to you.

Organized List

After you've allowed your mind to roam freely and you've jotted down a list of free associations, you try to stimulate your mind to find even more relationships that might be used for jokes.

This step is actually a patterned list of free associations. It's more organized. List people, places, things, events, words, cliches, and phrases that are similar or related to your subject, and a list of the same categories that are opposite. The opposites are, of course, related to your topic by their total difference.

I recommend that you make up a sheet of paper that is blocked off for these categories. That way you'll always have the areas clearly in front of you. I've enclosed a pre-printed sheet as an example, but you can design your form any way you desire.

On my pre-printed form I've listed a few of the ideas that I might jot down in each category. Your list should be much more extensive, because the same old caution applies—don't quit too soon. Work and think until you get a fairly representative number under each division. Some topics will be easier to analyze than others, but I recommend getting at least seven items in each section.

	SIMILAR	OPPOSITE
WORDS, PHRASES, CLICHES	"His bark is worse than his bite." Fetch, sit, HEEL, STAY. Man's best friend.	"I'm afraid of dogs." "I don't trust dogs." "I'm a cat lover."
EVENTS	Dog Days 1st litter When burglar broke in	Cat Show Alcoholics Anonymous Meetings (AA people are dry – dogs are wetters.)
THINGS	Leash Papers on floor Fireplugs Favorite Tree Dog Food	Other Pets Dog's natural enemies Dog's prey
PLACES	Kennel Dog House Pound	Stores that don't allow dogs. THE bedroom
PEOPLE	Pluto Lassie Pavlov Veterinarian Dog Next Door	Cats Dog Catcher Mail man.

The joke-writing benefits are exactly the same as we discussed with "free associations." The added advantage of this list is that it focuses your mind on specific areas. When you channel your thinking, your mind becomes much more productive. The more ideas you have to work with, the more and better jokes you will eventually generate.

Let's take a paragraph or two to reflect on what we've just done. Your first project was to freely associate any ideas you could think of that applied to your topic. You may have had some difficulty coming up with many ideas. However, being wary of quitting too soon, you continued. When you finally finished you thought you had every conceivable thought related to your subject. Then we categorized our thinking. We organized it more and again asked you to come up with related and opposite ideas. It may have been a struggle for awhile, but you completed the project. Your second list should have many more items on it than your first list. Several of them will be duplicates, but quite a few will be new items.

The point is, by organizing your thoughts and funneling your efforts, you were able to come up with new associations even though you were probably convinced after the first effort that there were no more ideas related to your topic.

All you did differently in the second project was channel your thinking. Rather than think of anything that was associated, you thought of anyTHING that was related, anyPLACE that was related, and so on.

It should be apparent to you now that preparation and organization work.

Take heart. We're getting closer to that moment when you can start writing jokes. Admittedly, it's taking us longer then it really ought to go through this procedure step by step because you have to spend a lot of time reading my commentary. With subsequent writing ventures, you'll whip through these preliminary steps in no time. All we've actually done so far is make two different lists.

That, however, is the good news. The bad news is that we have one more procedure to go through before we get to the fun part—the actual writing of the jokes.

Subdividing the Topic

In Chapter 9 I mentioned that for our purposes a monologue is considered to be 25 to 35 jokes long, and promised to explain why I arbitrarily chose that length. We've already touched on some of those reasons, but let's review them quickly here.

First of all, it forces you to do your preparatory work. Two or three dozen gags on one topic is a considerable task. Most of us typewriter jockeys would rather attack the joke writing, finish it, and dismiss it. Were we to do that, we might only write 6 to 8 jokes, which we might be satisfied with. However, since we began with a more challenging quota, we have to do the preliminary research to make the task accomplishable.

Second, it doesn't permit you to quit too soon. (Have you heard that before?) Writing can get a bit tough after writing the first 5 or 6 inspired jokes. The obvious jokes have been neatly typed, the inspired ones also, and we swear that there is nothing else funny about this particular topic. The goal of 25 to 35 jokes compels you to continue, and you'll surprise yourself with some of the clever material you can generate after you've guaranteed yourself that it couldn't be done.

Third, it makes your efforts more marketable because there is enough material there for the buyer to edit and still be left with a workable routine.

Fourth, the volume allows you to be more selective. If you're writing a finished presentation you can edit down to your best gags and be sure that you'll have enough.

None of the above logic, though, makes writing any less formidable. Anyone can write 5 or 6 jokes on a given topic, but not 25 to 35. The secret, then, is to subdivide your topic into 5 or 6 subtopics and write half a dozen jokes on each subtopic. The result: a monologue.

You arrive at your subtopics by analyzing your main topic. You note facts about it . . . you question it . . . you pull it apart searching for its components. Thinking of a topic, you generally have one or two half-written jokes somewhere in your head. Those may generate subtopics. Review your extensive list of related subjects, both your free-association and your organized list. There are probably several good subdivisions in there.

My main topic was "owning a dog." I broke it up into the following subtopics:

A) General (this is a catchall division allowing me to do one or two jokes that lead into the routine.)

B) Wetting on the rug (notice that came from the free association list.)

C) How big the dog was

D) Dog biting the mailman and other visitors

E) The dog chewing things around the house

Subdividing in this manner allows me to do a full routine on owning a dog. These are not the only subtopics about owning a dog; they're not the best, either. They are simply the ones that I chose to stimulate my mind to write 35 jokes about owning a dog. (Another benefit of this device is that if I were assigned tomorrow to write a routine on owning a dog, I could select different subtopics and write another full routine about the family pet.)

This division into subtopics is probably the most important part of writing a monologue— with the exception of writing the jokes. It will determine the tone of your monologue and the ease with which you write it.

Remember how much more productive your free-associating was when you organized and channeled it? The same applies here. If your subtopics are creative and well-thought-out, your jokes will be better and easier to write and your monologue will be more original.

Since you have already selected a topic, try now to think of areas that apply to it, but also strive to make them different and inspired.

Once you complete that, we can move on to the jokes. (Ain't this fun?)

11 GETTING THE JOKES FLOWING

All of our work to this point, with the exception of some of the exercises, has been preparatory. That's necessary. Boxers spend months preparing for an important fight. Football teams drill for the entire season. Baseball players are continually sharpening their skills. But that moment of truth always arrives: they have to face the opponent.

We've hit that moment of truth. Your opponent is the blank sheet of paper. It's a formidable foe. And, it's your battle, since neither the book nor I can write the jokes for you. However, we can do a little bit of coaching from the sidelines.

Now you should have with you a topic, a comprehensive list of references, and a set of subtopics. You want to convert them to a series of 25 to 35 gags that we'll later work into a monologue.

There is no need to write the routine in chronological order. If you can sit at a typewriter and begin with joke number one and proceed to joke number thirty-five, and it's easier that way, then do it. That's a tough assignment, though.

The extensive preparatory work we've been doing has all been toward one goal: to make the joke writing easier. Now we'll take advantage of that.

I recommend that you make an easy-to-read list of your subtopics and keep them in front of you while you're writing your gags. Keep a running tally of how many lines you've done on each subtopic, but don't limit yourself in any way with this scorekeeping: it's simply to stimulate your mind to write more and better jokes.

The joke-writing process now is the first one that we mentioned. You're going to roll thoughts and ideas through your mind with computer-like speed, selecting those two or three related items that you can word into a joke line. Your mind will be operating almost with a will and direction of its own. You simply step in when it stops and type out the joke that it has presented to you. At times this process will feel like aimless daydreaming— that's when the mind generates gags so quickly that you'll hardly be able to write or type fast enough to harvest the ideas. If your mind likes a certain subtopic and delivers more than the 5- or 6-line quota, allow it to continue. I've had subtopics that were so fertile I gathered enough gags from them to be monologues on their own. Then I expanded the other subtopics and created another routine from them.

Sometimes, though, after hitting a few good lines, the mind stops and needs more direction from you. That's when you can turn to your running tally sheet and say to your creative self, "We need more lines on this subtopic," and allow it to wander again.

If you remain reasonably faithful to your subtopics you will eventually generate your 30-some gags that are all related to the main topic. In Chapter 12 we'll discuss how to routine these into a smooth-flowing monologue.

Right now, though, the page is blank. The only remedy for that is to fill it with some jokes.

Inspiration probably produces the best and the quickest jokes. Set down any topic and gags that seem to pop into your head from the ether. Accept them and put them on the paper. Even if they are related to your topic but don't fall into any of your subtopics, don't be upset. Simply create another catchall subtopic called "General." Sometimes, again, I've had that area be so productive that I've written a complete monologue that had no relation to the one I started on.

Inspiration is usually stingy. You'll get a few lines with no exertion, but not many. Now you'll have to struggle to extract the lines from your mind. Following are a few techniques that might help.

Have Something to Say

Jokes are zany, bizarre, nonsensical, but in their own way, they have a point of view. They may be exaggerated, distorted, paradoxical, but they can be reduced to a certain logic. Most of them are saying something serious in a funny way. (There are some purely nonsensical lines, non sequiturs like, "It is better to walk with your back to the wind than to have your ear pinned under a manhole cover." I have no idea what that means, but it's funny and might get a laugh in a nightclub routine.)

As the gag-writer, though, you are beginning from scratch and you need a starting point. In the mental joke-writing process you have one thought, and you're auditioning and selecting other thoughts that roll quickly through your mind. It's too much of a burden to roll two sets of thoughts through your brain and select two at random that will produce a gag.

Even the nonsensical line that we just quoted probably had a starting point in the mind of the writer. The author said, "I'm going to create a completely nonsensical joke. I'll start with a traditional quote and come up with a funny-sounding phrase that has nothing to do with it."

The starting point for each gag is, "What do I want the gag to say?" The answer to that question doesn't have to be funny. The joke you create will be, but your statement is only the starting point.

In some of the exercises we did, we captioned photographs. If one hundred people captioned the same photo, you would get one hundred different gags. The starting point, though, was the photo. Wouldn't it be silly to enter a classroom and ask everyone there to write captions and not have any pictures? They would say, "Caption what?" It's just as silly to try to write a joke without first deciding what that joke is going to say.

Examples may help make this clearer. In joking about inflation I may want to say that it's getting so bad we may not be able to live with it. The resultant joke might be:

> "Whoever thought survival would one day be a status symbol?"

Or the writer might want to say that prices are like robbery.

She might write:

*"Supermarket prices are pure robbery. One store near
me even puts stockings over their heads of lettuce."*

Start with Factual Statements

We mentioned earlier that many gags are nothing more than
straight lines that have been captioned. Some of the exercises in
Chapter 8 deal with captioning. Most people find it a fairly simple creative exercise provided they have the raw materials to
work with—the photos or whatever.

By listing a series of factual statements you're furnishing
yourself with those raw materials. Then you begin rolling ideas,
many selected from your reference compilation, through your
mind until you strike a joke.

Again, the statements needn't be funny. They are the straight
lines. They are merely getting you started in looking for the
punchlines. Earlier you captioned photos: now you're captioning "word pictures."

Finding factual statements in current events topics is a matter of extracting phrases out of newspapers, magazines, or from
television reports. For example, were you to comment on the
Reagan-Carter election returns, you might list:

Carter conceded early.

The vote was a landslide.

Carter won only five states.

Carter conceded before the West Coast closed the polls.

Factual statements can also be listed about more general topics, too. For instance, suppose you're talking about how lazy
your husband is. The list of statements might read:

He sleeps on the sofa all day.

He never fixes anything.

He won't put out the trash.

Now the caption added might be:

> *"Jimmy Carter conceded very early. I guess he didn't*
> *want to lose both an election and a night's sleep in*
> *the same day."*

> *"My husband sleeps on the sofa all the time. One whole*
> *side of his body is covered with mohair burns."*

Sometimes you'll find that the factual statement prompts a punchline. Then you can vary the form. You needn't use the straight line and caption routine that strictly. Take, for example, the fact that Carter won only five states. That might suggest a line like the following:

> *"Now that Carter is out of office, he*
> *wants to travel around the country.*
> *He wants to visit all five states that*
> *liked him."*

Another good feature of captioning "word pictures" as opposed to photographs is that the words of the original statement can be changed in any way to suit your punchline. For example:

> *"We had a broken lock on the front door.*
> *The only way I could get my husband*
> *to fix it was to tell him my mother*
> *was coming to visit."*

None of these suggestions is an inviolable rule. They are all aids to get your mind thinking along the right track. If breaking, bending, or manipulating them helps you produce better gags, do it.

Ask Questions

This might be considered an offshoot of the previous ideas. Once you have something to say or a factual statement you want to caption, how do you go about it? You investigate it. Explore other areas of it. Why did it happen? Whom else does it affect? Who is pleased by it? Who is upset with it? What's the next logical step? There are limitless questions you can ask, and any one of them may prompt the punchline.

For instance, in the previous examples we stated that Jimmy

Carter conceded early. I asked myself why he would do that. One of the answers was because he wanted to get a good night's sleep. Hence the joke.

Sometimes, asking questions can give you a whole new approach or angle on a topic. For instance, working on jokes about the big earthquake that hit Los Angeles, I did routines on how much the earth moved, how scared I was, and so on, but then I wondered how it affected the stars. Then I could do a punchline for every famous Hollywood star. Did it get Jimmy Stewart so shook up that he stopped stuttering? Did it crack Glen Campbell's hair? (That was when we did a lot of Glen Campbell hair jokes.) How did it affect Raquel Welch? Mickey Rooney? Jackie Gleason? All of a sudden I've got a list of straight lines as long as Hollywood Boulevard. And come to think of it—how *did* it affect the people who cruise Hollywood Boulevard?

One of my favorite joke examples falls into this classification. A client called me to do some opening lines for her Las Vegas act. She had dislocated her shoulder and had to appear in Vegas wearing a large cast. The audience would be surprised and distracted by the cast, so we needed some lines that would explain it away quickly.

The first thing I did was ask myself what sort of bizarre activity could have caused the accident. Here is the opening line that resulted:

> *"Ladies and gentlemen, I know you're wondering how I got this cast. Well, if there are any of you out there who have just bought the book* The Joy of Sex, *there's a misprint on page 204."*

Exaggerate and Distort

Comedy is basically truth. A friend of mine does a joke about agents. He says, "If we get 90 percent of the money and they get 10 percent, how come we always have to go to their office?" That's a true statement. It's funny because besides being true, it's ironic.

Although comedy is based on truth, it's not that often that

true statements generate jokes without some sort of tampering by the humorist. One way to highlight the truth of a statement is to exaggerate or distort it out of its true proportions.

This is the same principle that caricature artists employ in making their drawings. They isolate a few features and distort them to false prominence. The resulting likeness isn't anatomically correct, but it doesn't destroy the recognizability; many times it enhances it. Some celebrities are easier to recognize from a caricature than they are from a photo.

Humorous exaggeration serves the same purpose, sometimes stating a case more powerfully than brilliant oratory.

The trick here is to allow your mind to play with the dimensions and the colors and all the physical attributes of the mental image until you create a funny picture. Sometimes you might even exaggerate and extend an idea out to its ultimate. For example, I previously quoted a joke about inflation ("Whoever thought survival would one day be a status symbol?") in which inflation was pushed to the point where only people rich enough to show off could stay alive.

Remember that we discussed in Chapter 3 how flexible the mind can be in distorting images and accepting them as reality. Audiences will accept distortion and not quarrel with your proportions, so long as you're funny.

Following are a few jokes I've written that have played tricks with proportion:

> "This friend of mine has so much flab
> on him that when he stands up, his feet
> disappear.

> "He was crossing the street the other
> day and was hit by a Volkswagen. They
> don't think there was any serious damage.
> Of course, they still haven't found
> the Volkswagen."

You can create zany mental pictures by adding colors. Let's use this same guy for some samples:

> "One day he wore a red, white, and blue
> shirt, stood on the corner, and a
> man threw some letters in his mouth.

"Once he wore a green shirt with white stripes and a bunch of kids played football on him."

Most of the above are distortion jokes, but you can get funny results with exaggeration, also.

"My dog is a bit vicious. If he likes you he doesn't lick your hand; he lets you keep it.

"The other day my husband told me to feed the dog. I said, 'He just ate. I can still smell the mailman on his breath.' "

Use Standard References and Expressions

Once I was doing an after-dinner speech before a group of personnel executives; during the meal I overheard two executives talking. One said something about running a reference check and they both chuckled. I asked what it was, and he told me that it was a process the company went through with some of the people they were about to hire: it was precautionary.

When I started my talk I said, "Your president called me and asked if I could speak tonight. I said I could and he said, 'I'll get back to you as soon as we run a reference check.' " That joke got applause and I don't even know what I said.

It always amazes me how two computer programmers can talk to one another and be perfectly intelligible, while a bystander might think they were talking a foreign language. All businesses have a jargon peculiar to them. Those phrases and expressions, if they're not too inside for your audience, make valuable fodder for your joke mill.

Also, almost any topic has a series of references connected with it. I have done hundreds of football monologues and every one probably has "Gatorade" in it at least once. If you're working for the military, you'll probably refer to eating something or other "on a shingle." Try writing a routine about ex-President Jerry Ford without mentioning his golf game.

There are innumerable general slogans and phrases familiar to everyone. Most advertising mottos can be used in gags, like

"Come fly with me," "Leave the driving to us," "We'll serve no wine before its time," or "You deserve a break today."

There are many popular catch phrases that may come in handy, too. I used to love to do "six-pack" jokes.

"I think I'll go write some jokes. I've got a pencil, paper, and a six-pack of erasers."

And practically everybody adopted the "industrial strength" slogan for their gags.

"I won't say I'm gaining too much weight, but my doctor put me on industrial-strength diet pills."

You can probably think of many more. The nice thing about them is that some advertising writers somewhere are creating more for us even as you read this.

Create Formula Jokes

We mentioned these briefly in Chapter 7. These are jokes that follow a standard pattern, for example, Carson's gimmick of saying it was cold out. The audience says, "How cold *was* it?" Then the formula is, "It was so cold that . . . "

There are limitless numbers of formula jokes. There is no way all of them could be listed in this chapter, but by listening you'll be able to pick up several for yourself and then plug in your own references. It's joke writing that's akin to painting by numbers.

I'll list just a few formula jokes so you'll have a better idea of what I mean.

There's a definition formula like the joke Bob Hope used during the war.

"You all know what a jeep is. That's a New York taxicab that's been drafted."

There's an initial formula, like the joke I did once when I emceed a company talent show for a business called PNB.

"Tonight, PNB stands for 'Please, no booing.' "

There's a formula that describes something in groups of three, the last one being the punchline.

"My brother-in-law has three speeds . . .
slow, slower, and 'okay, pallbearers,
you can set the body here.' "

These tips should get you started cranking out those 25 to 35 gags. It may be difficult at first but it gets easier the more you do. Again, I caution you that these suggestions are not commandments: they're ways to stimulate your creativity. Use them one at a time, or all together—whichever way gets your mind shoving ideas through your brain so that you can get those jokes on paper.

Once you get the gags written, we'll move on to organizing them into a smooth-flowing routine.

12 THE ART OF ROUTINING

If you've written 25 to 35 jokes on one topic, that's commendable. Many of my writer friends say that they don't enjoy writing but are proud of having written. Humorist Peter DeVries said, "I love being a writer. What I can't stand is the paperwork." So to have authored nearly three dozen gag lines on a given topic is something you can be proud of. However, it is not yet a monologue. It's like building a house, and you've just had the bricks delivered.

Now you have to arrange those jokes in a logical order so they will glide smoothly, like a narrative. There's nothing more tedious than reading or listening to a collection of disconnected one-liners. Yet it's exciting to read a funny story or listen to a skilled raconteur. Everything is flowing to a natural conclusion—to a high point—and each joke pulls you along with it.

Good routining also improves your lines because it allows you to be more concise. Each joke you write is not only complete unto itself, but can also serve as a set-up for the jokes to follow. Consequently, the gags that follow won't need as elaborate a set-up. Later in the chapter, we'll proceed step by step through a sample portion of a monologue and see how this applies.

Routining enhances the overall comedy effect by taking advantage of the natural peaks and valleys of comedy we discussed in Chapter 9. Johnny Carson kids about these peaks and valleys when his opening monologue isn't going well, but they actually do exist. They have to because each joke suffers in comparison to its neighbors. Each gag in a comic's routine cannot have the same degree of funniness: if each did, it would be monotonous. The softer jokes can make the strong jokes seem stronger, and some of the strong jokes can be used to help the softer ones. Also, some of the weaker jokes help the stronger jokes by providing the set-up for them.

Bob Hope takes advantage of this in his monologues as well as anyone. Study one of his routines; notice how each topic builds to a crescendo, and how Hope extracts laughs from weaker jokes based on the crescendo.

It reminds me of a crowd watching a fireworks display. There is anticipation as they watch the little speck of light propelled into the sky. There are "oohs" and "ahhs" as it explodes into a giant ball of light. There's even a thrill in watching the glowing particles of light drift back to earth. That's the way your comedy routine should operate. Just as varied rhythm in a fireworks display adds excitement, so your peaks and valleys should be staggered. Naturally, we want more peaks than valleys, but so long as we have to have the valleys we might as well take advantage of them.

There are no hard and fast rules to assembling a routine. It's pretty much a "seat of the pants" operation. Comedy is so subjective that in a group of six or eight jokes, few people will agree which is the "biggie" you should build to. However, the mechanics of routining are fairly simple.

First of all, just divide your jokes into their separate subtopics. Now try to determine a logical progression of subtopics. Sometimes this is predetermined for you. If you're doing a routine about taking your wife to the hospital to have a baby, you won't talk about how bad traffic was on the way until after you've done the gags about packing her suitcase. Other times, though, the subtopics fall in any logical order; then it's totally up to your discretion.

I use two methods for arranging the gags. You can use either one or invent your own.

The first method takes more time, but generally produces better results, especially if the monologue isn't cut and dried as far as the logic of its progression goes. I cut separate strips for each joke and then lay each subtopic out from first to last joke.

This makes the gags physically easier to arrange because they're unattached. You can play with them until you hit the order that satisfies you. Then I staple them together in readiness for the final retyping.

In the second method, I go through my entire collection of jokes and decide on the progression of subtopics. Then I go through and put a large circle in the margin for each joke that applies to subtopic one. Now the particular jokes I want are easily visible and I go back over those jokes and arrange them in logical order, numbering them as I go.

When I have arranged all the jokes in subtopic one, I circle those that apply to subtopic two, number them, and keep repeating the process until every gag is numbered. Then I retype from gag number one to the end.

This system is more difficult because it doesn't lend itself as easily to modification. Once you put that number in there, you really don't want to erase it and foul up your progression. When the gags are physically separate, modification is much simpler. I also find with this second method that I'll invariably miss a gag or two that should have been placed earlier in the routine. Then I have to devise some scheme of renumbering.

Obviously, I recommend the cut-and-staple procedure unless you're working by an open window on a windy day.

After you've arranged the jokes in logical progression and read through them again, you'll find that they just don't fit together properly. You wrote each joke as a separate entity, and you probably wrote them in no logical order. Now that they're in a sensible progression, some of the rough edges have to be smoothed out. You may have too many similar joke forms too close together. You may have a joke with an elaborate set-up that is no longer needed. You may have a good beginning joke that needs a set-up. All these problems can be taken care of with some minor rewrites.

For example, suppose you have these two jokes together:

> *"I have a friend who is so lazy he won't*
> *even go to a ball game until the second*
> *inning. That's so he won't have to stand*
> *for the National Anthem."*

> *"I have a friend who's so lazy he even*
> *married a pregnant woman."*

Obviously, the set-up line is too similar for both jokes that close together, and it's not needed twice. You could rewrite those two as follows:

> *"I have a friend who's so lazy he won't*
> *even go to a ball game until the second*
> *inning. That's so he won't have to stand*
> *for the National Anthem.*
>
> *"He even married a pregnant woman."*

However, this makes the second punchline a little too vague. It still needs some preamble. So I would add a different set-up line to vary the routine, like this:

> *"I have friend who's so lazy he won't*
> *even to go a ball game until the second*
> *inning. That's so he won't have to stand*
> *for the National Anthem.*
>
> *"He's never done anything for himself.*
> *He even married a pregnant woman."*

As I mentioned earlier you simply can't do a routine of six or eight jokes that all begin with "He's so lazy that . . . " However, if the joke is valid, the set-up lines can be adjusted or even dropped without affecting the humor content of the gags. This will become apparent as you reread your newly routined monologue.

You may also become aware of gaps in the routine. You'll see places where you just feel lines should be but aren't. For instance, suppose you're doing a routine about your lazy friend, and the bulk of the lines are about his inactivity around the house, except for one line about his sloth at the office. That should prompt you to do a few lines about his work that lead up to that line.

Here it's not a simple matter of rewording. You have to get back to the typewriter and generate a few more lines.

Probably the most glaring omissions will be in going from one subtopic to another. The change may seem abrupt. Bob Hope is noted for some of his transitions from one topic to another. He simply says, "Hey, but how 'bout those Yankees, huh." Henny Youngman almost makes a comedy routine out of his blends. In the middle of a roast of Milton Berle he wants to tell his standard wife jokes, so he says something like, "We all know Milton Berle has a wife, but how about *my* wife. My wife went to the doctor the other day. . . . " You won't be able, yet, to get away with that kind of blend.

The best way to make the transition from one subtopic to another is to find a gag that combines one element of each. That way you'll be able to introduce your new subtopic and proceed with your new jokes.

As an example, let's go back to my routine about owning a dog. One subtopic was how big the dog was and another about his biting people. After doing several jokes about the animal's size, I could use a line like the following:

> *"Do you have any idea what a dog that size eats? . . . Mailmen."*

Now I can talk about other people my pet has bitten.

For clarification, let's go through a portion of a monologue, starting with the roughly written first draft and on to the final routine. We'll discuss the reasons for the arrangement and for some of the changes that we made along the way. Since this is admittedly a seat-of-the-pants procedure, it might happen that you would have arranged the gags in a much different order. That's fine—in fact, it might be worth your while to try that.

Here are the gags as they were first jotted down:

1. A safe journey on the Schuylkill Expressway . . . That means you finish in the same car you started with.

2. There are always accidents on the Schuylkill Expressway. I saw a 12-car pile-up there the other day. Twelve-car pile-up . . . that means a woman signaled for a left-hand turn and eleven people believed her.

3. The Schuylkill Expressway . . . that's
a road that takes you from South Philadelphia to Valley Forge in twenty-five minutes
flat . . . whether you *want to* go or
not.

4. It's the only road in the world
that you can travel on from one end
to the other without once leaving the
scene of the accident.

5. If you want to speed your travel
time on the Schuylkill Expressway, just
move to the rear of the ambulance.

6. Actually our Schuylkill Expressway
is a famous road. It has been cited
by religious leaders all over the world.
It ranks second to World War II as a
cure for atheism.

7. I can always tell when I'm approaching
the Schuylkill Expressway. My St. Christ-
opher statue gets down from the dashboard
and climbs into the glove compartment.

8. Schuylkill Expressway . . . That's
an old Indian term meaning, "White man
drive with forked steering wheel."

Now let's go back and arrange this monologue in logical progression and discuss some of the reasons.

1. A PLEASANT TRIP
A ~~safe journey~~ on the Schuylkill Expressway

. . . that means you finish in the same

car you started with.

2. ~~There are always accidents on the~~ ~~Schuylkill Expressway~~. I saw a 12-car pile-up there the other day. ~~Twelve-car~~ the

way it happened was

~~pile-up . . . that means~~ a woman signaled

||

for a left-hand turn and ~~eleven~~ people believed her.

3. ~~The Schuylkill Expressway . . . that's~~

THAT

~~a~~ road ~~that~~ takes you from South Phila-delphia to Valley Forge in twenty-five minutes flat . . . whether you _want_ _to_ go or not.

4. It's the only road in the world that you can travel on from one end to the other without once leaving the scene of the accident.

5. If you want to speed your travel time on the Schuylkill Expressway, just move to the rear of the ambulance.

6. Actually our Schuylkill Expressway is a famous road. It has been cited by religious leaders all over the world.

It ranks second to World War II as a

cure for atheism.

7. I can always tell when I'm approaching

the Schuylkill Expressway. My St. Christ-

opher statue gets down from the dashboard

and climbs into the glove compartment.

8. Schuylkill Expressway . . . That's

an old Indian term meaning, "White man

drive with forked steering wheel."

To avoid confusion with two sets of numbers, I've arranged the new order alphabetically. I'll go through my arrangement and changes, discussing them as we go.

> **A.** This joke seemed to be the only one that had potential as an opener. Joke Number 8 did also, but it seemed kind of abrupt to begin with a definition before doing a small joke about the road.
>
> I changed it to "pleasant trip" because it might be easier to get into the routine that way. "I had a very pleasant trip over here on the Schuylkill Expressway . . . "—then do the joke line.
>
> **B.** I simply changed the format because otherwise my first three jokes would all have been the definition formula.

F. The first sentence was no longer necessary because the preceding jokes already established the road has a few accidents. This is a case where a joke is made more compact by routining.

In this gag, I dropped the definition formula because it has already been used enough in this short routine. It varies the routining a bit without hurting the gag.

G. This gag feels out of place in the routine. It either needs more jokes to establish the emergency procedures along the roadway, or it should be dropped. Let's drop it.

H. To me, this is the biggie that we've been building to. Now if it's as good as I expect it to be, then we might be able to add a joke or two after it to capitalize on the laugh this joke will generate. So I created the following trail-off jokes:

"Some of the potholes on there are big enough to be foxholes, anyway."

"The Pope blessed it, but he won't ride on it."

Now let's see how this section appears in its final form.

"I had a very pleasant trip over here on the Schuylkill Expressway. A pleasant trip on the Schuylkill Expressway . . . that means you finish in the same car you started with.

That road takes you from South Philadelphia to Valley Forge in twenty-five minutes flat . . .
whether you want to go or not.

Schuylkill Expressway . . . That's an old
Indian term meaning, "White man drive
with forked steering wheel."

I can always tell when I'm approaching
the Schuylkill Expressway. My St. Christ-
opher statue gets down from the dashboard
and climbs into the glove compartment.

It's the only road in the world that
you can travel on from one end to the
other without once leaving the scene
of the accident.

I saw a twelve-car pile-up on there the
other day. The way it happened was a
woman signaled for a left-hand turn
and eleven people believed her.

Actually, our Schuylkill Expressway
is a famous road. It has been cited
by religious leaders all over the world.
It ranks second to World War II as a
cure for atheism.

Some of the potholes on there are big
enough to be foxholes anyway.

The Pope blessed it, but he won't
ride on it."

The only thing remaining now is to generate a blend or transition line to our next subtopic. Let's assume that we'll be doing
material about your driving problems with the local police next.
We would then invent a line that has something to do with the
Expressway, but also includes the police. It might be one like
this:

> "Actually the Expressway is a safe road.
> Very few people ever get tickets on

there. The reason is the police are
afraid to drive on it."

Earlier we said having the jokes written was like having a bunch of bricks delivered to a construction site. It allows us just as much latitude, too. The resultant house might be ranch-style, colonial, or split-level. The humorist can do whatever she pleases with jokes, also, arranging them in any progression or form. It is important, though, to give them some flow because it makes them easier to read or to listen to. If you're trying to sell them, you want that buyer to be interested while reading. If you're presenting them yourself from the lectern, *boy* do you want that audience to be captivated.

I've cautioned you many times not to quit too soon. Until now that admonition applied to the quality of each joke and the quantity of all the jokes. Now it applies to the overall quality of the monologue. After struggling through three dozen lines and arranging them into a routine, the inclination is to be done with it. But now is when it needs some masterful strokes.

An artist friend of mine used to say that anyone can paint a picture, but it takes an *artist* to touch one up. I was privileged many times to see what he meant. Students brought in paintings for his criticism and advice. To my eye the artwork looked good, but the master would take a brush and make a few almost unnoticeable strokes—and the painting would be transformed. It would suddenly have a new energy, vitality, and reality that it lacked before.

The same applies to your comedy. Certainly composing and arranging 35 comedy lines is praiseworthy, but your work isn't done yet. You still have to add those deft brush strokes that change it from a good monologue to a work of art.

One producer that I've worked for had a devastating put down. Eager writers would bring in their latest efforts for his appraisal, and he would glance over it and say, "This isn't writing. It's typing." Going over your routine one more time with a critical eye will guarantee that it will be "writing."

I'll list a few weaknesses that you should look for and recommend a cure. But remember that comedy is a subjective art. In each individual joke, what one critic thinks is a weakness you may see as a strength. I have written gags that I loved and found out later that I was the only one who did love them. *You* have to be the ultimate judge of what leaves your typewriter. Before you can satisfy anyone else, buyer or audience, you have to be content with your material. So reread it pencil in hand and be aware of some of these possible shortcomings.

Jokes That Are Too Direct

Often comedy writers hit on a good combination of ideas and simply write the ideas down. The joke is funny, but it's not funny enough: it doesn't test the audience. There's not enough of a surprise element, and consequently the joke appears obvious.

Perhaps here we should discuss the nature of laughter and why it exists. I've done very little research in this field so I don't classify myself as an expert. However, I did read one explanation that has helped me in formulating jokes.

This hypothesis states that laughter originated as a cry of victory. Early cavemen would be involved in life and death struggles; once the battle was decided, the victor would be relieved of tension and let out a scream of glee. It seems to be valid. For instance, when you watch a prize fight, the boxer with the stupid grin on his face is probably the one who knows he is going to knock the other one senseless shortly. Either that or he's the one who knows he's defeated but is trying to feign victory with a false cry of conquest. (He's still going to get knocked senseless, but it's a nice last-ditch effort.)

In most sports, you see that laugh-like cry of triumph. But you're wondering what that has to do with comedy. Well, humor can be considered a duel of wits. I'll cop out again, stating that I'm not an expert. But keeping these principles in mind may help you write stronger jokes, whether the hypothesis holds or not. In this duel of wits, the comic throws out a straight line and everyone knows a joke is coming. The audience accepts this as a challenge and immediately begins formulating gags of their own. Before they have had a chance to get too far, the comic offers his punchline. The audience laughs because the tension of the battle is ended: the comic gave them the solution to the riddle.

There are jokes that we call "groaners." When the audience

hears them they groan instead of laugh. Why? Because they know the comic's punchline was a weak one. They know that if they had enough time, they would have come up with a better one. These are the gags that are too direct, or too obvious.

The ideal joke tosses out a straight line. It issues a challenge to the listener. Then just at the right time, it defeats the listener. A good punchline should make the listener stop for a fraction of a second, think, and then say, "Oh yes, I get the connection."

In rereading your monologue you want to find those areas where you can make the audience think for that split second.

My favorite example of this happened many years ago on "The Joey Bishop Show." It must have been a special occasion because the people on the show were dressed in tuxedos. Hugh Downs came onstage wearing a white dinner jacket; he certainly stood out.

Joey Bishop could have said, "You look like the Good Humor man," and it would have gotten a big laugh. Instead he put his hand in his pocket, took out some change, and said to Downs, "I'll take one chocolate and two vanillas." It got applause from the studio audience.

"You look like the Good Humor man" was the joke. However, it was too obvious—too direct. The other line said exactly the same thing. Bishop pretended to buy ice cream from Downs because he thought he was the Good Humor man, but he said it without actually saying it. He implied it. It was less direct, less obvious.

If there is any joke in your routine that appears too blatant, take some time to figure out a way of saying the same thing by implying it. It should improve the humor content.

Jokes That Are Too Obscure

This is the flip side of the previous admonition. It's the total reverse of it. In this case, the two comedy ideas are so far from obvious that they become untranslatable.

Rip Taylor has a line in his nightclub act that he uses after a line gets a minimal response. He says, "You're gonna think about that one when you get home and *LAUGH*." You do want your audience to think for a fraction of a second before catching your punchline, but you don't want them still thinking about it while they're motoring home. It's dangerous.

I went to a Hollywood restaurant once with a writer friend and the waiter was a part-time comedian who insisted on doing his act for us. When my sandwich arrived, there was a small chunk out of the piece of bread that looked like someone had taken a bite from it. I showed it to the waiter and said, "Did someone take a bite of my bread?" He said, "Oh no, we're just playing hockey in the kitchen." I'll give a hundred dollars to anyone who can tell me what that meant.

Surely, in the waiter's mind there was some connection between a missing bit of bread and a hockey game. However, he failed to convey the relationship to his listeners. Consequently, he had no joke. (He also had no tip.)

Let's investigate another example. I've sometimes used the following joke in my talks:

> *"In promoting my book last year, I traveled*
> *over 50,000 miles . . . which is not*
> *really a lot when you consider that*
> *my luggage traveled over 100,000."*

This gag is saying that my luggage was lost a lot; it didn't always go the same place I went. It says that by implying it, yet the meaning is perfectly clear. Everyone in the audience knows exactly what the punchline means.

Now let's study a rephrasing of that line:

> *"In promoting my book last year I traveled*
> *over 50,000 miles . . . not always with my luggage."*

Now the audience pauses, searches for the meaning, and can't really be certain of it. Does it mean I sometimes left my luggage home? Did I send it ahead? No one is really sure. Naturally, what it meant was that I was on one plane and my luggage was on another so I wasn't traveling "with my luggage." This particular wording, though, doesn't convey that idea clearly to the audience.

As the comics used to say, "I just tell 'em, folks. I don't explain 'em." No joke will work if you have to hand out a detailed explanation with it.

Spend some time reviewing your gags and make sure your meaning is clear.

You must also be sure that your meaning is clear to each particular audience. Earlier I quoted a gag in which I used the inside term, "reference check." It worked beautifully, but only for that particular crowd. That gag cannot be incorporated into a standard act, because no one else will know what it means.

This phenomenon occurs occasionally in television writing. Our staff will write a funny take-off of a commercial, but on investigating we find that we can't include it in the show because the commercial is regional: viewers on the East Coast won't know what we're talking about.

You have to be careful that all your phrases are universal, too. I've written a few jokes with the word "genuflect" in the punchline. I was surprised to learn how many people don't know what "genuflect" means. I thought I had written some beautiful jokes and they just looked at me like I was from another planet.

Jokes That Are Too Wordy

Shakespeare said, "Brevity is the soul of wit." That still applies today. Be stingy with your words. Say only as much as you must to effectively convey your idea. Why? Because each straight line or set-up that you offer the audience is a promise of a punchline to come. Your audience begins anticipating the reward at the end of it. The longer you make them wait, the more you have to deliver. If it's too long, they're all sitting there a bit impatiently saying, "Boy, this had better be good." Why create that kind of pressure for yourself?

Let's recall the analogy of an audience to a crowd watching a fireworks display. Think what happens when one of the fireworks is a dud. The audience follows its flight with anticipation, then when it fizzles they groan. Comedians don't want groans.

Let's rephrase a joke we quoted earlier about buying a puppy:

> *"My husband went out and bought a puppy.*
> *When he got it home, it wet in the living*
> *room. It wet in the dining room. It*
> *wet all over the house. He calls it*

> *a dog. I call it a bad kidney covered*
> *with fur."*

That long set-up is unnecessary. Everyone knows what puppies are famous for. There's a great old joke where someone says:

> *"I just got a dog."*
> *"Does it have papers?"*
> *"Yeah, but he never uses them."*

Everyone understands that joke even though there was no mention of the dog having accidents in the living room, dining room, and all over the house.

The worst problem with verbiage in a gag, though, is that it telegraphs the punchline. Because that last example dwells so long on the dog's bad habit, the audience sees the punchline coming. They anticipate it. And you also give them so much time that they just might compose a better punchline than the one you deliver. Make your point, but don't beat it to death.

Sometimes you'll find that a punchline needs a lot of set-up. Try as you might, you simply can't cut down the words. Here you have two options: A) make sure that the punchline you deliver is worth the extended buildup. B) Cut the buildup by delivering part of it in smaller, softer jokes. Here's a case where you might note that you have to add jokes to make your routine flow a bit more smoothly. Each joke you write can also act as a set-up for those to follow.

As an example, let's refer back to a joke we discussed in Chapter 9. It's a good gag, but the set-up is awkward and too long. It reads:

> *"You all know Jimmy likes to have a*
> *few drinks at these parties, and he*
> *always takes his glasses off after one*
> *too many. I was talking to his wife*
> *of twenty-eight years before dinner tonight and*
> *I said, 'I guess you can always tell*
> *when Jimmy's had one too many any time*
> *he comes home from work without his*
> *glasses.' She looked at me and said,*
> *'What glasses?'*

That's a lot of words to use to get to that punchline, but they're necessary to explain the humor. Let's explore now how we can get across the basic premise of the joke with shorter gags.

> *"Jimmy's been married to the same*
> *woman for twenty-eight years. Well . . . not really.*
> *After twenty-eight years of living with him, she's*
> *not quite the same woman."*

We get a laugh here and we let our listeners know that Jimmy has been married for twenty-eight years.

> *"And he really loves her . . . almost*
> *as much as he loves his drink."*

For those who aren't in on the joke, we inform them that Jimmy is often kidded about his drinking.

> *"You know he drinks quite a bit. Of*
> *course, nobody knew he drank until one*
> *day he came to work sober."*

This is a good laugh line, but it also establishes our premise that Jimmy drinks constantly.

> *"When he drinks a little too much, the*
> *first thing he does is take his glasses*
> *off. He figures as long as he can't*
> *see anything anyway why should he wear*
> *out the lenses."*

With this we get another response from the audience and we have set up our basic line with four laughs. Now you just continue on with the joke, except that you can drop the awkward phrase, "wife of twenty-eight years." It makes sense just to say, "I was talking to his wife before dinner, etc."

The joke now is cleaner. It's less wordy. Most importantly, the audience didn't have to sit through a long buildup to your punchline. Instead, they chuckled through it. They get less impatient that way and become more tolerant and more receptive to your joke.

Jokes That Don't Please You

This is kind of a catchall, copout category (I always try to cop out, don't I?), but it is valid, and important. Since comedy is a seat-of-the-pants operation, you have to trust your seat and your pants. You must listen to your own instincts.

You will run across gags that seem to fit all the criteria, but still they don't feel right to you. Others may say, "It's a great joke. Leave it alone." Still you feel dissatisfied with it. That discontent may be you telling yourself that you have a *better* joke in you. Listen to that voice and spend a bit more time improving or changing the line. You may surprise yourself with a 10-carat gem.

13 SHORTCUTS TO HUMOR

The author (me) and the reader (you) have to come to a meeting of the minds here. This book is written to tell you a bit about comedy writing. It can tell you the form your manuscripts should take; it can prepare your mind for writing humor; and it can help you market yourself and your material once it's written. But it can't write the jokes for you. Forgive me an unflattering metaphor: you're a horse that I've led to water, but you'll have to do your own drinking.

I'm not so naive as to think that my listing steps from one to whatever will magically produce fantastic lines the first time you sit down at the typewriter. You shouldn't be that naive either. (I feel it's safe to tell you that now because you're probably too far into the book to ask for your money back.)

If, after having tried a few of the exercises and struggling through the book's suggestions, you've discovered that comedy writing is not an easy task, then you've learned a valuable lesson. It's a lesson not all comedy buyers have learned.

I'm always amazed at how lightly people in the world of comedy treat its manufacture. Many a star we deal with thinks nothing of poking his head into the writers' office and saying, "Hey guys, I'm doing a banquet tonight. Can you write about 50 or 60 lines for me during lunch?" It shows a complete misunderstanding of—or disdain for—the creative process. These are some of the same people who complain how exhausting it is for them week in and week out to read lines written in a script.

Some Words of Encouragement

Fred Allen, the radio humorist, helped write most of his material. I was never a big fan of his as a youngster, but grew to love him when I heard this anecdote:

Fred Allen had come to the studio one day and heard another performer throwing a tantrum over the script he'd been handed. "These writers are trying to ruin me," the star bellowed. "This material stinks. I can't go on the air and say this stuff." But Allen asked him, "Where were you when these pages were blank?"

I've tried to outline a battle plan for you to attack the blankness of those pages. Presumably, the plan will simplify your writing, but it won't make it a mere mechanical function. You're still going to have to get your brain working. You're going to have to write and improve, write some more, and improve even more.

Some instructions require very little input from the beginner. If you purchase a tape recorder, the owner's manual will tell you to push this key to record and that key to play back. After you've read the manual once you're an expert tape recorder operator. Other instructions, though, demand more participation from the reader. A typing text will tell you to place your fingers on a-s-d-f-j-k-l-;. To type a "q" you move your left little finger up one row, and to type a "z" you move that same finger down one row. No one can quarrel with that, but it takes practice to get your fingers moving that way, and it takes quite a bit of repetition to develop any speed.

That's where this book has taken you so far. It has laid out the mechanics of writing jokes and routining monologues. Now you have to supply the creativity and the practice. It's almost axiomatic that the only way to learn how to type is to type, type, and type. Well, the only way to learn how to write is to write, write, and write.

If you have faithfully labored through the exercises and diligently attacked the assignments and not been totally satisfied with the results, don't be discouraged. It takes effort: you certainly wouldn't expect to read a book on typing and turn out 125 words per minute on your first try. Good humor writing requires a lot of imagination and a great deal of discipline. My suggestion is to relax, have fun with it along the way, and be delighted with the improvement that you'll see.

As you can see, I'm presuming that you may have had some trouble even after following each recommendation up to now. You've done your preparatory work religiously, followed the guidelines for getting the jokes flowing, and still you're puzzled. "I've got my references neatly listed, and I even have some funny combinations," you might say, "but how do I make the jokes funny?"

Following are a few ideas that I (a little presumptuously) call "shortcuts to humor." They're ideas that I've found help draw out the humor in a situation, and also help to intensify the comedy.

You can use these in conjunction with all the suggestions previously listed. They are more a slant or an angle that a joke can take. Keeping this list in mind can sometimes help you generate humorous combinations, or it can provide the wording for two ideas you already have.

I'll list them here and then we'll discuss them individually:

1. Reflect the truth
2. Relax tension
3. Shock
4. Attack authority
5. Involve the audience
6. Just be funny

Reflect the Truth

On "The Carol Burnett Show" we used to do a sketch once or twice a year that we called "Kitchen Commercials." You might remember it: Carol was a housewife haunted by television commercials that came to life. The Man from Glad would break through her walls, the Tidy Bowl man would speak to her from the toilet tank . . . Audiences loved these sketches, yet the lines weren't that funny. They were simply direct quotes from TV commercials. People laughed because they recognized them. You see the same phenomenon when an impressionist turns around and does the voice of a star. People howl and applaud even though the entertainer didn't say anything humorous. They spark because they *recognize* the celebrity.

That's the value that you can bring to a joke when it's not only funny, but truthful. The audience perceives that truth and identifies with it.

A comedian whom I worked with a few years back used to work primarily in one city. He was born and raised there, and knew all the local customs—as did most of his audience. He would do a ten-minute chunk in his act that had absolutely no funny lines in it, yet it would bring screams from the audience. It was purely reminiscences of childhood.

He would do lines like:

> *"Remember the candy ice cream that came*
> *in those little tin dishes with the*
> *spoon that always bent?"*

The audience would howl.

> *"How about those long pieces of paper*
> *with the candy dots stuck to them?"*

More laughter. Why? Because the audience *did* remember them and responded with a laugh of recognition.

For contrast, try to imagine writing jokes where you create new types of candy. You could concoct some pretty zany combinations that would generate bizarre lines. Probably none of them would get the audience response that these got, though, because these were true.

Your truth can even be a simple statement. Jack Benny once got laughs by saying this to his studio audience:

> *"I don't know why I'm being so funny.*
> *You all got in for free."*

That's basically a statement of fact and the audience recognized that.

George Carlin does some wonderful routines with words. He loves to analyze and play with the idiosyncrasies of language. Basically, though, he is dealing with the truth of the statements. He is seeing a literal meaning in them that most of us overlook. Most of our idioms have those two meanings—the literal and that implied by common usage. We get so used to the common usage that we can totally ignore the literal meaning.

One of Carlin's bits deals with the stilted language of the airlines.

> *"The stewardess asks, 'Would you like*
> *to get on the plane now?'*
> *'No thanks, I'd rather get in the plane.' "*

He doesn't want to fly to Pittsburgh sitting on the wing. He'd rather be inside where the seats are; it's more comfortable and secure.

> *"And then the stewardess announces*
> *'We're preparing now for our final de-*
> *scent.' Oh God, I hope not.*
> *I'd like to make another descent next*
> *week sometime, or the week after that.*
> *But I don't want this one to be my final*
> *descent."*

I've paraphrased Carlin in these quotes, but you can see how he plays with the literal meanings in those statements.

I heard another comic do pretty much the same thing when he said that we have a way of substituting distance for time.

> *"How far do you drive to work?"*
> *"Oh, about 15 minutes."*

That makes perfect sense to us, but it doesn't work in reverse.

> *"Excuse me, sir, could you give me the time?"*
> *"Oh sure," (checking his watch) "I have*
> *about three miles."*

It's ironic and it's fanciful, but it's basically true. We laugh because we recognize the truth in there—and also the dumbness of it. We're laughing at ourselves because we use and accept that language.

Your truth can also be exaggerated or extended out to its logical conclusion. You needn't limit yourself to reflections of fact. Your true pronouncement can be distorted, twisted, extended, or shortened—played with in any way so long as it remains recognizable.

> *"Inflation is getting terrible.*
> *I went to the supermarket today*
> *and put a down payment on a leg*
> *of lamb."*

It's true that inflation is getting worse, although we don't yet buy meat the same way we buy houses. However, we've extended the reality of the inflation situation out to its ludicrous limit; the audience will still see the truth in this.

Relax Tension

Nothing can ease tension in an audience so easily as comedy, and a tense situation can give you the greatest straight lines. This particular phenomenon is especially useful for ad-libs—those spontaneous lines that audiences love. Should something happen to upset an audience, almost any line will get laughs. If a waiter drops a tray of dishes while an entertainer is onstage, the performer can get laughs with anything. The crowd has been upset, tension has been created, and they're waiting for the comic to relieve it.

I remember seeing a very good comic perform one night, but his biggest laugh was unplanned. He was working in a small club that had rented its upstairs room for a private party. In the middle of his act, the folks above must have started dancing a polka. The noise coming through the ceiling was frightening. The comic said, "What's going on up there?" Someone from the audience volunteered, "It's a wedding party." The comic said, "Can't they wait till they get home?"

The ad-lib is so surefire that some comics even create their own situations. I once saw George Gobel do an ad-lib that I suspect was planned. In the middle of a song, he began choking sightly. He said, "I think I swallowed a fly," and called offstage, "Can you get me a glass of water, please?" Gobel coughed a bit more, and then said, "Oh never mind. Let him walk down."

If you perform your own material, sooner or later something upsetting will happen. People drop things, lights blink on and off, sound systems go crazy, hecklers shout out the wrong thing. It can be annoying, but it can also be a sent-from-heaven straight line. You'll fare better if you treat it as a set-up and provide an off-the-cuff punchline. It isn't that difficult because, as we've said, almost any line will do.

Once I emceed an early evening banquet. The sound system wasn't working properly, and each time I approached the microphone it whistled shrilly. I backed away and it stopped. I approached it and it whistled. I backed away, it stopped: I went near and it whistled. The audience was laughing heartily at my misfortune. Finally one of the proprietors balanced the system so that it worked, and at last I took the microphone without it rebelling. My opening line was "Well, when you hold a banquet at 6 o'clock, a guy doesn't always have a chance to shower first."

The audience loved this because they appreciated the situation was totally beyond my control. It was annoying and it was making me appear the fool, yet I took the joke and played it back on myself. That dismissed that incident and we could get on with the show.

Many years ago there was a documentary on TV about Shelly Berman's career. The camera was on Berman doing a monologue, when a backstage phone rang. Berman was furious: he stormed backstage and tore the phone off the wall. The cameras showed everything. Some people contend that this hurt his career. That I don't know, and I don't mean to demean him because I'm sure the film didn't take all the factors into account. I mention this here only to show the difference in reaction. Had he joked it away, the audience would have appreciated his humor, but by throwing a tantrum, he made a tense situation even more tense.

As a writer, you can use this device by creating your own tension and then relieving it. I saw one comic do this beautifully in his nightclub routine. Right near the opening, he said:

> *"This is the cheapest club I've ever*
> *worked in."*

Right away the audience got a bit tense thinking they were in the middle of a management-labor feud.

> *"This place is owned by a father and*
> *son and you see them walking up and*
> *down the aisles every so often (which*
> *was true). They're checking up on my*

> *act. I'll show you how cheap they are.*
> *First the father comes out of that office*
> *back there with a big cigar, walks around*
> *a little while, then goes back in the*
> *office. Then the son comes out of the*
> *office back there with a big cigar and*
> *walks around. It's the same cigar."*

Now the audience knows they've been put on. They're relieved. They laugh.

The late Godfrey Cambridge was popular just when black comedians had begun working regularly to white audiences. He was a short rotund man, and he had a great opening line for his act:

> *"My name is Godfrey Cambridge. I'm 6*
> *foot 2 and weigh 180 pounds. Anybody*
> *who doesn't believe that is prejudiced."*

It exposed any latent racism in the crowd, dismissed it, and cleared the way to simply get on with the entertainment.

A writer can be aware of an already existing situation and capitalize on it for humor content. Back in the days when the government hadn't yet admitted to the hostilities in Vietnam and were still insisting that American troops were only there as military advisors, Bob Hope got a big laugh with this opening line:

> *"Hi. Welcome, advisors."*

Shock

Part of a comedian's entertainment value is that he can say and do things that normal people either can't or won't do. He's the naughty boy in school. His behavior *shocks* normal people like ourselves. A comic like Jerry Lewis relies on this heavily. He acts the buffoon on stage, shocking people by doing and saying crazy things that ordinary people are too inhibited to try.

Even dignified performers like Bob Hope and Johnny Carson gather a few laughs from this device. People are surprised that they would dare say certain things about the President of the United States. It stuns them.

Most of Don Rickles's act depends on shock value. He insults perfect strangers. Normal people don't say those things to anyone but their closest friends. Consequently we laugh not only at Rickles's wit, but at his audacity, too.

Dirty jokes, also, depend on shock value. If you dissect an off-color story sometime you may find that there is nothing inherently funny in it, except that someone would use those words in public.

There's no need to list examples here because almost all insult and off-color humor and general buffoonery falls into this category.

Attack Authority

This really is an offshoot of the "shock" category, except that it's a bit gentler. Basically, it's insult humor, but the comic is on much safer ground because chances are the audience will side with him. He's ribbing someone who the audience will agree deserves to be kidded: the boss.

Bob Hope did this many times while entertaining servicemen overseas. He always appeared to be more one of the enlisted men than one of the generals.

Allow me to cite an example from my own experience again. I was doing a retirement party for one of our supervisors who was a big cigar smoker. I kidded him by calling them cheap cigars.

> "Everybody likes a boss who smokes cheap cigars . . . you can always tell when he's in the area."

> "He's not the only stinking supervisor we have in the plant. He's one of the few with a valid excuse."

I've talked a lot about roasts, where I got my early comedy-writing experience. Well, at one affair some people decided to write their own roast. It was so devastating that the guest of honor walked out in the middle, offended.

There *is* a way to do insult humor, make it funny and enjoyable, and not antagonize anyone. Bob Hope kids politicians constantly and yet can have dinner with the President the next day.

It may seem contradictory that you can use insult humor without irritating anyone, but it can be done if you apply the following guidelines.

1. Kid about things that are fabricated, or obviously not true. At one party I ribbed a guy who prided himself on his drinking prowess. I said, "When he retires we're going to light a permanent flame in his honor. We're going to set fire to his breath." The man didn't drink excessively; he talked about it excessively. There is no way I would do that line about someone who had a serious drinking problem.

2. Kid about things people kid themselves about. The joke I quoted above applies here, too. This man liked to joke about his drinking feats; I went along with him.

The emcee at one company roast introduced a man who was about 5 foot 6 and had 13 children—but he introduced him as being 6 foot 1. Then when the roastee got to the microphone, the emcee explained that he was 6 foot 1 when he got married. This was a "short" joke, but it was permissible because this particular guy was always kidding himself about his height; there was no risk of offense.

3. Kid about things that are of no consequence. I'll stick with examples from these company roasts because a writer walks a fine line here. We were ribbing people who were good friends, and we didn't want to hurt them. One supervisor had a powerful telephone voice and could be heard all over the office. A speaker said of him, "He's the only fellow you can hang up on without losing volume." That line doesn't belittle his work, his personality, or his family—it kids him about something that doesn't really matter.

By using those guidelines, and a bit of common sense, you can do insult humor without really insulting anyone. A safe rule of thumb, though, is when in doubt about a joke, drop it. It's easier to write a new joke than it is to get new friends.

Now back to our shortcuts to humor.

Involve the Audience

Your listeners will always enjoy humor more if they are made a part of it. Localizing your comedy will always multiply its humor content. The audience members feel like they're sharing the stage with you.

A speaker friend of mine sometimes starts his talk by saying something like:

> *"Your chairman (he mentions the name)*
> *called me about doing this talk. I gladly*
> *accepted the charges."*

You've just poked fun at one of the audience's own. It gets laughs.

Instead of using jokes that begin with "Two guys were walking down the street," find out the names of some people in the audience who fit into the story, and tell it about them.

You can also localize by using the names of places in the area . . . suburban towns, eating places, the local lovers lane. All of these devices bring the audience into the performance.

Even if you don't know that many specifics about them you can still draw your audience into the routine. Slappy White used to tell a story that illustrates this point perfectly:

> *"I just read in Reader's Digest that*
> *one out of every four people in the*
> *United States is mentally unbalanced.*
> *Think of that . . . one out of every four.*
> *You don't have to take my word for it,*
> *you can prove this for yourself. Here's*
> *what I want you to do. Think of three*
> *of your best friends."*

Now the people at each table laugh and look around, even point fingers at their friends. He goes on:

> *"Do they seem all right to you?"*

Again, the people at each table are relating to each other. They have the feeling that Slappy is talking directly to their group. Then he finishes:

> *"Because if they do, you must be the one."*

It works every time because the people become involved.

Just Be Funny

Obviously, this is a catchall category designed to get me off the hook for anything I omitted in the preceding ones. It's included to convey the message that if you have something that's funny, it doesn't have to be pigeonholed into any other area. Just use it.

My writer friends used to discuss the famous Abbott and Costello "Who's on First" routine. Some contended that the premise was weak, that it was impossible to have a team with such outlandish names—it was too much of a coincidence, and it was unbelievable that the double meaning could run that long. Yet, every time I hear that routine I laugh. If you think it's funny, I say do it whether the premise holds up or not.

14 WRITING TO YOUR AUDIENCE

I've referred once or twice to a sign in a producer's office that read, "There are few good judges of comedy. And even they don't agree."

That sign was wrong. There is only one ultimate judge of comedy and that is the audience: the rest of us are merely guessing. Some of the pros are better guessers than others, but even the best cross their fingers and hope that the audience responds.

Making People Laugh

Carpentry is an exact science. It can be creative, but it's always exact. If you take out a tape measure and mark off the distance from point A to point B, that's how long the board should be that you're going to put in that space. Comedy is different. You can't measure how long a pause should be or exactly how to make a voice inflection. It's a seat-of-the-pants operation.

Almost any time I speak about comedy to writers or performers, I ask the following two questions:

1) What is a joke?

2) What does every entertainer have in common?

I suggest that you think about those questions and come up with some answers before going on.

Surely there are learned and technical definitions of a joke, but my homemade one is practical and applies: a joke is anything that makes people laugh. It can be a series of words, a look, a shrug of the shoulders, even a moment of silence—but if it makes people laugh, it's a joke.

I worked on "The Jim Nabors Hour" for two years and one of the biggest laughs I remember came from Ronnie Schell, playing the inebriated boarder; he told Frank Sutton to close his eyes because he had a birthday present for him. Frank shut his eyes and everyone else on stage turned to see what Ronnie would produce. Ronnie paused a moment and then shrugged his shoulders as if to say, "I don't have anything." It's difficult to believe from telling it, but it was hilarious and got tremendous audience response. That's a joke whether it fulfills the dictionary definition or not.

And now for the answer to the second question: What does every entertainer have in common? Entertainers have to have an audience; there is no way a person can perform without one. Some people might contend that a filmmaker doesn't have a crowd in the editing room, or that an author writing a book does it alone. That's true, but it *is* done for the benefit of an audience eventually. No one would make a movie if it were guaranteed never to be shown, nor would anyone begin a book that was to have no readers.

The answers to these two questions are very important because they highlight *people*. A joke makes *people* laugh. An entertainer performs for *people*. The audience is supreme.

An audience is tremendously important in humor because it becomes a participant. There is no humor until audience members get involved. You've often heard the question, "If a tree falls in the woods and there is no one around to hear it, does it make a noise?" I don't know. I do know, though, that if you tell a joke and it gets no laugh, it's not a joke. There is really no humor until the listeners ratify the comic's input with laughter.

A comic once told me how much he envied singers. He thought they had the easy life—they could sing a song over and over again, and they had access to the greatest writers in the world, for free. Even a novice vocalist can sing Cole Porter or Jerome Kern. But where is a young comic to get top-notch comedy material? The same comedian complained, too, that if a singer does a bad job of singing a song, he'll still get applause when he's finished. But if a comedian tells a bad joke, he doesn't get automatic laughs—quite the contrary.

The audience doesn't have to participate in a song. The vocalist can warble away as badly as he pleases, the crowd can talk to one another at their tables; when they realize the song is coming to its conclusion, they turn politely and applaud. Certainly, some singers pull an audience into the performance and make them get involved in the show. They're great entertainers. Nevertheless, even the bad ones get polite clapping. A comedian *needs* the attention of the audience. They *have* to listen, and the laughter generated *has* to be spontaneous, otherwise it's worthless.

True humor is a partnership. It's equal parts humorist and audience. Sadly, many writers and performers overlook this. As a young comedy writer I often traveled with comics to study audience response. I was confused by the comics who came backstage and complained, "Nobody could make that crowd laugh." I wondered why people would get dressed up and come to an expensive nightclub in order *not* to be entertained.

Actually, they didn't. They were willing to do their part. The comic didn't do his.

I've found that's a big difference between writing for nightclub comics and writing for television. In a nightclub you get instantaneous, honest appraisal. Either that crowd laughs or it doesn't. I've told you about jokes I loved that got no response. After rewording it, relocating it, delivering it differently, it *still* didn't get a laugh, and we had to admit that it just wasn't working, and take it out of the act.

In television, it's too easy to blame someone else. "The actor didn't say the line right." "The director had the wrong shot." "The studio audience was too interested in the cameras." There are a hundred and one different excuses that the writer falls back on—consequently we never improve our writing. Why should we? It wasn't our fault.

If You Ignore Them, They Won't Laugh

Steve Martin's entire act is practically a parody of show business. Ironically, he gets a lot of laughs making fun of the profession he's in, comedically biting the hand that feeds him. On one of his records he has a routine that illustrates the principle of audience participation beautifully. Martin does this routine in his own inimitable style; I'll weakly paraphrase it just to get the point across.

He tells the audience that he has heard there's a plumbers' convention in town, and he's found out they're at the show that night. So he asks the audience's indulgence while he tells what he promises is a hilarious plumber joke. The jokes goes on and on and finally ends with a punchline something like, "I said a Watson wrench, dummy, not a number 10 wrench." Then he laughs crazily to himself and waits for the audience to join in. Naturally he gets no big response, so he covers by explaining, "I guess that busload of plumbers must have been delayed or something." Take my word for it, it's a funny routine, and it shows how important the audience is to a comic. Martin's bit is a total put-on, but presumably there *are* jokes that only plumbers would appreciate. I've told you about a gag I did that only personnel executives understood—I told the joke not even knowing what I was saying, but it worked.

As a writer, you have to admit the audience's importance to your writing, and include them. You really have no choice. If you ignore them, they won't laugh. If they don't laugh, you have no product.

It's like a man who wants to make a million dollars from oil wells. Does he go out and simply start digging holes in hope one of them will produce? Certainly not. The earth is a participant in his venture; it will eventually supply his wealth. He must study the earth, discover where oil is likely to be found—*then* he drills to produce the gusher.

The humorist must treat the audience as a participant, because it will supply *his* reward. Therefore, the writer must study the audience and find out where mirth is to be mined.

A few years back I visited my home town, Philadelphia. It was right after the Philadelphia Flyers hockey team had won the Stanley Cup. My nephews and nieces had posters of all the different players hanging in their rooms. Several friends gave me replicas of the Stanley Cup as a memento of my visit. My brother even played a recording of Kate Smith singing the National Anthem, because that year each time Kate Smith sang at the game, the Flyers won.   The entire city had "Flyer Fever."

A few weeks later Bob Hope was appearing at the Valley Forge Music Fair outside Philadelphia. I wrote a bunch of material from what I had learned about the Flyers. The audience went crazy. Just mentioning the Flyers sent them screaming, and if it was funny, it was magnified that much more. Hope was amazed at the reaction, but I didn't have the nerve to ask for a raise. It was too easy.

As a writer, how do you capitalize on audience participation? Again, we're back to the preparatory work. You have to become something of an investigator. Particularize and isolate your audience. Ask the following three questions:

1) What applies to them?
2) How does it apply to them?
3) What do they know?

What Applies

Find out what the people you're going to talk to are talking about themselves. What's happening in their city? If you're talking to a business or professional group, what is happening in their line of work?

If you're doing material for a college campus, find out who the big sports rivals are and what happened in the rivalry this year. Did this college win or lose? Was it a decisive victory or a close call? Find out the good restaurants and the real dives. What's the name of the notorious necking spot?

If you or your comic client are visiting a city, what are the headlines? Has the mayor been up to anything strange lately? What's the weather been like? How are the local teams doing this year?

If you're working for a particular group of people, uncover some of the inside politics. What is *the* topic of conversation among the members of the group?

I once did a show for a group of insurance people in Vancouver, British Columbia. I casually mentioned to one of my hosts that I had never seen so many unusual license plates. He laughed and explained that in British Columbia, insurance agents distributed auto licenses and they all took care to get the unique numbers for themselves. At the banquet I mentioned that you could tell it was an insurance agents' convention—outside was a parking lot full of the most beautiful license plates in Canada.

That was an accidental discovery, but writers shouldn't generally rely on serendipity. Ask someone in the organization to supply you with some newspapers, bulletins, or his own ideas about what's going on within the organization.

If there are two jokes of equal value, one that applies to your audience can get ten times the laughter of the other. It's worth doing some research.

How It Applies to Them

If you're doing material for a convention of farmers, you can write jokes about the President's farm policy, right? Right, but you'd better find out how it affects the farmers and what their position is on the policy. If they're "pro" and you do jokes that are "con," you might be in trouble.

If you're working for a college that is de-emphasizing football, you'd better find out where the students stand before you compose your gags.

Some folks may argue that this makes you a fence-straddler: it sounds like a wishy-washy position to take. But it really isn't. You're simply trying to find the mind of the audience and then use that to make your gags work. Often, you can tell the same joke in a slightly different way to generate a response.

Here's a joke I've heard that can be told at either a Republican or Democratic gathering.

> "A man asked a politician why he was a
> Republican and he responded by saying, "My
> Daddy was a Republican, and his Grandaddy
> before him." The man asked, 'If your
> Daddy was a jackass and his Grandaddy
> before him, what would that make you?'
> The politican replied, 'A Democrat.' "

Simply reverse the parties and you have a joke fit for either group. You're not really taking a stand pro or con, you're just kidding.

Here's another example. Let's suppose Alpha Manufacturing Company and Beta Manufacturing Company are fierce competitors. This is a story you can tell to Alpha.

> *"A very rich gentleman wanted to get his three sons started with businesses of their own, so he asked the oldest son what he wanted. The boy said he wanted an oil company, so the man bought him Exxon. The second son was a bit younger. He said he liked movies, so the man bought him MGM. The third son was much younger and he loved Mickey Mouse. He wanted anything that was Mickey Mouse, so the man bought him Beta Manufacturing."*

Obviously, the story works just as well when you're appearing before Beta employees—provided you remember to change the punchline.

There are other ways of manipulating a joke so that it doesn't reflect back on you. In writing a newspaper column, I have to maintain political impartiality, otherwise I'd lose half my readers with one offensive gag. Impartiality can be accomplished by using such handles as "It's rumored that . . . " or "Some people say that . . . " "Some Democrats are wishing that . . . " "Some Republicans are hoping that . . . "

The bottom line is, as a humorist you're involved with an audience. What does it benefit you to do lines that won't amuse them? Either convert lines so they're less offensive, or drop the routine and write a different one.

In any case, it pays you to find out which way an audience thinks on each issue you're going to speak or write about.

What They Know

This may sound silly, but it's so obvious that it's often overlooked. For a joke line to work, people have to know what you're talking about.

One danger in asking people in an organization what's going on is that they may tell you, you'll write up a fistfull of good jokes—then you find out the night of the banquet that the only people who are aware of what you've been told is going on are the president and corresponding secretary of the organization. The general membership never heard of it.

Audiences vary from region to region. Some products aren't available all over the country. People on the East Coast have rarely heard of the May Company, on the West Coast they don't know about Wanamaker's. Philadelphia has hoagie sandwiches; in other parts of the country a hoagie might be a "hero" or a "submarine."

These are all just random examples of how a line that makes perfect sense to you may be completely unintelligible to a different audience. You must either know the frame of reference of each audience or use topics that are understood by all.

I've already told how we had to drop commercial take-offs from "The Carol Burnett Show" because the commercials we were spoofing were regional.

In writing topical one-liners for comedians who travel all over the country, we get most of our inspiration from the Los Angeles papers, but we check to make sure the rest of the country is aware of the topic.

This phenomenon really hit home a few years ago when the Bob Hope staff had to write gags for the trip to Red China. It was very hard to try to figure out what these people knew about the western world and what they didn't. Did they know what the Love Boat was? Would they understand a Billy Graham reference? Suppose a joke had the name Frank Sinatra or Muhammad Ali in it . . . which ones would they recognize? However, we were fairly safe because most of Hope's jokes were told through an interpreter. If they didn't work, the interpreter was the one with egg on his face.

Most of the above cautions apply to specific audiences. What do you do when you're writing for a general audience? You have to work to general frames of reference. You have to come up with ideas the entire nation is aware of.

Bob Hope deals in headlines that affect the entire nation. Erma Bombeck deals in generalities that apply to every homemaker in the North, South, East, and West. Bill Cosby reminisces about childhood.

The gags are much easier to come by the more particularized your audience is, but the same principles apply even if your audience is potentially the whole world.

15 KEEPING A COMEDY NOTEBOOK

One Saturday morning I woke around 7 o'clock, dressed, and rushed over to my tennis club for my weekly five hours of doubles. Normally, I shower afterward and relax by watching whatever inane sports are on television. This particular Saturday, though, I had to hurry and do a newspaper column. I couldn't think of a single topic to write about.

This is typical of most writers: when the deadline nears, the mind goes blank. However, the reason I was so rushed this day was because I wanted to watch the Wimbledon matches on television. John McEnroe was in them and, aside from his brilliant tennis, he always provides excitement with his shenanigans. The front page of the morning newspaper showed a photo of McEnroe being the "brat of Wimbledon." All that the club members talked about during our tennis recesses was the mischievous monkeyshines of McEnroe at the sedate and proper Wimbledon tournament.

All this was right in front of my nose and I couldn't think of anything to write about. McEnroe at Wimbledon cried out for satire and I didn't see it.

One thing you should have learned by now is that a large part of comedy writing is preparation. It won't write the jokes for you, but when time comes to compose the gags, preparation will make your life easier and you'll finish much sooner.

Had I been prepared that Saturday morning, I could have written an entire newspaper column while luxuriating in my bubblebath. In fact, 12 gags on McEnroe's Wimbledon antics might have been dashed off in the six-minute drive from the tennis club to my home. Had I been truly alert, the 12 gags might have been written by companions as they discussed Wimbledon during our tennis breaks.

We've talked a great deal about preparation, but most of it has been devoted to preparing the topic. A joke, as we all know by now, is a combination of two different ideas—which needn't necessarily be on the same topic, so long as they are related in some way. In fact, relating a standard topic to a current news item gives it a particular zest: it makes the joke as fresh as that news item.

Ideas are the raw material that jokes are made from. You can *never* have too many of them. Also, you can never *remember* all of them. You can't trust your faculty of recall to serve you well as the deadline nears. My overlooking the McEnroe topic is sad testimony to that.

While blocking this chapter out in my head this morning, I visited my barber. While I was there, the phone rang constantly. The barber had to keep assigning different times to his customers. There was no way he could keep each appointment in his head, so he kept an appointment book by the phone and jotted down each reservation as it was made.

Why then should gag writers expect to keep all their ideas in their heads ready for immediate recall any time they need them? They can't, but many of us try.

It is only logical that any and all ideas that you come by should be jotted down for future reference. They may generate entire topics, or they may provide the punchline for a joke you need. In any case, it is much more dependable if they are written down than if they are simply assigned a corner of your brain. There they are too easily misplaced.

I keep a notebook of current topics. Each day, while reading the papers, I jot down items that have special prominence. They may be selected from the front page, the entertainment section, the sports page, the business section, or even the comics. During the course of the day, I engage in conversation with a number of people. I might jot down any topic that many people are talking about. This could be a new movie under discussion or a TV show that everyone watched.

At the time I write this chapter my list of current topics looks something like this:

Cheese distributed to the poor

Crackers distributed to the needy

Rain and mud slides in California

Reagan reinstates the draft

Cold spell across the nation

$500,000 paid for one golf win

McEnroe and Connors fight on tennis court

In addition to newsworthy topics I might keep a list of everyday observations. Certain things that are noteworthy might happen to me while I'm driving on the freeway. Salesclerks in department stores may be more rude or more cheerful than usual. Anything that strikes me as different is fed into the notebook.

Now with this added ammunition I'm much better prepared to write a column or compose jokes. These items, coupled with the preparation of the given topic, provide a tremendous amount of fodder for my gags.

For example, the idea of distributing overabundant cheese to the poor struck me as ironic. On that topic I wrote:

> *"The cheese is being distributed by the
> government, but only to the poor. In
> other words, you get your cheese only
> if you can prove you don't have a cracker
> to put it on."*

That joke is composed of two ideas that both came from the topic itself. However, a week or so later, I was writing on Reagan's reinstatement of the draft. In looking over my notes I saw the older topic of distributing cheese, and later crackers, to the needy. Combining those two elements I wrote:

> *"Our government is really being nice
> to the poor of this nation. They've given
> them cheese and crackers and now a nice
> new khaki suit to wear."*

Your notebook can take any form you choose. Mine is a simple little pocket-sized loose-leaf book that I keep on my desk. As ideas present themselves, I simply enter them with a date and a short capsulization. Other writers keep a weekly or monthly diary and make entries under the appropriate date. When I first began in Hollywood I saw one writer who kept a large sheet of paper on which he made his entries, taped to the office wall. This way all topics were visible with a glance; no page-turning was necessary. As topics became too dated to use, he simply crossed them out with a single line. You may develop your own handy system. Any procedure is acceptable so long as it works for you.

A writer friend of mine here in Los Angeles, John Lewis, has a system that is much more elaborate. It isn't that much more work than mine to keep current, it's simply better organized. I recommend it.

John keeps a loose-leaf binder with several separate categories. For instance, he may have sections devoted to the areas that we've just discussed—current topics and everyday ideas. However, he also has a page where he'll list any intriguing commercials he sees on TV or hears on radio. He has a page devoted to movie and television stars, and beside them he may make an entry about something they're noted for: Sammy Davis, Jr., may have the amount of jewelry he wears written next to his name; other stars may be in the news for some noteworthy reason or other. John also devotes a page to movie titles and comments—some movies get a lot of press. He may tally the runaway hits and the worst bombs. He lists TV shows, which he may gather from *TV Guide*, and keep a commentary on which are doing well and which poorly in the ratings, who has quit which show and so on. Finally, John keeps a page of clever sayings and phrases.

This isn't a tremendous amount of work, because once you do your initial research it's a matter of making a few entries each day. But such a collection can be a terrific time-saver.

When Opportunity Strikes

If I were to ask you right now to write 15 take-offs of television commercials, you would be hard put even to think of that many memorable commercials, let alone write jokes about them. But by simply turning to the right page in the notebook, you'll have all your research already done for you.

Each rain season we have mudslides in California. A natural joke-writing slant is about how the slides affect the stars. Yet each time I come to that point, I have to think of stars. I always come up with the same ones . . . Sammy Davis, Jr., Dean Martin, Dolly Parton, Jackie Gleason. It would be really valuable to have a list of stars on hand to select for my straight lines, along with little notations about them.

Sometimes in writing about certain topics, television shows become straight lines. For instance, when a writer's strike hits, it's logical to do jokes on how it affects current shows. But I have to grab a copy of *TV Guide* and read through the program listings before I can begin the gag writing. Why don't I have a list handy?

These are only the obvious applications of such a notebook, but there will be some inspiring fringe benefits, too. A notebook can provide brilliant ideas for gags on topics that don't seem to have any relationship to some of these lists. But when you *find* that relationship, you create a truly original gag.

A comedy writer's notebook will make each of your assignments a bit easier. In the long run, it will make your comedy writing faster and better. As we've said so many times, you learn to write by writing. Each time you write you learn more about writing. Your mind becomes accustomed to it.

Using a prompter like the lists you collect in your writer's notebook will teach you to associate ideas and to do it fast. That's what the ideal humorist does.

Someone once asked Mel Brooks's Two-Thousand-Year-Old Man who he thought was the greatest comedy team in the history of film. Brooks answered:

> *"I would have to say Wilt and Neville*
> *Chamberlain. What a hysterical team.*
> *Neville would read the Nuremberg Pact,*
> *then Wilt would stuff him through a*
> *basket."*

What a weird combination—Wilt and Neville Chamberlain. Can

you imagine how many different names went through Brooks's mind before hitting that one?

I've worked with many comedy writers who have astoundingly quick minds. When a straight line is delivered, they can select a name from history that fits perfectly in the punchline. These gagsters are innately brilliant, but some of their mental dexterity comes from having done it over and over again.

Woody Allen's off-the-cuff remarks always amaze me. An interviewer once asked Woody what gave him the biggest thrill in life. He said, "Jumping naked into a vat of cold Roosevelt dimes." Where did that idea come from? Another questioner asked what his greatest sin was. Allen confessed, "Having impure thoughts about Art Linkletter."

We should all aim for the comedic brilliance of Woody Allen. If you haven't attained that mental quickness yet, start by keeping a writer's notebook.

16 SKETCH WRITING

As a novice television writer, one of the most difficult transitions for me to make was from writing one-line monologue material to sketch humor. The inclination among one-line writers is simply to string a series of jokes together to form a sketch, but it's not that easy.

Certainly a sketch is a collection of jokes, but it is much more. Remember the bricks metaphor? Gags are the bricks from which sketches are fashioned, but a pile of bricks at a construction site doesn't make a decent dwelling. You can't simply mortar the bricks together, either—that just forms a collection of glued-together bricks. You need a master plan to build a house. The building blocks must be assembled in an orderly, well-designed fashion. I suppose the difference between a gag writer and a sketch writer is like the difference between a mason and an architect.

What we said earlier applies, though. It's easier to learn the sketch form, and you'll be better at it if you're schooled in the basics of joke writing.

Professional writers always say that a sketch needs a beginning, a middle, and an end. That definition never tells *me* much because anything that occupies time and space has a beginning, a middle, and an end, and a good sketch should do a great deal more than just occupy time and space. The beginning-middle-and-end precept is merely a simplistic way of saying that a sketch has to be more than a collection of gags.

Every rule has an exception, and some readers may spot them immediately. Johnny Carson does sketches that are simply interviews with Ed McMahon. Bob and Ray do some brilliant pieces of comedy that are merely strings of gags. Mel Brooks's Two-Thousand-Year-Old Man is hilarious, but it's nothing more than a series of one-liners. Most of these, with the exception of some of Bob and Ray's material, are dialogue comedy—monologue material done by two people. It can be done on television, but only sparingly. One of the greatest sketch shows in TV history was the "Sid Caesar" show, but a complete rundown each week of nothing but interview spots, even though Caesar did them brilliantly, wouldn't have sustained the show. Solid sketches are required.

A good sketch needs:

    1) A premise
    2) Some complications
    3) An ending

or in other words, a beginning, a middle, and an end. Let's take a look at each part of a sketch.

A Premise

Just as the starting point for joke writing is having something to say, likewise the starting point for sketch writing is having some sort of message. This seems axiomatic, but even solid writers forget it.

Many times ideas that are pitched for sketches are not premises at all, but costumes or places. The head writer hears things like, "Have Tim Conway dressed in a cowboy suit. It'll be hilarious." That's a costume. Tim is a terrific comic, but if you dress him in a cowboy suit and put him in front of a television camera, he still has to do something.

Writers suggest, "Put Carol Burnett in the complaint department of a department store and it'll be a riot." That's a place. Who will she be dealing with there, and what will her attitude be?

Something that just seems to lend itself to crazy antics isn't enough to make a sketch. The craziness has to be programmed and directed. There has to be a reason for it to take place. It must have impetus that leads it in an orderly progression. It needs a premise.

If you have a threatening sheriff give Harvey Korman only 20 minutes to get out of town or be lynched, and the stagecoach driver is Tim Conway's old man who does everything slower than molasses, *then* you have a beginning. You have a premise.

If you set up Carol Burnett as the complaint person in a department store and add a long line of irate customers, with the man at the front of the line Carol's husband who wants a divorce, you have the beginning of a sketch. You have a premise.

A premise consists of one or two sentences that tell you what the playlet is about. A gambler threatened with a life-or-death proposal who then has to hurry a slow old coot in order not to be killed tells me a lot more about a sketch than "Tim is in a cowboy suit."

Each of the sketches you begin to write should be easily explained and should sound interesting in one or two sentences. That's a hint that you've found a beginning: a premise.

In writing your sketch, you should get to your premise quickly, and it should generally be delivered almost like a punchline. It should be concise, clear, and explain what the sketch is all about. I like to call this the "Uh-Oh Factor." It's that point in the sketch where the action is moving along nicely, and then suddenly you introduce one or two lines that cause the audience to say, "Uh-Oh, what are they ever going to do now?"

This point was illustrated graphically in each of the old "I Love Lucy" shows. In almost every one of them there would be that moment where audience members would actually shout out "uh-oh" when Lucy began her shenanigans. That's what should happen in a sketch.

To show you what I mean, let me just give you some quick examples of sketches we did on "The Carol Burnett Show." In one story we had Harvey Korman with Carol, his wife, seated at a restaurant bar having a drink while waiting for their table. We revealed that Harvey had been in prison for some time and was just paroled. He was a free man at last, but with the least little bit of trouble he would be back behind bars for another 20 years. Just then, Carol shouted to the huge bartender, "Hey, Fathead, do you call this a *dry* martini," and the audience thought, "Uh-oh, this guy's in trouble now."

In another sketch we had Carol being welcomed home from the hospital by her friends. It became apparent that she was hospitalized with a nervous breakdown from getting too involved in soap operas. But now she was totally cured. As she said, "I don't care if Bruce marries Wanda or not." A girlfriend said, "Bruce is dead." Carol's eyes widened in shock—and everyone thought "Uh-oh, she's hooked on soap operas again."

On "The New Bill Cosby Show," we had Peter Sellers and Lily Tomlin seated side by side on an airplane. The pilot announced that the plane was in serious trouble. After some general hysteria, Sellers turned calmly to Tomlin and asked if she were sitting in the right seat. "What difference does that make at a time like this?" she wanted to know. Sellers said, "Because I think *your* life is flashing before *my* eyes." The audience immediately said, "Uh-oh, what an embarrassing situation this could be."

Any sketch you compose should have that moment in it, fairly close to the beginning.

Again, there are exceptions. One fantastic bit on the Burnett show featured a family saying goodbye to a relative at the airport. They talked about what a good time they had had and what a pleasure it was entertaining him. They said their emotional goodbyes—then his plane was delayed. They had to go through the procedure once more. The plane was delayed again and again until the departure became a violent family argument and they couldn't wait to get rid of the jerk. In this case, the premise was concealed for awhile and revealed gradually, but still the audience knew rather quickly what the sketch was about.

More important . . .it *was* about *something*. It had a beginning. It had a premise.

Some Complications

Once your premise is set forth, you have to make something happen. If your premise has presented a predicament, the audience is going to want you to try to solve it. If you've postulated a goal to be accomplished, you have to introduce some complications to that goal. Obviously you can't pose a premise and then jump abruptly to the ending. You need some action.

Sometimes your action can be episodic, a series of jokes that happen one right after the other. We did a sketch where Tim Conway and Harvey Korman were Revolutionary War soldiers surrounded by the enemy. They had a solitary cannon. Harvey proposed that he would decoy the enemy into the open, and then Tim would destroy them with one perfectly timed and aimed cannon shot. Harvey charged into the enemy lines and Tim discovered that the cannonball was bigger than the mouth of the cannon. ("Uh-oh, Harvey's in trouble now.") Harvey came back into the picture a little worn for his ordeal. He got the cannonball into the cannon, then charged courageously back into the enemy lines. Now Tim tried to clean the cannon and lost the brush. Then he didn't have a match. Then he tilted the cannon and the cannonball rolled away. And so on and so on.

We duplicated this premise later with Ken Berry as a cavalry officer in a cabin with Conway. They were surrounded by Indians. Ken would decoy the Indians while Tim lit a fuse to a barrel of dynamite and rolled it down the hill. While Ken was in jeopardy, Tim discovered the barrel wouldn't fit through the doorway. The sketch again proceeded in episodic fashion.

The action can develop naturally. In the case of the family saying goodbye to the relative at the airport, the situation progressed from sadness at his leaving to impatience, then to name-calling, to fist fights, and finally, when his plane was actually ready to depart, back to the emotional, loving goodbye.

The action can be almost any sort that you can invent. The point is that your premise has to be strong enough to drive and sustain this action.

We had a delightful premise on the Carol Burnett show that stymied us for awhile because of this. The premise was that two gentlemen are vacationing in Hawaii. One has lost ten dollars and is brooding over it. The other tries to reason with him, saying it's silly to ruin a costly vacation because of a ten-dollar loss. The brooder says, "That's easy for you to say. It wasn't your ten bucks." So the second man takes ten dollars from his wallet and sets fire to it. "Now," he says, "we've both lost ten dollars. Let's forget it and have a good time." The brooder relents, cheers up, and takes a pack of cigarettes out of his pocket and says, "Hey, look. I found my ten dollars."

Most of the writers loved the premise. The general consensus, though, was that there was no place to go with it. Once the man discovered his ten dollars, the sketch was over. It was difficult to have that premise sustain enough action to keep a sketch going.

The writers liked the beginning so much, though, that they decided to give it a few hours of thought before abandoning it. Eventually, we did find a natural progression that made for a delightful sketch.

I'm printing this sketch in its entirety at the end of the chapter so you can see how a sketch is written and the form it should take on paper. However, why not take the premise and play with it a bit to see if you can come up with enough complications to sustain the sketch? (Here's a hint: solve the immediate problem and search for a complication to that. Then solve that difficulty but find a problem it can cause. Keep going till the ending.)

Endings

Everything up to now has been fairly easy. Endings are the really hard part of sketch writing. It's like jumping off a building— the jump and the fall are relatively harmless. It's the sudden stop that does the damage.

A sketch is like an elongated or acted-out story joke. If you've ever told (or listened to) a joke, you know that the most important part is the ending. So it is with sketches.

Endings take the most effort in writing, and are the cause of most rewrite time in a variety show office. If you ever want to be believable as a head writer on a variety show, all you need do is look pensive and say after reading a sketch, "The ending could be a little stronger."

If the head writer of the "The Carol Burnett Show" reads this book, he may be mortified to learn that my writing partner and I often wrote two endings for a sketch and handed in the *weaker* one. That way, when it was handed back for a stronger ending, we had one already prepared and hidden in a drawer.

The big problem is that the ending has to be sure-fire. It has to be the big laugh. Along the way, you can allow gags to slide by because if one doesn't provide the laugh, the next one will. However, you only have one ending: it had better work.

A good ending should progress naturally out of the sketch's action. That poses trouble for the writer, because the ending should be a logical conclusion of the sketch—and yet be unpredictable.

For instance, in the cannon sketch we've discussed, the ending should deal with the cannon. Perhaps Harvey finally takes Tim, stuffs him into the cannon, and fires him at the enemy.

A poor ending would be if after doing this entire sketch about the troubles of firing the cannon, Arnold Palmer walks on the set with a golf club, does a HILARIOUS line about a lost golf ball, and walks off to tremendous laughter. You've got a star, a great joke, and an audience convulsed with laughter—but you don't have an ending for your sketch.

To generate the ending, review the plot points of your sketch. Discover which way they go, then reverse the direction, twist the thrust, extend it, bend it, break it . . . do something unique with it, but have the ending be a natural result of the sketch itself.

Your ending should also tie the sketch into a neat little package. It should almost be so definitive that it couldn't go any further even if you wanted it to.

Trying to be definitive can get you into trouble, however. A recurring problem we had on the Burnett show was that many of the sketches ended with death. A character would get shot accidentally, or someone would be bumped out a window. This is because in sketches containing comedic physical abuse, any physical shtick you write can be topped—you can always write another disaster after that one. The only ultimate is death. We used to make certain that the sketch deaths were genuinely comedic and not in bad taste—but we still tried to find different endings.

Your endings *should* have a finality of some sort to them.

An exception to this is the kind of ending that flip-flops a sketch back on itself. In an ending like this, the last line of the sketch is actually the beginning of a new sketch. For example, in a sketch about a strange psychiatrist who torments his patients, the guy finally breaks down and tearfully admits that he's crazy and can't help himself. The patient leaves and the shrink composes himself, goes to his desk, and says to his nurse, "Send in the next patient, please." You know that he's going to do the same thing all over again.

Sometimes when this device is used, the (hypothetical) new sketch is magnified by the ending. For example, you have a woman who can't train the family dog. The entire sketch is about the woman chasing the dog and both of them destroying the house. Finally the woman finds a way of getting rid of the dog. She sits and rests, and just then her husband comes home with a gorilla on a leash. You know she'll have the same problems—only ten times worse.

These types of endings work occasionally, used sparingly. They're cheating, because the audience realizes that you haven't really solved the predicament; you simply start it all over again. It can be as annoying as being asked a riddle, and, when you give up and demand the answer, simply being presented with another riddle.

You must be careful, too, that your ending doesn't destroy the sketch; trick endings will sometimes do this. Often writers spend so much time working on the sketch ending that they forget what the sketch is about. Suppose that you have a hilarious sketch about a husband and wife who are attacked by little green men. They shoot and throw things at the attackers. When the green men leave, the husband says to the wife, "Our kids really have a good time with Halloween, don't they?" Even if that were a riotous ending, it would destroy the credibility of the sketch: the parents wouldn't fight so violently if they knew those were their own kids dressed for Halloween.

After you decide on your ending, reread the sketch with that ending in mind, to be sure it's compatible with the body of the sketch.

Let me tell you about a sketch ending that we had to rewrite for the Burnett show. It points out how difficult endings can be, how strange sketch logic can become—and also that you can get the joke you're after if you don't quit too soon.

This sketch featured Carol and Tim as a husband and wife in a motel room. After turning out the lights, Carol felt a bug in the bed. Tim had to get up and do something about it. The audience never saw the insect, but the thing kept becoming more and more of a threat and Carol became more and more hysterical. Finally, after a lot of good comedy, Tim managed to get the insect out of the room. But now Carol was sad that they took the creature away from his family. Maybe the bug had young children that were waiting for him to come home to them. Carol forced Tim to go out and get the insect and bring it back.

Here's where we need the ending. The first choice was that as soon as Tim stepped out the door, we heard a squishing sound: end of insect.

Most of us objected to this because it just had a bad feeling about it. It was too sad. It was too cruel. This is what's strange about sketch comedy logic: each week we shot Tim, pushed Harvey out windows, threw people off cliffs—but we couldn't kill a bug that was too small for the eye to see. It sounds weird, but it made sense.

Understand, it wasn't the censors who fought us on this. It was the writers themselves who refused to write it in.

Now another peculiar phenomenon occurred. Some of the writers wanted to get the rewrite over with and they began to argue for killing the bug. "Nobody cares about bugs," "We never see him on camera," "We kill people, why can't we kill insects?" (What a sad commentary that writers would sacrifice an innocent insect just to get home in time for dinner.)

Finally someone threw the perfect ending that broke up the entire room. We typed it in and it was one of the best endings we've ever had. (Well, at least it got us home before dinner was over.)

The ending was: Tim went outside the room, then came back and reported to Carol that the insect had joined a bunch of other insects, probably his family, and that they all looked very happy. Carol bought the story and was delighted. As Tim walked around the bed to climb back in, he turned his back to the camera, and we saw a four-foot lizard clinging to his back.

Idea Sources

Where do you get ideas for sketches? Who knows? F.A. Rockwell has written a book entitled *How to Write Plots That Sell* (available in paperback from Henry Regnery Co., 180 North Michigan Avenue, Chicago IL 60601). This is a worthwhile book for all creative writers; it lists ways of stimulating the mind to come up with usable plots.

A staff writer has an advantage over a freelancer in that he or she can brainstorm sketch premises. Most variety show staffs spend many hours en masse "pitching" ideas. ("Pitching" is where we just throw random observations to the room for discussion, hoping some workable ideas will result.) Most of the writing is done by individual teams, but a good deal of the pitching or brainstorming is done with eight to ten writers in a room.

The premises can be launched from any springboard. The King and Queen sketches we did on "The Carol Burnett Show" came from an off-color joke. The basic premise for the ten-dollar bill sketch reprinted here came from a hassle I had on an outing with my children. They were upset about something or other, and were pouting so much that the trip was in danger of being spoiled. I decided I would do something grandiose like burn a bill to show that nothing trivial should ruin a trip—then the thought struck me that suppose I did, and their problem was suddenly solved? I would end up brooding because *I* would have lost good money for nothing.

Most of a staff's ideas come from everyday occurrences dressed up in sketch form. One writer came into a pitch session and told us about having gone to a restaurant the night before where his waitress was always accompanied by another young woman who said and did nothing. She just followed the waitress around. He asked what was going on and the waitress said, "Oh, this is my 'puppy.' " That was their word for someone who was being trained.

We all loved the idea and kicked it around. The resultant sketch was Harvey Korman holding up a bank, but the teller takes a good deal of time to hand over the cash because she's training a new teller. Harvey also is breaking in Tim Conway, a new bank robber. At the end of the sketch, a policeman has the drop on the crooks—but they get away because the policeman is training a new cop.

A sketch, like a joke, is a combination of two or more ideas. It must be written more delicately, though, because you're asking the audience to invest more time in it. Remember that the longer you go, the better the pay-off has to be. Sketches go for some time, so they have to entertain along the way *and* have a strong punchline.

I've reprinted a couple of sketches we did for "The Carol Burnett Show" so you can see the writing style and the format they're typed in. These are favorites of mine, but more importantly, they went over well on the show.

Study these sketches and enjoy them.

THE HOLLOW HERO

MUSIC: PLAYON

SOUND: CROWD ROAR

(ON A PARADE GROUND A LINE OF BRITISH SOLDIERS ARE STANDING AT ATTENTION. ONE SOLDIER (BIRL) IS STANDING IN FRONT OF THE QUEEN (CAROL) WITH THE KING (HARVEY) BY HER SIDE. SHE PINS A MEDAL ON HIS CHEST. THEY SHAKE HANDS. CAROL AND HARVEY NOW MOVE ON TO THE NEXT SOLDIER (TIM). SHE MAKES A SMALL GESTURE TO HIM AND SMILES)

(SHE TAKES THE MEDAL FROM HARVEY. SHE STARTS TO PIN IT ON TIM'S CHEST)

> CAROL
> Private Newberry, for your distinguished heroism, in
> the face of the enemy, far above and beyond the call
> of duty, we, as your King and Queen, are proud to
> present to you, in the presence of your fellow country-
> men . . .

(INDICATING THE AUDIENCE WITH A QUEENLY SWEEP OF HER ROYAL HAND)
> . . . gathered here and the millions of viewers at
> home . . . the highest honor this nation can be-
> stow . . . the Perks Medallion.

TIM
I don't want your medal.

CAROL

(NOT SURE SHE HEARD RIGHT)
I beg your pardon?

TIM
I don't want it.

CAROL
What?!!!

TIM
Stick it in your ear.

(CAROL GIVES HARVEY A PUZZLED LOOK. "WHAT DO I DO NOW?" HAR-
VEY PULLS HER BACK GENTLY AND THEY BOTH TURN SO TIM CAN'T
HEAR THEM)

HARVEY
What did he say?

TIM
He said, "Stick it in my ear."

HARVEY
Don't do it.

CAROL
I shan't.

(THEY TURN BACK TO TIM)
You must take the medal.

(SHE STARTS TO PIN IT ON HIM AGAIN. TIM PUTS HIS HAND UP AND
STOPS HER)

                    TIM

(PUSHING IT BACK AT HER)
         No.

                    CAROL

(PUSHING IT BACK AT HIM)
         Yes.

                    TIM

(PUSHING IT BACK AT HER)
         No.

                    CAROL

(PUSHING IT BACK AT HIM)
         Yes.

                    TIM
         No!

(HARVEY CLEARS HIS THROAT TO ATTRACT HER ATTENTION. SHE
LOOKS AT HIM. HE SHAKES HIS HEAD VERY SLIGHTLY AND CAROL
STOPS. CAROL STEPS ASIDE AS HARVEY STEPS IN FRONT OF TIM. HE
GIVES HIM A FRIENDLY SMILE THEN LOSES HIS TEMPER AND GRABS
HIM BY THE LAPELS)

                    HARVEY
         Listen you . . . you . . .

(CAROL CLEARS HER THROAT TO ATTRACT HIS ATTENTION AND THEN
SHAKES HER HEAD. SHE THEN MOTIONS HIM WITH HER HEAD TO COME
BACK WHERE THEY CAN TALK PRIVATELY. HARVEY LETS TIM GO AND HE
AND CAROL TURN THEIR BACKS TO TIM)

                    CAROL
         Let me handle this.

(HARVEY NODS WITH DIGNITY AND BACKS AWAY. CAROL AGAIN AP-
PROACHES TIM)
Young man, every soldier wants a medal.

TIM
I don't. I want a pony.

CAROL
A what?

TIM
A pony . . . you know . . . a little horse.

(HE GIVES HER A LOOK LIKE SHE'S STUPID. CAROL LOOKS AT HARVEY
AND GIVES HIM THE MOTION THAT THEY SHOULD TALK PRIVATELY.
THEY TURN THEIR BACKS TO TIM)

CAROL
He wants a pony.

HARVEY
A what?

CAROL
A pony . . . you know . . . a little horse.

(SHE GIVES HIM A LOOK LIKE HE'S STUPID)

HARVEY
How about if I have him beheaded?

CAROL
Good idea.

(THEY TURN BACK TO TIM)
Young man, how would you like to have a pony with
no head?

                    HARVEY

(TO CAROL, QUICKLY)
        Pssssssssst.

(HE GIVES HER THE MOTION WITH HIS HEAD. THEY TURN AWAY FROM
TIM AGAIN)
        I meant have **him** beheaded . . . not the pony.

                    CAROL
        We can't do that.

                    HARVEY
        Why?

                    CAROL
        He's the biggest hero this country has ever had.

                    HARVEY
        What did he do?

                    CAROL
        He saved the lives of his entire platoon by swallowing
        a live hand grenade before it went off.

                    HARVEY
        Really.

                    CAROL
        Really! That brave man has no internal organs.

                    HARVEY

(NOT BELIEVING HER)
        Get out of here.

(SHE MOTIONS WITH HER HEAD AS IF TO SAY "WATCH." SHE TURNS
BACK TO TIM AND OPENS HIS MOUTH. SHE THEN YELLS DOWN INTO HIS
THROAT)

CAROL
Hello!

(ECHO)
Hello . . . hello . . . hello . . . hello . . .

(HARVEY MOTIONS HER BACK WITH HIS HEAD. THEY TURN AWAY FROM TIM)

HARVEY
I say we give him the pony.

CAROL
Right.

(SHE CLAPS HER HANDS TWICE REGALLY. A SOLDIER (STAN) BRINGS IN A PONY AND STANDS AT ATTENTION WITH THE PONY IN FRONT OF TIM)
Private Newberry, for your distinguished heroism in the face of the enemy . . . far above and beyond the call of duty, we as your King and Queen, are proud to present you with the highest honor this nation can bestow . . . a pony.

(TIM LOOKS DOWN AT THE PONY FOR A LONG BEAT THEN BACK AT CAROL)

TIM
I don't want that pony.

CAROL
I beg your pardon?

TIM
I want a blue one.

CAROL
You what?

TIM
I want a blue one . . . you know, like the sky.

CAROL

(WAVES PONY OFF)

(STARTING SLOWLY AND BUILDING TO NEAR HYSTERIA)
You're crazy. You know that? You're crazy. We're
standing out here in the hot sun trying to give you a
medal . . . engraved and everything. You don't want
that . . . you want this . . . then you don't want
this . . . because you want that. I'm out here busting
my royal bustle trying to please you and you say you
don't want this pony 'cause you want a blue pony.
Well, lemme tell you something, you hollowed out little creep . . . there's no such thing as a blue pony.

TIM
In that case, I'll take the medal.

(CAROL LOOKS LIKE SHE WILL HAVE A STROKE. THE FRUSTRATION AND
RAGE SLOWLY RISES WITHIN HER. HER HANDS COME UP AND SHE
STARTS TO GO FOR HIS THROAT)

HARVEY

(STOPPING HER)
Pssssssssst.

(HE MOTIONS FOR HER WTH HIS HEAD. CAROL STOPS HER ADVANCE ON
TIM AND JOINS HARVEY WITH THEIR BACKS TO TIM. HARVEY WHISPERS
SOMETHING IN CAROL'S EAR)

(CAROL NODS AND TURNS BACK TO TIM AS HARVEY, WHISTLING AND
BEING AS NONCHALANT AS POSSIBLE, SNEAKS AROUND BEHIND TIM,
GETS DOWN ON HIS KNEES, AND CAROL SHOVES TIM BACKWARDS
OVER HARVEY)

SOUND: BODY FALL

(HARVEY THEN GETS UP, LEAVING TIM SPRAWLING ON THE GROUND. HE ESCORTS CAROL OFF STAGE WITH REGAL DIGNITY)

MUSIC: PLAYOFF

(APPLAUSE)

ROOT OF ALL EVIL

MUSIC: PLAYON

(DICK AND TONY ARE SITTING AT A BAR. BOTH ARE DRESSED IN HAWAI- IAN SHIRTS, THEY'RE IN THE MIDDLE OF THEIR VACATION. TONY IS DE- PRESSED)

> DICK
> You're gonna spoil our whole Hawaiian vacation over that lousy ten bucks.

> TONY
> Look. I don't like losing ten bucks of my hard-earned money no matter where we are.

> DICK
> Now that is dumb. That is really dumb. You spend all this money to come over here and it's wasted be- cause you lost a lousy ten bucks.

> TONY
> Sure . . . but if it happened to you you'd probably cut your throat.

> DICK
> It would not mean **that** . . .

(SNAPPING HIS FINGERS)
   . . . to me.

> TONY
> It would if it was your ten bucks.

> DICK
> Ten bucks isn't what this is all about. It's the fact that you're letting it bother you, and letting it ruin our vacation.

> TONY
> I guess if you lost ten dollars, you'd just forget about it.

> DICK
> Absolutely right.

> TONY
> Like hell you would!

> DICK
> Alright.

(DICK TAKES HIS WALLET OUT AND REMOVES A TEN DOLLAR BILL)
   I just wanna show you something.

(HE HOLDS UP A TEN DOLLAR BILL)
   This is a ten dollar bill, right?

> TONY
> Yeah.

> DICK
> Watch this.

> TONY

(HE TAKES OUT A CIGARETTE LIGHTER AND SETS FIRE TO THE BILL)

> TONY
> Hey, what are you doing?

> DICK
> Just watch.

(THE BILL GOES UP IN SMOKE)
> There. Ten dollars of my money up in smoke.

(HE LETS IT BURN OUT IN THE ASHTRAY)

(BRUSHING HIS HANDS WITH FINALITY)
> . . . doesn't bother me in the least.

> TONY
> Boy, you really are a nut.

(HE TAKES OUT A PACK OF CIGARETTES)
> Hey . . .

(HE TAKES A BILL OUT OF THE CELLOPHANE AND SHOWS IT)
> There's my ten dollars.

(DICK JUST STARES AT HIM IN DISBELIEF)
> Sure, I remember putting it in there so I wouldn't lose
> it when we were playing miniature golf.

(NOW TONY FEELS BETTER)
> Aw, now I can enjoy Hawaii . . . come on, let's go
> shoot some pool.

> DICK
> Hey . . . how about giving me the ten bucks?

> TONY
> What for?

> DICK
> I just burned ten dollars.

TONY
You wanna set fire to money, that's your problem.

DICK
But I did it for you.

TONY
Thank you. Now let's go before all the tables are
gone.

DICK

(VERY GRUMPY)
I'm not going anywhere.

TONY
What's wrong with you?

DICK
I'm out ten bucks is what's wrong with me.

TONY
Didn't you just tell me that ten bucks doesn't mean
anything?

DICK
Yeah.

TONY
Well, now I'm telling you.

DICK
Wait a minute. That's different. I didn't do something
stupid like lose the money.

TONY
Oh, you did something smart, like set fire to it.

                    DICK
All I know is you were out ten bucks, now **I'm** out ten
bucks.

                    TONY
Alright, tell you what I'll do . . . you're making such
a big stink over this, I'll split the difference. I'll give
you five bucks.

                    DICK

(HE DOESN'T LIKE THAT IDEA)
          Five . . . ?

(BUT HE DECIDES TO SETTLE FOR IT)
          Okay.

                    TONY
Let me get change for the ten. Bartender.

(BARTENDER (DON) COMES OVER)

(TONY HANDS HIM THE BILL)
          Can you break this into fives for me?

(DON TAKES THE BILL AND GOES TO THE CASH REGISTER)

                    DON
          Sure.

(HE NOW TURNS BACK AFTER CLOSING THE CASH REGISTER)

(COUNTING OUT FOUR BILLS)
          Here you go . . . five . . . ten . . . fif-
          teen . . . twenty . . .

DON MOVES OUT OF THE PICTURE)

(TONY AND DICK SIT THERE FOR A BEAT LIKE THE CAT THAT ATE THE CA-
NARY . . .)

(BOTH ARE WONDERING IF THEY REALLY GOT AWAY WITH THIS. NEI-
THER ONE IS MOVING TOO MUCH FOR FEAR THEY MIGHT BLOW THE
WHOLE SCAM. TONY EVEN MOVES HIS HANDS A BIT TO COVER THE
MONEY, VERY DISCREETLY SO THAT NO ONE LOOKING CAN TELL THEY
GOT MORE THAN THEY SHOULD HAVE GOTTEN. A SMILE CROSSES BOTH
THEIR FACES)

(TONY NOW PICKS UP THE MONEY. DICK STARTS RUBBING HIS HANDS
TOGETHER IN ANTICIPATION OF THE WINDFALL)

                    TONY

(HANDING DICK ONE BILL)
        There's your five.

(HE FOLDS THE REST AND PUTS IT IN HIS POCKET)

(DICK IS DUMBFOUNDED)

                    DICK
        Hey . . .

                    TONY
        What?

                    DICK
        Where's the rest of my money?

                    TONY
        I gave you five.

                    DICK
        Yeah, but you got fifteen.

                    TONY
        It was my ten.

DICK
Oh no, it was my ten.

TONY

(DUMPING THE ASHTRAY)
There's your ten.

DICK
Forget that ten. You just got twenty from the bartend-er. The fifteen you got in your pocket and this five.

(DICK LAYS HIS FIVE ON THE BAR)

TONY
Hey, you're the one that was saying money didn't mean anything.

DICK
It didn't then. It does now. You owe me five bucks.

TONY
You know you're ruining our whole vacation with this money thing.

DICK
I want another five.

TONY
If I give you another five, can we forget the money and just have a good time?

DICK
Put another fiver down there and I'll never mention money to you again . . . believe me.

TONY
I don't know why I'm doing this . . .

(HE TAKES ONE OF THE FIVES OUT OF HIS POCKET)
    . . . but anything to keep you quiet. There.

(HE PUTS THE FIVE ON THE BAR NEXT TO DICK'S OTHER FIVE)
    Now can we just be friends and have a good time?

(HE HOLDS OUT HIS HAND FOR A HANDSHAKE)

                    DICK
        Okay, buddy.

(THEY SHAKE HANDS)

(WHILE THEIR HANDS ARE CLASPED, DON COMES INTO SCENE)

DON
        Hey, I gave you ten dollars too much before.

(HE TAKES THE TWO FIVES OFF THE BAR AND MOVES OFF)

(DICK QUICKLY GRABS TONY'S HAND)

                    DICK
        Give me five dollars.

                    TONY

(TRYING TO WRESTLE HIS HAND FREE)
        Let go of me, will you?

                    DICK
        Give me five dollars.

                    TONY
        It's **my** money!

                    DICK
        It's not your money. It's my money.

(VICKI, AS A BEGGAR LADY, COMES IN WITH A HANDFUL OF SCRAGGLY
FLOWERS)

                    VICKI
Flowers for your lady. Help the poor.

                    TONY
Wait a second. Here's the answer. Let's give the ten
bucks to someone who really needs it.

                    DICK
Good idea. I'll go along with that.

                    TONY

(STARTS TO HAND HER THE MONEY)
Here you are, my good woman.

                    DICK
Hold it. Hold it.

                    TONY
Now what?

                    DICK
You always want to be the big man, don't you? I
should give her five dollars of that money.

                    TONY

(HANDING DICK THE TWO FIVES)
Here, give her the whole thing if you want.

                    DICK

(HANDING HER THE MONEY)
This is for you, dear. May this make your life a little
fuller in these troublesome times.

VICKI
Oh, thank you, sir . . . thank you . . .

(SHE BEGINS TO SOB A BIT AND THROWS HER ARMS AROUND HIM, HUG-
GING HIM AND PATTING HIM)
Blessings on you. You are so generous. Thank you,
sir. May all your days be happy. Thank you.

(SHE TURNS AND LEAVES)

(DICK IS DELIGHTED WITH HIMSELF)

TONY

(A LITTLE BIT SURLY BECAUSE THE MONEY IS GONE)
Are you happy now?

DICK
Yes, I'm very happy. Nothing is as rewarding as gen-
erosity. In fact, I'm going to continue that generosity.
I'm going to buy you a drink. Bartender . . .

DON
Yes, sir.

DICK
Two more here, please.

DON
Right.

(DICK REACHES INSIDE HIS COAT FOR HIS WALLET. IT'S NOT THERE. HE
FEELS AROUND FOR A BIT. THEN THE AWARENESS COMES OVER HIS
FACE)

DICK
She took my wallet . . . and my watch
. . stop, thief.

(HE RUNS OUT AFTER HER)

(DON BRINGS TWO DRINKS, SETS THEM DOWN, AND HOLDS UP THE CASH REGISTER TAPE)

>   DON
> Hey, you got a double star on your receipt. Both these drinks are on the house.

(TONY LOOKS AROUND TO MAKE SURE DICK CAN'T SEE, AND POURS DICK'S INTO HIS OWN GLASS)

(HE RAISES HIS GLASS TO DON)

>   TONY
> Cheers.

MUSIC: PLAYOFF

(APPLAUSE)

Intro to No Frills Airline

>   VICKI
> Not too long ago, many of the commercial airlines introduced a new low cost fare which was nicknamed the "No Frills Plan." Simply put, it meant that you gave up some of the little extras like movies, cocktails, stereo, and if you wanted lunch, you had to bring your own. Tonight, we'd like to bring you **our** version of the "No Frills Plan."

MUSIC: BRIDGE

NO FRILL AIRLINE

(SET: INT. AIRLINER)

(NANCY AND BIRL CROSS THROUGH)

(HARVEY IS BEHIND THEM, FOLLOWED BY TIM. THEY ARE BOTH CHECK-
ING THEIR BOARDING PASSES AGAINST THE SEAT NUMBERS)

>   HARVEY
> Two A . . . Two B . . . Three A . . . Three B . . .
> Here I am.

>   TIM
> Hey, there's mine. I'm right in back of you. I'm in the
> no frills section.

>   HARVEY

(NOT INTERESTED)
>   Fine.

>   TIM
> Save a lot of money back there. And you know what
> they say. The back of the plane gets there the same
> time as the front.

>   HARVEY
> That's wonderful.

(HARVEY STANDS IN AISLE AND STARTS REMOVING COAT. AS TIM
SQUEEZES BY HIM, HE TRIPS)

>   TIM

(LOOKING DOWN)
>   Oops. Watch it. That rug ends right there.

(HARVEY OPENS THE OVERBOARD COMPARTMENT AND STARTS LAYING
HIS JACKET OUT IN IT AS TIM STARTS REMOVING HIS JACKET)
>   Of course, you don't get any food or anything . . .

(HOLDING UP BROWN BAG)

. . . that's why I brought this. Besides I never saw a
meal yet worth forty bucks. But everything else is the
same.

(HE OPENS HIS OVERHEAD COMPARTMENT TO PUT HIS JACKET AWAY.
IN IT WE SEE A SPARE TIRE. A JACK AND LUG WRENCH FALL OUT. HE
CATCHES THEM JUST IN TIME AND SHOVES THEM BACK IN THE COM-
PARTMENT)
Well, we don't have to worry about a flat.

(HARVEY SITS AND TIM SITS WHILE HOLDING HIS JACKET IN HIS LAP)

(LEANING UP TO HARVEY)
It's not just the money, you know. It's safer, too.

HARVEY
Good.

TIM
Never heard of a plane backing into a mountain yet.

HARVEY

(PUTTING HIM IN HIS PLACE)
Do you mind . . . please.

TIM

(TO HIMSELF)
Harrumph . . . rich people.

(CAROL NOW ENTERS AS THE STEWARDESS. SHE IS CARRYING A PIL-
LOW)

CAROL

(TO HARVEY)
Comfortable, sir? Would you like a pillow?

HARVEY
Yes, please.

(CAROL PUTS THE PILLOW IN BACK OF HIS NECK)

CAROL
How's that?

HARVEY

(NOT SURE)
Well . . . it's better.

CAROL

(TO TIM)
May I take your coat, sir?

TIM
Oh, yeah . . . great.

(TIM GIVES HARVEY A SNOTTY LOOK. HE GOT BETTER SERVICE)

(CAROL TAKES TIM'S COAT AND FOLDS IT NEATLY, THEN ROLLS IT UP IN
A BALL AND PUTS IT DOWN BEHIND HARVEY'S BACK)

CAROL
How's that?

HARVEY
Much better. Thank you.

(TIM NOW TRIES TO GET COMFORTABLE IN HIS VERY UPRIGHT SEAT. AS
HE DOES THIS HE STRETCHES HIS LEGS OUT INTO THE AISLE AND INTO
THE NEXT SECTION)

CAROL

(TO TIM)
You're in the no frills section, right?

TIM
Yes, and you know what they say. The back of the
plane gets there the same . . .

(CAROL STOMPS ON HIS FOOT)

SOUND: CRUNCH

CAROL
Then get your feet off of our rug.

TIM

(PULLING HIS FOOT BACK)
Yes, ma'am. Sorry.

CAROL

(SPEAKING TO THE ENTIRE PLANE)
May I have your attention, please?

(SHE TAKES THE SAMPLE OXYGEN MASK FROM THE COMPARTMENT
ABOVE HARVEY'S HEAD)
Our cabin is pressurized for your comfort. It is very
unlikely that there will be any sudden change in the
cabin pressure, but in the rare event that this does
happen, our emergency procedure will be as follows . . .

(CAROL WHISPERS TO BONNIE)

(CAROL THEN BENDS DOWN AND WHISPERS IN HARVEY'S EAR. TIM
TRIES TO LISTEN IN BUT CAN'T)

TIM

(TO HARVEY)
What did she say? I didn't hear that . . . what did
she say?

(TIM STARTS MOVING UP TO HARVEY'S AREA AS HE SPEAKS. CAROL RE-
TURNS)

CAROL
I said . . . "Keep your feet off our rug."

(SHE KICKS TIM IN THE SHINS)

SOUND: CRUNCH

(FORCING HIM TO RETURN TO HIS SEAT, HOLDING HIS LEG IN PAIN)

(SWEETLY TO HARVEY)
Is your seat belt fastened, sir?

HARVEY
Oh, no. I'll take care of it right away.

(HARVEY BEGINS FASTENING HIS BELT AS TIM STARTS LOOKING
AROUND FOR HIS)

CAROL

(TO HARVEY)
Thank you.

(CAROL STARTS TO WALK AWAY)

TIM

(STOPPING HER)
Ah . . . Miss . . .

CAROL
What???

TIM
My seat belt isn't fastened.

> CAROL
> Well, so?

> TIM
> In fact, I don't even have a seat belt.

> CAROL
> Noodge!!

(SHE WALKS BACK TO TIM, REACHES IN BACK OF HIS SEAT AND PULLS OUT A ROPE WHICH SHE QUICKLY WRAPS AROUND HIS CHEST SEVERAL TIMES AND THEN MAKES ONE FINAL PASS AROUND HIS NECK)

> ERNIE (V.O.)
> Stewardesses, prepare for takeoff.

(CAROL SITS IN A VACANT SEAT AND FASTENS HER BELT. HARVEY LEANS ACROSS TO WINDOW, TAPS ON IT AND WAVES GOODBYE TO SOMEONE. TIM WATCHES THIS AND IMITATES HIM. HE REACHES OVER AND STARTS TO TAP ON WINDOW. THERE IS NO GLASS IN HIS WINDOW AND HIS HAND GOES THROUGH)

SOUND: ENGINES REVVING UP FOR TAKEOFF

(AS TIM CONTINUES TO FEEL AROUND FOR THE VACANT GLASS, WE SEE SMOKE FROM THE ENGINE BEGIN POURING IN HIS FACE. THIS IS FOLLOWED BY DUST, CANDY WRAPPERS AND MISCELLANEOUS PAPER. HE QUICKLY UNWRAPS THE ROPE THAT IS AROUND HIM, TAKES THE SEAT CUSHION FROM THE NEXT SEAT AND STUFFS IT IN THE WINDOW OPENING. HE NOW SETTLES BACK IN HIS SEAT AS BEST HE CAN AS THE PLANE TAKES OFF AND REACHES CRUISING ALTITUDE. CAROL UNFASTENS HER BELT, GOES BRIEFLY OUT OF SHOT AND COMES BACK IN WITH SEVERAL SETS OF EARPHONES IN PLASTIC BAGS)

(SHE GOES TO BONNIE, RANDY, IN FRONT OF HARVEY)

> CAROL
> Do you want to hear some music?

BONNIE
Yes, please.

CAROL
That'll be two dollars each.

(THEY GIVE HER THE MONEY)

CAROL

(TO HARVEY)
How about you, sir. Some music?

HARVEY
I'd love it.

CAROL
Two dollars, please.

(HARVEY GIVES HER THE MONEY AND SHE GIVES HIM THE EARPHONES. SHE NOW MOVES BACK TO TIM)

(TO TIM)
Would you like to hear some music?

TIM

(SURPRISED AND ANXIOUS)
Why, yes. Wonderful.

(HE HOLDS UP TWO DOLLARS AS CAROL BEGINS SINGING)

CAROL

(SINGING)
OFF WE GO, INTO THE WILD BLUE YONDER . . .
CRASH!!

(TALKING)
>That'll be two dollars, please.

(SHE TAKES THE BILLS FROM TIM AND EXITS)

>ERNIE (V.O.)
>Folks, if you will look out the right side of the airplane you will see that we are passing over the Grand Canyon.

(TIM LEANS OVER TO HARVEY)

>TIM
>Well, so far your forty bucks got you over the Grand Canyon about a foot and a half ahead of me.

(HARVEY GIVES HIM A FROZEN STARE. TIM THEN LEANS WAY OVER AND STARTS LOOKING OUT OF HARVEY'S WINDOW. HARVEY SEES THIS AND LOOKS OUT THE WINDOW HIMSELF WHILE COVERING AS MUCH OF IT AS HE CAN WITH HIS HANDS SO THAT TIM CANNOT SEE. TIM SHRUGS, GIVES UP AND SITS BACK DOWN)

(CAROL NOW ENTERS WITH AN ARMLOAD OF PAPERS AND MAGAZINES)

>CAROL

(TO HARVEY)
>Would you like something to read, sir?

>HARVEY
>What do you have there?

>CAROL
>Well, I have **Fortune, Newsweek, Time, Playboy, The New York Times** and **The Wall Street Journal.**

>HARVEY
>Oh, good, I'll take the **Wall Street Journal.**

(CAROL HANDS HIM THE PAPER. CAROL STARTS BACK UP THE AISLE
AWAY FROM TIM)

TIM

(CALLING HER)
Ah . . . Miss. . . .

CAROL
What?

TIM
I might read a little something.

CAROL
Hokay. For the no frills section we have **The Wichi-
ta Gazette, The Opthamologists' Journal**
and **The Mushroom Growers' Weekly.**

TIM
Hmmm. Well, let's see what's happening with those
mushrooms.

(CAROL SLAPS HIM WITH THE PAPER WHICH HE OPENS)

HARVEY
Well, I think I'll get a little shut-eye.

CAROL
Oh, let me help you.

(SHE PUSHES THE BUTTON ON THE SIDE OF HIS SEAT. THE SEAT BACK
GOES BACK INTO TIM'S LAP, CRUSHING THE PAPER AGAINST HIM SO
THAT IT AND HARVEY'S SEAT ARE LITERALLY UP UNDER HIS CHIN. TIM
CAREFULLY WORKS HIS FINGERS LOOSE FROM UNDER THE SEAT AND
UP OVER THE TOP OF THE SEAT)

HARVEY
On second thought, maybe I'll have a drink first.

(HE PUSHES THE BUTTON ON THE SIDE OF HIS SEAT, BRINGING IT
QUICKLY TO THE UPRIGHT POSITION. TIM IS PROPELLED UP AND OVER
HARVEY'S SEAT AND DOWN INTO HIS LAP.

                    CAROL

(TO TIM)
        No, no. No sneaking up here.

(TIM CLIMBS OUT OF HARVEY'S LAP AND GOES BACK TO HIS OWN SEAT)

                    TIM
        Sorry. Just passing through.

(HE NOW SITS BACK DOWN)

                    CAROL

(TO HARVEY)
        I'll be serving lunch shortly. Would you care for the
        beef or the turkey?

                    HARVEY
        I think I'll have the turkey.

                    TIM
        Hah . . . now you're going to see what you get for
        your forty bucks . . .

(TIM TAKES OUT HIS LITTLE BROWN BAG)
        By the time you get your lunch, I'll be into my second
        package of Twinkies . . .

(CAROL ENTERS AND PUTS THE TRAY OF FOOD IN FRONT OF HARVEY)
        Oh sure, it's fast, but is it good?

(HE SITS BACK AND TAKES OUT A SMALL SANDWICH AND COFFEE IN A
PAPER CUP WITH A LID ON IT. TIM JUST GETS IT ALL OPEN IN FRONT OF
HIM WHEN . . .)

ERNIE (V.O.)
Ladies and gentlemen, this is your captain speaking.
We're expecting some very slight turbulence. I'd like
to suggest that you fasten your seat belts loosely.
Thank you.

HARVEY
Maybe you'd better take the food back.

CAROL
Oh, no, that announcement is just a precaution. We
always check with the pilot, before serving.

(TIM STARTS TO TAKE A BITE OUT OF HIS SANDWICH WHEN HIS SEAT
STARTS BOUNCING UP AND DOWN VIOLENTLY)
If it were going to be anything serious, we wouldn't
even serve food or drink.

(TIM CONTINUES TO BOUNCE UP AND DOWN)

(DEMONSTRATING WITH HER HAND)
It'll probably be just a little rocking motion or an up
and down movement. You won't even feel it.

(TIM NOW STANDS UP WITH QUITE SOME DIFFICULTY BECAUSE OF ALL
THE TURBULENCE. HE STEPS FORWARD INTO THE FIRST CLASS SEC-
TION OF THE PLANE AND THERE IS NO TURBULENCE)

CAROL
What are you doing up here?

TIM
Miss, how come it's so rough back there and it's so
smooth up here?

CAROL
Will you please get back in the no frills section?

TIM
Yes, ma'am . . .

(AS SOON AS HE STEPS BACK IN HIS OWN SECTION THE TURBULENCE STARTS UP AGAIN. AND HE CAN HARDLY STAND UP. HE MANAGES TO GET BACK IN HIS SEAT)

CAROL
Would you like a little wine?

HARVEY
Yes, good idea.

(CAROL EXITS. TIM STOPS BOUNCING UP AND DOWN, DECIDES IT'S OVER AND BEGINS CAREFULLY WORKING THE TOP OFF THE COFFEE CONTAINER SO AS NOT TO SPILL IT)

(CAROL RE-ENTERS WITH A BOTTLE OF WINE AND A GLASS)

CAROL

(SHOWING HARVEY THE BOTTLE)
Sparkling Burgundy. Okay?

HARVEY
Perfect.

(TIM TAKES OUT A PAPER CUP AND HE AND CAROL START TO POUR AT THE SAME TIME. AT THAT INSTANT TIM'S SEAT STARTS BOUNCING UP AND DOWN AGAIN, SPILLING COFFEE ALL OVER HIM. CAROL POURS AND NOTHING HAPPENS. SHE FILLS THE GLASS AND HANDS IT TO HARVEY. TIM STOPS BOUNCING UP AND DOWN. HARVEY SWIRLS THE WINE IN HIS GLASS AND TAKES A SIP. TIM WATCHES HIM, SWIRLS THE COFFEE IN THE PAPER CARTON AND STARTS TO SIP. HE SEES THAT ALL THE COFFEE HAS SPILLED OUT AND HE TURNS THE CARTON UPSIDE DOWN. NOTHING COMES OUT)

(CAROL LOOKS AT HER WATCH)

CAROL

(TO HARVEY)
Say, you're not getting off at Chicago, are you?

HARVEY
No, I'm going straight through to New York.

TIM
I'm getting off at Chicago.

CAROL
Well, you'd better get your things together and come
with me.

(AS HE BEGINS GATHERING HIS BELONGINGS SHE PASSES HIM AND
GOES TO A DOOR IN BACK OF HIS SEAT. TIM GETS UP AND FOLLOWS
HER)

TIM
What time do we land?

(CAROL OPENS THE DOOR)

SOUND: WIND

CAROL
Land?

(SHE GIVES HIM A SHOVE OUT THE DOOR. HE GOES BY WINDOWS WITH
PILLOW)

MUSIC: PLAYOFF

(APPLAUSE)

17 SITCOM WRITING

"Sitcom" is short for situation comedy. That is, a television show, generally a half-hour long, that has a story, like "The Mary Tyler Moore Show," "Taxi," "Barney Miller." A comedy variety show, by contrast, is made up of divergent sketches and characters, like "The Carol Burnett Show," "Laugh-In," or "Barbara Mandrell."

Most comedy variety shows are staff-written, while sitcoms buy from freelancers.

Let's see how most freelance scripts are purchased for a sitcom. Everyone reading this will have heard or read of an exception to this scenario and exceptions do exist, but ninety-nine percent of the shows assigned to freelance writers follow this typical pattern.

The producer's biggest problem at the beginning of each session is getting scripts working and finished on schedule. Each season dependable writers are taken off the open market. Show staffs change, and many freelancers are either tied up doing pilots or on the staff of another weekly series. The producer generally has to find new people to write scripts for his show.

Consequently, the producer reads many speculative scripts submitted by agents—even unsolicited scripts. Some producers only read scripts submitted through a qualified agent; others read anything that crosses the desk. Certain writers impress the producer and a story conference will be arranged.

The story conference is a frightening ordeal. The author enters a room full of apparent adversaries—the producers, the story editors, and the script supervisors. There might be up to six people who refuse to be impressed with any of your accomplishments, and each of them probably has veto power. Your task is to dazzle them with your brilliance.

It's frightening for the staff people, too, because they are usually interviewing a stranger. They may buy a story from you and then be dependent on you to make their lives easier . . . or at least, not to make their lives too much more difficult.

They would love to purchase a good story from you and have a well-written first draft turned in within a reasonable time. However, they're not sure.

The meeting invariably begins with a bit of small talk, some bad jokes, occasionally a terrific joke, and then someone says, "Okay, what have you got?" That's the signal for the author to start "pitching" his story lines. "Pitching" is a TV word for brainstorming: ideas are thrown to the creative minds to be discussed, discarded, changed, or simply ridiculed.

The well-prepared freelancer will have several storylines worked out for presentation. She may present these orally, or hand out a sheet of paper that the producers can read, or that she may read aloud. There's no set formula; this is one of the few areas where producers try to make the author feel comfortable. The freelancer should have some of this material on paper— even if it's only a paragraph or two—so that she can leave a document with the buyers if they show any interest.

This can be the most discouraging part of the meeting. Let me present a playlet to show you exactly what I mean.
SETTING: Any television situation comedy producers' office. The room can be any size, but there will always be one less chair than is needed. Present will be two producers, two story editors, and two script consultants. One will be in tennis clothes, one in jeans and a tee-shirt, one in expensive slacks and sweater, and all will have their feet up on the desk. We'll omit the small talk and begin with the phrase . . . .

PRODUCER A
Okay, what have you got?

(Several of the buyers take their feet off the desk and sit up, leaning forward attentively.)

FREELANCER
I have this one story where Carol and Marge are both dating the same guy, but they don't know . . . .

PRODUCER B
Hold it. We have a story that's very similar to that working right now.

FREELANCER
Okay. I've got one where they're dating a guy who's starring in a minstrel show.

PRODUCER A
Is this guy going to be in black-face during the show?

FREELANCER
Well, yeah, I've got this hilarious scene where . . . .

PRODUCER B
"All in the Family" has a big show with that joke and we can't do another one.

PRODUCER A
What else have you got?

FREELANCER
I have this story where the girls find a submarine.

PRODUCER A

We've got a submarine story already.

FREELANCER

Okay, they're all sitting around at
dinner.

PRODUCER B

Sorry. The network says we can't
do any eating scenes.

FREELANCER

I've got one you'll love. Marge
finds out that she's going to need
braces . . . .

*(She pauses, waiting for someone to voice an objection. When
none is forthcoming, her eyes light up and she continues with
increased fervor.)*

Now, she really hates this at first,
you see, but then she goes there
and finds out she's in love with
the orthodontist. But after the
first visit he discovers that it's really Carol's teeth that need
straightening. Marge tries to find
ways of keeping Carol from visiting "her" doctor, and also some
reason for seeing him herself
even though her teeth are fine.

*(Now there is a long pregnant pause. Everyone is searching for
a reason to shoot it down. Finally someone says . . . .)*

PRODUCER B

I like it.

*(Now the author really gets caught up in the enthusiasm. She
senses the sale.)*

FREELANCER

I think it can be a really funny
show. I've got this great scene in
the dentist's chair where . . . .

PRODUCER A

I don't like dentist shows.

FREELANCER

Hey, I can make him a chiroprac-
tor. Yeah, that's even funnier.

PRODUCER A

How about if she falls in love
with a bullfighter?

FREELANCER

A bullfighter?

PRODUCER B

That's good. Then we can do that
scene we had to take out of the
other show.

FREELANCER

A bullfighter?

PRODUCER B

We have another meeting right
now, but we like this. Try and
write up an outline of this same
story, except make him a bullfighter. Okay?

FREELANCER

(Writing resignedly in her notebook.)

Okay, a bullfighter.

*She leaves, and eventually will show up back in the office
with a four-page outline about a bullfighter.*

We exaggerated the story conference a bit, but they *can* sometimes seem this bizarre. Nevertheless, the author made a sale. Her outline will be revised, probably extensively, and the notes reviewed with her at a subsequent meeting.

She will then write a complete first draft, which again will be discussed during a meeting at which she's present. Then she'll turn in her final draft.

This is the "final" draft for her only. After the second draft, she will have no more to do with writing the script, but it will be changed considerably before it airs. Those changes will be made by the show's writing staff without consulting her.

The playlet shows some of the problems that a freelance writer has in selling a story to a sitcom. The author has no idea what taboos the network or the show itself might have. I actually did pitch a story once only to find that the network didn't want this particular star to be shown eating. The freelancer also has no way of knowing what stories are in the works or have already been done.

When you consider a show like "M*A*S*H," which has been on for years and has produced 26 different stories each year, you have to figure that the odds are against you coming up with anything they haven't done.

Our playlet also demonstrates why the writer should live near where the show is produced. (We'll talk more about that later in the chapter.)

The scenario does have a happy ending because the freelancer ends up with a sale. She got a story assignment for two reasons. First, the powers that be liked her writing style so they arranged a story meeting. Second, they liked one of her story ideas.

If you have an established reputation, it may be easy to get a story conference. If you don't, the buyer is going to want to see a sample of your writing. The relentless schedule of television makes producing a weekly series hectic. Even under ideal conditions, some say it is impossible. Consequently, no one wants anything that's going to make the task yet more difficult. The producers want reasonable assurance that any script assignment they hand out is going to be professionally executed. They'll want to know whether you can handle a storyline and dialogue before they contract with you for a freelance script.

You will need a sample of your work. You needn't write for a specific show; any sitcom writing will serve the purpose. Therefore, it's to your benefit to write for those shows that you enjoy. Having watched a show regularly, you'll know the characters better and it will be easier for you to write for them.

Most people'll pick the better shows to write spec scripts for. We generally see sample scripts written for "M*A*S*H", "Barney Miller," "Taxi" and a few others. This makes the producer's task easier, too, because he's familiar with the show and the characters and can understand the writing. It's difficult to evaluate a script written for a show you've never seen, because you don't know what those characters are like.

All producers read scripts in search of new talent, but not many of them like to. Most of them read into a script only until they find one or two glaring errors, then close it and move on to the next script in the stack. It's thus in your interest not to make any boo-boos. Since you're trying to demonstrate your expertise, your script should also show that you're aware of the everyday realities of television production.

Be Careful with Characters

One fact of television life is that the producer has to do a show with stars. These stars deliver an audience for the show, they get paid handsomely, and they expect to *be* the star of the show. It's incredibly difficult to produce a show that features a new character who's funnier than all the regulars.

We often read scripts like this because writers create a character who fits right into the show. The writing may be hilarious, but you simply can't do that to a cast—and keep your job.

Certainly, you've seen shows where a new character was introduced, was funny, and stole the show from the regulars. "Maude" was a spinoff of a very funny "All in the Family" episode. Laverne and Shirley were orginally guests on a "Happy Days" episode. Robin Williams created Mork on a "Happy Days" episode. Generally, shows featuring new characters are thought through by the production company and written by the staff. It's presumptuous for a beginner to try to create a spinoff the first time in the batter's box.

The best way to show off your skills is to stay with the characters and format of established shows.

Watch the Budget

Another fact of TV production is that there is never enough money in the budget to do the show. Budgets are constant foes to creativity; your script should reflect your awareness of this.

Study the shows you want to write for and notice the sets. "All in the Family" was acted largely in the Bunker living room and kitchen. "Three's Company" is taped in the apartment and the corner bar. "Barney Miller" is done almost exclusively in the squad room or in Barney's office—there's very little outside shooting. "Taxi" has some exterior scenes, but they're filmed without dialogue and are pretty much stock shots of the city.

Any new sets that are introduced cost money, and there is never enough of that. Keep your scripts as uncomplicated as possible as far as sets and shooting costs go. Try to limit your writing to the sets you've seen repeatedly.

When I was working on "Laugh-In," one of the writers turned in a sight gag that said simply, "A man is seated in a room with polka-dot wallpaper. He leaves, slams the door, and all the polka dots fall off the wall." It was a great visual joke because it was so unexpected. We shot the joke, but the wall was an elaborate construction. Each polka dot was a plastic disk held on the wall by a protruding piece of metal. All of these pieces of metal were connected to a longer piece of metal behind the wall. Prop men were ready to trigger all the pieces of metal just as the actor slammed the door. This pulled all the pieces of metal through little holes in the wall and the polka dots fell to the floor. The joke lasted perhaps ten seconds and the wall cost $4,000.

Another time we did a sketch for "The Carol Burnett Show" that totally destroyed a kitchen. It involved a lot of special effects and prepared props and reportedly cost $10,000. The producers okayed the sketch, but were determined to get it in one take. My partner and I watched the taping on a monitor in our office. It worked beautifully, but as soon as it was over we called the associate producer—the guy who handled all the money on the show—and told him we weren't satisfied with it and would like to do it again. We were just playing a joke, but I've never heard a phone hung up louder in my life.

As a producer, I've turned in scripts that had so many sets they wouldn't physically fit on the stage we had to work with. I had to blush a bit and do some fancy rewriting before the show was taped. There is no way a writer can be aware of stage size or other particular limitations, but his script should show a general appreciation of television production.

Some shows, of course, have exterior shooting, a number of different sets, and even incredible car destruction scenes. Others don't. You can blow up a car on "Dukes of Hazzard," but you won't sell that to "Barney Miller." You have to observe what is acceptable on each show. If you're in doubt, play it conservatively: you want to avoid those errors that tell the reader to discard the script and move on to the next.

Don't Destroy the Premise

Another cold fact of television existence is that the producer is paid quite nicely to put together a show each week. He would like to continue producing that show for the rest of the season and for many seasons to come. A producer may complain bitterly about the star and the network and the show itself, but he has no quarrel with the paycheck and wants to keep it coming: there is no percentage in offering the producer a script that is going to destroy his show.

That sounds stupid, but it happens regularly: writers will try to sell stories that will ruin the premise a show turns around. Someone may pitch a story where a madman breaks into the precinct and kills Barney Miller. It may be a tremendous episode and the writing may be superb—but what are you going to do next week? Some authors want the Jeffersons to go bankrupt and move back to the ghetto. Some want Hawkeye to get his discharge from the service. You can't do it.

(As we go to press, "M*A*S*H" is indeed going to discharge Hawkeye next season; the show has agreed to a limited run that will end the series. Hawkeye will leave the service and the war will be brought to an end. This reinforces my point: any idea like this will *end* the series.)

Sitcoms usually wind up at the end of the half-hour exactly where they started. "Soap" had a continuing storyline, but most shows remain relatively unchanged. The Jeffersons might be threatened with bankruptcy, but will wind up in the same apartment at the end of the show. Jack Tripper and his "Three's Company" roommates may be temporarily evicted but will be back in the same apartment next week.

If your script is to show your talents—and be read—it had better not wreck the premise of the show.

Maintain Established Characterization

A perennial complaint from comedy writers is that characters are too closely guarded by their creators. A classic line from "My Favorite Martian" production days illustrates this. A script was criticized because "A Martian wouldn't say that." How on earth did this particular producer ever find out what a Martian *would* say?

Nevertheless, the creators of shows, and the actors portraying those roles, have established characters that have personalities and prejudices and beliefs. Any dialogue you write should reflect that characterization, not oppose it.

You're trying to sell scripts. You're building a reputation so that you can eventually create shows and characters of your own. Until you establish that reputation, it's unwise to attack the windmills of television. Archie Bunker may not always say the right thing, but if it comes down to an argument between you and Carroll O'Connor about what Archie should say, I think Mr. O'Connor is going to win.

Remember, too, that you're not just writing gags now. In writing good sitcom dialogue, your joke-writing principles must be altered somewhat. The people you're writing for usually aren't inherently funny people like George Burns or Joan Rivers: you are now writing for *characters*.

George Burns and Joan Rivers are on stage to make you laugh. That is what they do for a living; that is what the audience expects. Even outlandish set-ups seem logical from them. However, sitcom characters aren't onscreen to make us laugh. (The actors may be, but the characters aren't.) They are there to react to the situation in their own ways. The writers try to make them react so that it will be funny and will make the audience laugh, but that is not a character's primary goal.

The difference may seem subtle and nitpicking, but it is very important. For example, some boxing enthusiasts argue that boxing isn't as violent as football, while the football devotees counter that the primary objective in boxing is to knock an opponent senseless, but that football's violence is unintended.

A stand-up comedian comes out like a one-punch boxer. He intends to "knock you senseless" with dynamite material. Everyone expects it, so he can wind up and throw his most devastating routines at you. The actor in a situation comedy, though, has to be more subtle. He acts. He is a character in a situation and his dialogue and reactions must arise from that situation. *His* dynamite material has to refer to the circumstances.

Obviously, both circumstance and material have to be funny. From the writer's standpoint, though, the fun has to be approached from a different angle. Story, plot, and character are supreme in a sitcom, and they dictate the humor.

Make It Believable

In good sitcom writing, jokes move the story forward: they are consistent with the storyline and with the characters. The Marx Brothers film *Monkey Business* begins on shipboard with dialogue that says something like this:

> SEAMAN: *Captain, there are four crewmen trapped in the hold below deck.*
> CAPTAIN: *How do you know there are four of them?*
> SEAMAN: *They're singing "Sweet Adeline."*

The Marx Brother's peculiar zaniness marked them more as comedians than comic actors. Their inimitable antics allowed them to violate rules. This particular line got a big laugh, so it accomplished its purpose, but let's study it in relation to our discussion of sitcom writing.

The line is unbelievable: it doesn't flow from the situation. If a panic-stricken crewman approached his captain with news of an emergency, the captain would want to know what the problem was. Could the emergency be controlled or would it spread to the rest of the ship? What was being done about it? But the captain asks how the seaman knows there are four trapped men. Why? Simply to set up the punchline, "They're singing 'Sweet Adeline.' "

In this instance, the joke took precedence over the situation. The Marx Brothers were unparalleled jokesters, so this was acceptable in their film—but it shouldn't be in writing situation comedy dialogue. You shouldn't force even a good joke in where it doesn't belong.

Test this theory out for yourself by watching some sitcoms— both those you like and those you don't. Analyze them to see why you prefer some to others. You might be surprised to find that the jokes are just as powerful in the one as they are in the other—the difference may be that the gags are sometimes out of place: they might be funny but unbelievable under the given circumstances.

Let's let the Marx Brothers off the hook by citing a modern-day example. This is from "Three's Company," a show consistently rated in the Top Ten. It's also a show that I produced for a year, so I'm not keeping my own head off the chopping block while attacking fellow writers. This particular episode illustrates how a good joke can be forced into an implausible situation. Let me briefly give you the background to the scene:

Chrissy is dating a policeman. Through some mix-up she and Jack are handcuffed together, and because Chrissy's friend has been guilty of other minor rule infractions, he will get in serious trouble if his superiors discover that civilians have his handcuffs.

When the policeman's commanding sergeant comes to the apartment, Jack and Chrissy, still handcuffed, hide in the bathroom. For some reason the officer barges in there and Chrissy pretends she's showering—while Jack, still handcuffed to her, hides behind the curtain. The policeman, embarrassed, excuses himself, and leaves. Conveniently (for the writers), though, he leaves his hat in the bathroom. As Janet shows him to the door, he remembers his hat.

Here's the questionable scene: the sergeant goes right back into the bathroom and almost catches Chrissy and Jack hand-

cuffed together. Chrissy quickly grabs a towel while Jack franti-
cally maneuvers to stay behind the towel.

The physical sight gags were hilarious. The audience, the final judge of comedy, agreed. What argument do we have with a
scene that gets loud laughter from the viewers?

Well, it's not consistent with the characters, so it destroys
credibility. Jack and Chrissy's situation is funny because
they're in jeopardy, but sooner or later the audience is going to
recognize that that jeopardy should never have happened: it
was forced. It was unreal.

To begin with, the officer would never go into a closed bathroom without knocking. Circumstances didn't warrant it. (Let's
excuse that for the moment, though.) Once he gets in there and
finds a woman showering, the sergeant would NEVER go back
in without knocking. Janet is there with him. He could politely
ask her to retrieve his hat. Obviously, though, if Janet goes in,
Jack and Chrissy have nothing to hide from her, so all their
comic antics would be lost. It's the same reason the captain
said, "How do you know there are four of them?"

When you watch shows like "Taxi," or "The Mary Tyler Moore
Show," or even "M*A*S*H"—where Hawkeye can get away with
some non sequiturs because of his character—you'll find that
the comedy appears natural and always seems to flow from the
story.

Apply these guidelines to your own dialogue writing:

Map Out Your Storyline and Scene: You'll know exactly
where you're going and what you want to accomplish in each
scene. This will keep your dialogue from rambling and your
writing uniformly tight and compact. By following a roadmap,
you'll find that each line of your dialogue will be relevant and will
have a purpose.

Ask Yourself What Normally Would Follow: All comedy
writers are afraid of being predictable—yet that is exactly what
you must be in writing dialogue. Well-defined characters should
come across as real people. There is a predictability in the conversation of real people. If you question that, ask directions
from someone. If they know the way, they'll tell you—and invariably include the phrase, "You can't miss it." (Fred Allen once
said of a certain actor that if he was playing the part of a drown-

ing man he couldn't ad-lib the word, "Help.")

Your dialogue has to convey that predictability. It can be done with ingenuity; that's the skill of the writer. But if someone breaks into a room and shouts, "My God, the maid has just been murdered," the next line of dialogue is not, "Where did you get those beautiful shoes?"

Ask yourself what the people in you story would say—and then compose it for them.

Base Your Jokes on Character and Situation: Once you know where your scenario is going, and what has to be conveyed to the audience, you can create your jokes, sight gags, physical shtick, or whatever. But remember that it must be consistent with the situation and must flow from your characters. Don't force a joke in merely for the laugh. Analyze the story and have that generate the humor.

Sitcom Structure

The above suggestions will help your sitcom writing be consistent, but the other important selling point is the story. Let's discuss that for a while.

A situation comedy basically is a story. It has jokes in it, but they're a by-product. As we discussed earlier, when you sell a sitcom, you don't go to the producer and tell him jokes: you tell him a story. If the story is worthwhile, the jokes will follow.

So you must have a good strong plot. What is a plot? It's a well-defined goal, with complications along the way, eventually resolving itself. That can also be called a good beginning, middle, and end.

That should sound familiar to you. It's basically the same formula as for sketch writing. Sketch form is similar to sitcom, film, or novel form. The difference is largely in scope. With a sketch you generally investigate one incident and remain with it. With the larger forms, like a half-hour story or a 90-minute film, you can write about other characters and events surrounding your main plot. The basic plot form, though, remains constant: goal or premise, complications and a resolution—beginning, middle, and end.

The goal is what your story is about. It's what your hero hopes to accomplish. It's the direction you start your audiences' minds along. At the beginning it generally seems fairly innocuous and straightforward . . . but then we get further into our story.

Now we introduce the complications—the obstacles to the goal. Obviously, without these we have a fairly weak story. If Rocky had said, "I'm going to beat Apollo Creed," then went out and beat him, *Rocky* would have been a dumb movie.

It's the inventiveness of the complications that makes a story both interesting and funny. Mary Tyler Moore, as Dick Van Dykes's wife, meets an old friend she hasn't seen in ages and invites him over to dinner—she wants to fix him up with Rosemarie. Rosemarie dresses in her sexiest gown and determines to come on strong. So far it's fairly simple. But when the gentleman shows up, he's in a Roman collar. Jack Tripper on "Three's Company" has to earn money in a hurry to pay the rent, so he takes a job as a male model. No problem. When he gets to the studio, he finds out it's pornography they're photographing.

The complication requires a solution, but the solution can lead to other complications. For instance, Rosemarie's solution is to leave her fur coat on all through dinner so the priest won't see her provocative dress. That presents *another* complication—how to act nonchalant while eating dinner in a full-length mink coat. Jack decides to take the modeling assignment but never take off all his clothes—which, of course, presents complications in getting the pictures shot.

These false resolutions can continue as long as they're funny and for as long as you have time. Some motion pictures are just the process of complication and false resolution repeated over and over again.

Eventually, of course, the story should actually resolve. All the problems disappear and happiness is restored—but that's easier said than done. As we discovered in sketch writing, the ending can sometimes be the most difficult part. In writing a story you create a dilemma. Often, it's easier to create a complication than it is to untangle one—it's easier to mix up a Rubik's cube than it is to solve one.

Unlike a sketch ending, the sitcom ending needn't be as strong a punchline. However, it does have to have certain attributes of the punchline. It has to give the audience the feeling that the story was worth watching. It must be strong and believable enough to justify the half-hour that preceded it. You don't want a groaner.

My partner and I once sold a script to a CBS show called "Joe and Sons." The producers needed scripts in a hurry, so they hired us largely on our reputation and allowed us some latitude with our storyline. We had a beginning and a middle, but had no idea how the thing was going to end. (We don't always follow the advice we write in our books.) We had practically written ourselves into a corner because we created a dilemma from which there seemed to be no escape.

We got to our office one day and vowed to finish the script come what may. We had to find a resolution. I inserted a sheet of paper into the typewriter and numbered it page 28.

Then the phone rang. It was the producers of "Joe and Sons." "Stop typing," they said. "We just got word that we're canceled." I turned off the power on the electric typewriter. "Send us whatever you have, so we can pay you for the script." Naturally, we did just that, but today we feel cheated because we never *did* find out how that story ended.

It's advisable to have a complete story mapped out in your head and outlined before beginning the dialogue: writing is so much easier when you know where you're going.

Many years ago I was traveling to a summer resort in New Jersey to visit my sister and her family. My mom and dad were traveling with me. I grew up in Philadelphia, but once I crossed the bridge into Jersey, I was in a foreign country. I could get from the Walt Whitman Bridge to point A in Jersey and I could get from the Walt Whitman Bridge to point B in Jersey, but if I had to travel from point A to point B, I was lost: I had to go back to the bridge and start over again.

So on this trip, I asked my Mom if she had the explicit directions. She assured me she did. I traveled over the Walt Whitman Bridge—which is eight lanes wide and empties into about twenty different branches—and said, "Okay, Mom, which way now?" She said, "Follow the white line."

There were twenty white lines to follow. I was lost before we even started. That's the situation you'll get into if you begin a story without some idea of the ending.

In *selling* a story, though, the ending isn't that important. What will interest the buyer most is that first complication. If the problem you present is fascinating enough, they know that jokes and a resolution will follow. Your sales pitch should present the goal and build to the interesting complication. They'll buy that.

Creating Ideas

Where do we find obstacles to the goal? The same place we find jokes—who knows? You can stimulate your mind pretty much the same way you do for jokes: ask questions and make statements. What is the worst thing that can happen as your hero pursues his goal? Who else might get involved? What could possibly go wrong? The answer to these queries might present the plot points you're searching for.

Analyze and dissect your situation thoroughly. The different elements and themes you uncover may trigger some plot complications you can use.

Writing a sitcom is like writing a short screenplay: you should know characterization and plotting very well. The field is much too extensive for me to touch on anything but the highlights in this volume, but there are many excellent books available. One fairly recent book by Syd Field, *Screenplay, The Foundations of Screenwriting*, has become a bible for students of screenwriting. It's published in paperback by Dell Publishing Co.

A Word of Encouragement, A Word of Caution

Before leaving this subject, I would like to defend the industry—and also give the reader a realistic view of selling sitcoms for television.

Producers sometimes are bum-rapped for promoting a closed industry. It's not true. We need stories, we need ideas, and we need writers. We are open to all of them. Nevertheless, it's very rare that a story idea is purchased from anyone who doesn't live in the production company's immediate vicinity.

As I demonstrated earlier in the playlet, producers sometimes buy a show the author didn't intend to sell. He pitches one story, it's changed to something else, and finally he writes an outline about something he never even heard of before. It evolved from the meeting.

The outline he writes may go through the same metamorphosis, so that the author's first draft bears little resemblance to the outline, and the second draft may be even further removed from the first draft.

When the author watches the show on television, the only thing he may recognize is his name on the credits.

The writer is involved with and consents to many of these changes, and some happen after he is absent from the project, but the point is that producers don't buy a single story idea or storyline. They purchase an ongoing project.

Whether this process is the most efficient or not is irrelevant: it's just the way things happen in television. My partner and I once sold a script about a young boy minding a plant for a friend who was going out of town. The boy's parents mistakenly thought it was a marijuana plant, and pulled a leaf off to sniff it. The producers objected to mutilating a plant the youngster was so fond of. We dropped that from our draft.

When we saw the show on the air one of the characters was so scared the police would find the plant that he ate the entire thing. We weren't permitted to pluck a single leaf—but in rewriting, the plant was completely destroyed. That's how thinking varies from day to day.

Obviously, producers aren't going to pay top dollar to someone so far removed from the project that he or she can't participate. In so doing, they are in effect buying an idea that's unchangeable, and so it's worthless to them.

The same principle applies to the purchase of variety show sketches, but for a different reason. There are strict rules covering payment for such purchases and they're not inexpensive. Most variety shows have a staff on salary, so there's no percentage in buying a single idea that may change many times when a group of writers is already being paid to come up with ideas.

You can write sketches, though, for other media than television—for example, local theatrical or radio shows—whereas the sitcom can only be successfully produced on television.

Most writers dream of creating a new show and selling it to television as a series. That's done many times a year because each new season brings new weekly series. However, the odds are against this happening to a newcomer. Most pilots, because they are so expensive, are assigned only to writers and producers with proven credits. Again, it's an area of constant change. Hardly any pilot idea is purchased, scripted, produced, and put on the air without many network meetings and modifications. It's an ongoing process and the reputable professionals have to be close by at all times.

Then why even discuss sitcom writing if it's such an impossibility. Why should a beginning writer even attempt this form?

It's *not* an impossibility. I've had great success in handing out assignments to first-time sitcom writers, and many of the people my partner and I brought into the Writers Guild are now scripting weekly series. I simply feel that a writer can work more efficiently and wisely if she recognizes the percentages. A person can waste much energy trying to create a pilot for TV when the more prudent path is to write for established shows, create a reputation, and use that to sell a pilot.

Second, a beginning writer should attempt the sitcom because all writing is beneficial. We learn from our work. Writing spec scripts—even those that won't sell—teaches you to write ones that will. And by writing, you'll have those showcase scripts that you'll eventually need if you're serious about writing TV sitcoms anyway.

Remember, the two best ways to learn your craft are to practice it and to observe what others are doing. Watch TV, study what's being produced, and write.

PART THREE

BUILDING YOUR CAREER

Nothing in the world can take the place of perseverance. Talent will not; nothing in the world is more common than men with talent. Genius will not; unrewarded genius is almost a proverb. Education will not; the world is full of educated derelicts. Perseverance and determination alone are omnipotent. The slogan "Press On" has solved and always will solve the problems of the human race.

—Calvin Coolidge

18 THE PROPER ATTITUDE

The overriding question lurking behind every other question beginning writers ask is, "How do I get into comedy writing?" The answer is so simple and obvious that some readers may rebel—they may feel I'm trying to get off the hook with a pat answer. But I'm not. You get into comedy writing the same way you get into anything else you want in life: be good at it.

I *warned* you that you might take exception to that oversimplification. Some readers expect me to give Step One, Step Two, Step Three, and bingo! They'll be on the staff of a television show. They want *me* to do all the work.

It's Not the Breaks

The way to succeed in anything is to be good. Excel at what you do.

I remember the excitement that John McEnroe stirred up a few years ago in his first Wimbledon tournament. If I remember correctly, he made it to the quarter-finals. He was a schoolboy sensation who shocked the tennis world. Sportscasters interviewed him condescendingly. He was an unknown who got lucky at the greatest tennis tournament of the year. He obviously was playing way over his head. They figured they'd better interview him now because he'd probably never be heard of again.

Well, John McEnroe has been heard of again. For years now,

he's ranked among the big three of tennis, finally winning the Wimbledon title and establishing himself as the Number One tennis player in the world.

No one put John McEnroe in the top spot. His racket did his marketing for him. He didn't have to tell people how good he was. He showed them. He beat the best tennis players in the world and thus *became* one of the best tennis players of the world.

The point is this: anyone who has the skills of John McEnroe would have to be as successful as he is. That expertise can't be hidden.

A few years back there was another athlete whom no one believed in. He wanted a shot at the heavyweight boxing championship of the world, but no one thought he was qualified. This youngster had won the Olympic gold medal as a light heavyweight, but Sonny Liston, the reigning heavyweight champ, was considered unbeatable. Nevertheless, Cassius Clay—who later changed his name to Muhammad Ali—talked and shouted his way into a championship fight. Only one sportswriter in the entire nation picked Clay to win.

Then he became "The Greatest." Admittedly, that's by his own definition, but many boxing aficionados feel that Muhammad Ali may have been the greatest heavyweight champion of all time. When did he change from the kid who had no chance to the greatest of all time? He never did. He was good enough when he got the shot at Sonny Liston. He knew it, but the rest of the world didn't. He convinced them.

The proficiency of both McEnroe and Ali did their marketing for them. Their talent could not be denied. They both had to become tops in their fields.

Consider this for a minute, though. Imagine McEnroe saying, "Boy, if someone would just get me into Wimbledon, I'd really practice hard and try to win that tournament." Picture the young Cassius Clay saying, "I don't want to work real hard unless I'm sure I'll be able to get a championship fight." You would never have heard of either one again. They had to be good to get where they got and they have to be good to stay there.

"How do I get to be a tennis champion?" Be good.

"How do I get to become a boxing champ?" Be good.

"How do I get into writing?" Be good.

There's a myth around that hidden somewhere in the United States are people much more talented than the big names. Someone somewhere has a voice better than Sinatra's, but Frank just got lucky. The guy in the next office writes better than Neil Simon, but no one has discovered him yet.

That simply isn't true.

Here's another story. I worked on a televison show where a performer who was not one of my favorites put on a private show for everyone connected with the show. This didn't thrill me. It had been a long day and I wanted to go home.

Professional courtesy dictated that I stay for the show. Well, by the end of the performance the man had a convert. He had a jaded show-business audience enthralled. He deserved the superstar status he enjoyed.

Somewhere, someone feels that they could have had his success if they'd only had the same breaks. They're wrong. If they have his showmanship, his talent, and his vivacity, they won't need breaks. Someone will find them.

This point is very important for beginners to understand for two reasons: first, it tells you that you have to do the work. No one else can or should do it for you. If John McEnroe were a mediocre tennis player, but his uncle was a bigshot who managed to pull strings and get him into the Wimbledon tournament, would he be famous today?

Second, it tells you that if you do perfect your skills, you won't have to depend on breaks: someone will find you.

Breaks are tremendously overrated. They're nothing but everyday, ordinary circumstances. They don't officially become "breaks" until after the fact. Every name performer talks about his or her "big break." However, if that particular break didn't occur right then, it would have occurred later. If Cassius Clay hadn't gotten that contract to fight Sonny Liston, at another time he would have fought whoever was then current champ and still have been "The Greatest."

To me, it's like taking a ride from point A to point B in the family car. You take a certain route and you arrive at point B. Then you say, "I turned left at 22nd and Siegel. If that corner had been road-blocked, I never would have arrived." Nonsense. You would have taken an alternate route. The same is true of so-called breaks.

Let me tell you about two young writers many years ago who read an article on comedy writing that I wrote. They both asked me for assistance in their careers. Their material was promising, so I worked with them.

I asked the first writer to send me a set quota of material each week; this was a way of getting her to polish her skills with just a touch of encouragement from me. But the material never arrived. Excuse after excuse was offered with the promise that she would get on it next week or next month.

Several months later I was asked to recommend some good young monologue writers for two top television variety shows. There was no way I could suggest this young lady because I had no idea whether she was ready or not.

The other writer asked for my help and I wrote him a fairly standard letter telling him to try this and that. (I've sent similar letters many times and never received a reply because the correspondent doesn't want to do that much work.) This gentleman wrote back and said, "I've done all that. What do I do next?"

I didn't know. I'd never gotten this far before. I did give him some advice—and he followed it. His work improved, and eventually I recommended him for an assignment on the "Dinah" show, which he got. From there he moved on to "The Dean Martin Show," and now he works for Bob Hope.

Why did the second writer progress from show to show? Because I recommended him? I wish I could command that much respect in the industry. It was because he was good.

How do you get into comedy writing? Be good. It's not an oversimplification.

The next question, obviously, is "How do I go about being good?" You work as hard at your craft now as you would if you had the success that you hope for. You write and you listen and read as if you were the producer of a major television show. You perfect your skills now so that when the circumstances—not the breaks—present themselves, you can deliver.

I hope this hasn't made attaining a career in comedy writing sound easy. It's not; it's simply not complicated. There's a difference. If you come to me with a desire to play the piano, I'd advise taking lessons. That's not complicated, but it doesn't make your learning process easy.

Don't misunderstand this point, either. Once you're good, success probably won't be immediate. It takes a while for others to recognize your skills. To become successful you not only have to be good at what you do, you have to convince others. It takes perseverance for you to keep convincing them. You'll have to show them over and over again before it finally sinks in. That's the marketing of your talent.

Acquiring the skill is the easiest part because you're totally in control. You depend on no one else. If it takes six hours of practice a day for three years to become a proficient jazz drummer, you can arrange your life to do that. Convincing others of your proficiency, though, can be frustrating because you're not in charge. They are.

Once, playing a silly parlor game, I learned a lesson that may benefit you. Some friends and I were taking a test that consisted of names of colors printed in contrasting inks—the word "blue" might be printed in red, and the word "yellow" in green, and so on. There were about sixty words in this list, and the test was taken by going through the list calling out the color of the ink. Someone would time you and your speed would supposedly tell something about your personality.

Several of us took the test and I had a very fast time. When we read the results, it said that my speed indicated I was careless with details. Naturally, I objected, but people said it was true because in going so quickly I probably made several mistakes. "I made no mistakes," I argued. They smiled patronizingly. Now I was a bit angered and determined to prove my point.

I took the test again with comparable speed while someone checked my accuracy. He stopped me in the middle and said, "You just made four mistakes on this line alone." I said, "I'm not on that line. I'm on the line below it." Again the patronizing smiles. Now I was near fury. "If I can do the test in 30 seconds and this man does it in 60 seconds, how can he possibly test my accuracy?"

Finally, to prevent me from going into a rage, my friends wrote down the correct answers on a separate piece of paper, I did the test at the same speed, and made *no* errors.

You needn't applaud. I'm not telling the story to boast at my prowess in calling out colors spelling other colors. What I did learn was that often in life we will be evaluated and judged by people less qualified than ourselves. And that's frustrating.

You'll work hard at your craft. You'll assemble a showcase of your writing. You'll present it to someone who knows less about humor than you do. Authority doesn't always indicate ability or good judgment. You'll be rejected for the wrong reasons. You'll have to try again.

During this journey toward success, you'll receive many unjustified "no's." It's not really unfair: it's a fact of life. You must remember, though, that it only takes one justified "yes" to erase all those "no's." You don't have to have everyone accept your writing—just the people who know what they're doing.

Nevertheless, it's disappointing and irritating to have good efforts rejected. I almost blew my stack because somebody told me I couldn't do a puzzle in a newspaper. If you really want to make a success of humor writing, it will help if you approach the challenge with a realistic attitude.

It Won't Happen Overnight

Some aspirants have what I call "Send the Limo" syndrome. I recognize it because I had it for two years. Writers send a few pages of material out and sit home and wait for some Hollywood mogul to reply by sending a chauffeured limousine to whisk them away to Tinseltown. It's a fantasy we all have hidden in the back of our minds.

It's not going to happen and you do yourself a disservice in expecting it because your disappointment could be fatal to your enthusiasm. The frustration could lead to the abandonment of a promising career when the first few queries don't bring dramatic results.

A worthwhile career will build slowly and solidly. It will have its share of minor victories and slight defeats. It probably will *not* explode in a dazzling burst of triumph.

Why? Because first of all, if the person you sent your material to is at all important, he will have seen some pretty fantastic material before. He's not going to be knocked off his feet—not even if your writing is way above average quality.

Secondly, most of the people you will submit your material to don't really know good stuff when they see it. I include myself in that indictment. Remember that there are very few good judges of comedy. The rest of us are only guessing.

I've read sketches and sitcom scripts I hated, then on tape night watched them go through the roof. I've read material that amazed me with its brilliance; on tape night it sat there like a lump.

I wrote a sketch for Bill Cosby that I was convinced bordered on genius. Seeing this masterpiece taped before a live, laughing audience was going to be one of the highlights of my career. I stood in the wings (so I could go onstage quickly when the audience called out, "Author, author") and watched the sketch die a horrible, silent death. I was crushed and confused—then convulsed with laughter when an old gentleman in the audience turned to his wife and said matter-of-factly, "It was a good idea."

We just plain, flat-out don't know, so an experienced comedy writer is reluctant to get too exuberant about any material until it's been tested before the ultimate jury, the audience.

Why a Career Takes Time

Most prominent people in show business aren't in the habit of discovering new talent. They deal mostly in proven commodities. Las Vegas, for example, is the reputed show business capitol of the world. Do producers look for new acts to put in their showrooms? No. They want established people with proven marketability.

To impress a producer you have to be better than the talent that's already available. "Better?" you ask. That's right—*better*. Why? Well, let's look at it from the buyer's point of view. He knows what the certified talent can deliver. He's worked with them before and knows their output is good, consistent, on time, dependable. They're easy to work with and will accept changes readily. Whatever the pluses and minuses are, he is used to them. *You* are still a question mark. Can you write fast? Can you deliver under pressure? Can you take editorial criticism? These are all unknowns. So long as you're *just as good* as the other guy, why shouldn't he go with the proven talent?

The only way you can gain an edge over this competitor is to be *better* than he is. Now you're offering the buyer something in exchange for the risk he's taking. You have to continue doing this until your reputation is established and *you* become the proven talent.

The defense is penetrable, but don't expect to do it with one sampling of your material. This is not to say that because it took me nearly a decade to make it into television, you must put in an apprenticeship that long. You might do it in a month if you have what it takes, but no matter how long it takes, it will be easier for you to break in if you approach it with a realistic attitude. Expect rejection. Don't allow any negativism to shake your confidence.

Once I did some writing for a national telethon. It was taped in Hollywood to raise money for a Presidential candidate. (I won't tell you which one because I don't want to alienate any of you. We writers are so insecure . . .)

Telethons are a vision in chaos. They run most of the day and guests come and go at any and all times. The schedule falls apart within the first hour of the telecast.

I sat backstage with another writer—a well-known creative talent and a good friend of many stars—waiting to be called should any of the guests want something written.

A popular comic came in and talked to us for a while. It was the first time I had been introduced to him. We started trading lines, and the comic laughed at everything I told him. They were lines I'd written for another client, but he loved each of them. He laughed so hard at some of my material that he had tears in his eyes. Then he wiped them dry, turned to the more established writer and said, "Geez, you got to write some new material for me."

I'm not telling that story to be boastful because this other writer could certainly write funny stuff. I tell it only to show what new writers are up against. I regaled this comedian with terrific lines, but still he turned to the "name" writer.

There is no justice to any of this, only reality. Years later—and I never could determine at what exact point—I somehow changed from the newcomer to the established pro. Powerful people now listened to my comments and gave them weight.

A few years ago, some young writers on one of my writing staffs were upset because none of their material seemed to be getting on the show. They were afraid they weren't writing well. I did something devious to prove to them that their writing was fine.

With their permission, I took one of their sketches and re-typed the first page with my name as author. This was sent to the powers that be—and they made a few comments and ac-cepted the sketch.

Be Realistic About What You're Worth

We all have to serve an apprenticeship and deal with the cold facts of life. Among those cold facts is compensation. Samuel Johnson once said that no man except a blockhead would write for anything except money. Now, money is one of my favorite re-wards for hours spent at the typewriter, but young careers can sometimes be hurt by asking for too much too soon. As you car-ry out your apprenticeship, your skills will grow—as will your re-muneration. But your skills should grow faster.

A novice writer may read in the paper that so and so makes $1,000 a page for his monologue material. Now a comic who works weekends for $50 a night asks the young writer for some material. "Okay," the writer agrees, "but it'll cost you a thou-sand bucks a page." No sale.

First of all, any salary you read in the paper you should divide by two. We all lie. (Someday I hope to make as much money as I tell my friends I make.)

There's a great show business story about that point, which I'd like to pass on to you. A certain Hollywood writer was walking along Wilshire Boulevard and saw the movie he had written playing in a theatre. He casually walked in and asked the man-ager how the film was doing box-officewise. The manager screamed, "This is the worst movie we ever had in here. It's kill-ing us. I may go absolutely broke." The writer said "How much did you take in?" The manager moaned, "So far we did three dol-lars." The poor author was broken-hearted. He slumped over to Nate and Al's delicatessen for some lunch. While he was sitting there another writer came in and said, "Hey, I see your film is over at the Wilshire. How's it doing at the box office?" The guy said, "I don't want to talk about it." The other writer said, "Come on. How's it doing?" The author said, "No." The other scribe persisted, "Come on, I'm a good buddy. How's your film doing?" The writer said, "Okay. It did six dollars."

So divide every figure by at least two. Let's even assume the top writer really got $500 a page for his monologues—that's no measure of price for the apprentice writer. The other gentleman may be so successful and so busy that he discourages monologue assignments. He may charge an exorbitant rate just to avoid getting any. That practice certainly isn't in the best interests of the beginner.

During an apprenticeship and while your career is blossoming, you'll need experience and credits more than you need top dollar for your work. If you work hard and constantly improve, the money will come. At this stage, though, perfecting your craft should take precedence over accounting figures.

Remember, the first step in marketing your wares is to be good.

19 GETTING YOUR CAREER GOING

Becoming a barber is easy. You find a barber school in the Yellow Pages, investigate, take the required courses, get your certificate, and open your shop. Becoming a brain surgeon is uncomplicated. You study pre-med, then go to medical school, serve your internship, have your diploma framed, and perform your first operation.

Yes, I'm making light of this and don't mean to offend any barbers or brain surgeons reading this book, but there's no real mystery to taking up either occupation. The requisite steps can be outlined by any qualified counselor. Comedy writing is not that simple. There's no listing in the Yellow Pages. Want ads don't advertise for humorists.

Each new venture into comedy writing is a journey over uncharted land. You can't follow a road map because there are no paved highways leading to comedy writing careers. At the beginning, you're in a wilderness and you have to find the escape route.

No two professional humorists I've talked with have ever arrived at their careers by the same route. No two have ever followed any pre-designed paths. There simply are none.

Very little literature is available about a career in humor. That's why this book was written—because comedy writers have had no place to turn. There are writers' organizations, magazines, and instructional books, but few are devoted exclusively to humor; in fact, few of them deal with humor at all.

Your journey toward a career in humor writing will be an adventure, like the home computer programs that are listed as "adventures." These are disks or tapes that you insert in your computer; they place the operator in a situation. Then, by deduction and experimentation, you try to reach a destination or accomplish a goal. Aficionados tell me that some of these adventures take from nine months to a year to solve.

Your comedy writing adventure may be like that. You already have a goal, but how do you begin to accomplish it? Pretty much the same way as the home computer operator: by trial and error.

Your first task is research. You'll want to know more about this business you're trying to enter. You want to read books on the subject, and magazines or newspapers that deal with comedy, and you'll want to talk to people who are associated with the business.

The nice thing about the research is that it's all interlocking. It's like solving a jigsaw puzzle. Each time you find the correct place for a piece, you not only have solved that segment of the puzzle, but you've given yourself information you need to solve *other* segments. So you can jump into this research almost anywhere and it will lead you to the next logical step.

If you have a book on comedy, it may refer you to periodicals that deal with humor. Should you discover a periodical, it may suggest reading particular books. Suppose you know someone who deals in comedy? They may be aware of magazines and books you might be interested in.

Suppose you know of none of these. How do you begin your research? At the library. The librarian can be helpful in finding periodicals, associations, or books on your subject. However, sometimes you benefit more from doing the research for yourself. A glance through the reference section may uncover some books or ideas that neither you nor the librarian would have considered. Leafing through different areas of the card catalog may present new thoughts to your mind.

It's amazing how knowledge is intertwined and how quickly information can be compiled merely by starting somewhere. It's almost as easy as unraveling a sweater. Grab any loose thread and pull.

Where do you start? Anywhere. I recommend my own publication, *Round Table*, a gathering place for comedy writers and humorists (P.O. Box 13, King of Prussia PA 19406), because it is truly a dialogue form of publication. *Round Table* encourages reader input, so that subscribers may benefit from each other's experiences. However, a copy of the weekly *Variety* may begin your research chain. It doesn't matter where you start unraveling a sweater, so long as you keep on pulling.

Personal Contact

The dialogue aspect of your research is important. Your investigation will produce the names of many people who are in the comedy business. Call or write and ask for an appointment. You may be surprised to discover how friendly and helpful these people can be.

When I began my career, I toyed with contacting a gentleman whom I didn't know, but knew of. I composed several letters—only to destroy them, thinking it presumptuous of me to write and ask for guidance. Finally, I worked up the courage. I received a phone call in response to my letter and we met a few days later. This gentleman became a true champion of my work, the man who picked my spirits up when things didn't go well, and my best friend to this day. He has been responsible for more of my success than any other person. All this was the outcome of a letter I was afraid to write.

This gentleman is not only my biggest booster, he also was influential in another important letter that I wrote. Phyllis Diller once canceled a scheduled interview appointment with him—he's a journalist—but left her home address so he could send a list of questions she would answer by return mail. I intercepted the address and sent a letter introducing myself—along with several pages of jokes. Phyllis replied with a check buying many of my submissions.

Not only have I written for Phyllis ever since, she helped launch my TV writing career, and introduced me and my work to many other people who have become clients of mine.

I'm a big advocate of letter writing. Most people who are interested in the same things you're interested in delight in talking about them. Not everyone will answer your letters: some will answer only with a polite, non-committal reply. But some people you write to may become helpful pen pals and friends.

Over twenty-five years ago I wrote to television and radio personality Peter Lind Hayes. He wrote back listing a few television writing friends of his who might be able to help me. I contacted a few of them and learned a great deal. Peter also suggested that I write some monologues to him in the form of a letter: he read these on his shows, giving me full credit. This exposure led to contacts and sales for me.

When I landed my first job in television, I wrote to Hayes thanking him for his help along the way. I received a beautiful response which said in effect that he had received and replied to many letters asking for advice, but this was the first letter he could remember that offered thanks. (Just last year I met Hayes for the first time, introduced myself and reminded him of our correspondence.)

Don't Expect Too Much

As we discussed in the previous chapter, your letter writing will produce better results if you are totally realistic in your approach. People are generally gracious with their knowledge and often are happy to share it with others. Many will even read samples of your material and might even offer constructive criticism; it's unfair, though, to expect much more of them.

All of us hope that someone will adopt us, sell our material, or get a job for us—but they won't, they can't, and they shouldn't. Why? Because those are your duties. No one else can really accomplish that for you. It's not only improper for you to ask that of someone else, it would be a disservice to you if they did.

Getting a person one job does her no good unless she has the ability to continue on from that one to the next. If you are that talented, your material will get the job for you.

Your letter of inquiry should ask only for an exchange of ideas, and perhaps that they read some of your samples. Requesting too much can turn the reader off.

Didn't I just say, though, that Phyllis Diller did all the things for me I've said a person shouldn't do? Yes and no. She did many nice things for me, but it was after we had worked together for several years. She already knew what I could do—and had done.

Remember, as a beginning writer, you're faced with the chore of finding out as much about the business as you can. Each bit of information you uncover will lead to several more pieces of knowledge. Some of this material will be tremendously helpful; some will have minimal value and you'll have to discard it. But it's an interesting adventure, one which will educate you and help your skills to grow.

That's also why it's unfair for others to supersede this process. *To get the full benefit of it, you must go through it yourself.*

The Value of Networking

I didn't mean for this chapter to be so autobiographical, but I can attest to the value of this process: I used it to get my career going. Recently, I used it again. I've become interested in public speaking, but know little about the speaking business. So I began my research. I discovered a few books and newsletters on speaking. That led to other publications and eventually to some names. I wrote and called people I met through my reading. In short, I have lunched and dined with many of the top speakers in the nation. I've been a guest in their homes and they in mine. Through contacts I've made, I've landed speaking engagements and have even been invited to conduct a seminar at a National Speakers Association Convention. I went from knowing nothing at all to conducting a speaker's workshop all in the space of one year.

Through this method of research I met and spent three enjoyable days visiting with "Doc" Blakely, one of the top humorous speakers on the circuit. He told me a story that applies to all of this. The anecdote touched me so much that I would like to pass it on to you. (If "Doc" doesn't mind my paraphrasing.) "Doc" told me:

When I first got interested in speaking I went to visit a man who lived near my home town who was a fantastic and funny speaker. I told him I wanted to do that kind of work, too, and asked if he could help me in any way. He patiently listened to me and graciously listened to a tape of one of my talks. He seemed to like my work so I asked if he could help me in any way. He asked what he would get in return. I offered him a price and he wanted more. I offered him a percentage of my income for a year and he still wanted more. Now I started to get a bit scared. I finally asked how much he wanted. He said, "You're going to make it as a speaker. You're going to work hard and be very good someday. When you arrive, some youngster is going to come to you and want help. My price for helping you is you have got to promise me you'll help them."

(I love that story just as it stands, but there's an ending that makes it even more intriguing. This gentleman died not too long after helping "Doc" get started, and left a very young son behind. Many years later that boy—not knowing anything about this story—came to "Doc" Blakely to ask advice on becoming a speaker.)

Rejection

Sometime during the course of your factfinding, you're going to have to submit some of your material for scrutiny. This can be a frightening experience because of the overwhelming fear of rejection: so much hard work and so much of yourself goes into your writing that it's painful to see it turned down. Yet we all have that fear in us because we've already admitted that we don't know comedy—we're only guessing. The guy who's reading it can always guess differently than the guy who wrote it.

The most terrifying experience is to have to sit in a room and watch someone read a sketch or a monologue you've just written. Silence can take on a whole new coloration while that's happening. I always pick that moment to go out and get myself a cup of coffee or search for the nearest (or farthest) men's room.

It's also difficult to have to read someone's work who's sitting there gazing intently into your face for any expression of approval or rejection. It's always better to have the author leave you quietly with his material so that you can read it, digest it, and think of some excuse for rejecting it besides, "It's simply not funny."

Most head writers have that unwritten law. They dance around a rejection with explanations like, "I don't think the characters really come alive," or "The premise is too unbelievable." Generally, they'll say anything except it's not funny.

Bill Cosby once did a routine about the corner bar his father would sometimes visit. He talked about his macho dad having a few drinks before heading home for dinner, and how he, a youngster, was sent to get his dad home. "Mom says you gotta get home right now or she's coming after you." None of the other men in the bar would say a word in ridicule. They all knew *they could be next.*

That's the way writers feel about saying, "It's not funny."

Facing possible or even probable rejection can frequently discourage a beginning writer from submitting material. It shouldn't. Shakespeare advised us well and succinctly when he said, "Doubts are traitors and make us lose the good we oft might win by fearing to attempt."

Rejection is part of any writer's life. It should be accepted and understood. Often a turndown is an economic reality, not a critique of your submission. Publishing houses, for example, can only produce so many books each year. For the sake of discussion, let's presume the one you send your novel to can publish twenty. Does it then follow that they will only get twenty quality submissions? Of course not. They will get many representative manuscripts. They will only accept twenty and reject the rest.

Rejection is part of life, period. A painful duty of a television producer is casting. One actor is needed and 15 hopefuls show up for auditions. The producer selects one for the role, but the others may be equally competent. In watching ballgames on TV, I often hear the cliche, "It's a shame one of the teams has to lose." It's a pity some of our manuscripts have to be rejected, but they do. If God didn't want us to receive rejections, he wouldn't have invented the self-addressed, stamped envelope.

The beginning writer must also learn not to take rejection personally. It is not a comment on the quality of your material so much as it is a comment on *the person* judging your material. Yet again, we remind ourselves that we're only guessing. When you wrote your material, you made an educated guess that it was funny. Whoever reads it and dismisses it as unsuitable is guessing that it isn't funny. He may just be a lousy guesser.

All writers experience these setbacks. When I first started, I seriously toyed with the idea of writing, but making my real hobby collecting rejection notices. Some were truly disappointing, some were just funny. One stands out. I assembled several pages of monologue material and sent it to nightclub comic Joe E. Lewis. I received back a sheet of memo notepaper from the Fontainebleau Hotel in Florida that had written on it, "I already have a writer." Signed Joe E. Lewis.

As a cocky young jokesmith, though, I adopted an attitude that served me well through those apprentice years: *I* wasn't losing out when someone turned down my material—*he* was. Whether that arrogance later proved accurate or not didn't matter. It kept me going.

You must remember, too, that rejection is a negative and has no real meaning. It doesn't change anything you're doing. You still continue to strive for acceptance.

When Thomas Edison was struggling to perfect the light bulb, he tried many substances unsuccessfully. Someone once asked him how many he tried, and Edison told him about 3000. The gentleman said, "You tried 3000 elements and failed? You know no more now than when you started." Edison corrected him. "You're wrong. I know 3000 things that don't work."

Rejections are not obstacles to a career: they're simply things that won't work. So we fear them for no reason. They can do us no harm.

Fearing rejection can harm us. It can keep us from continuing. That's why it's essential to see how impotent rejection is.

Does anyone know or care how many filaments Edison tried unsuccessfully before finding the right combination? Whether it was one or one million is immaterial because the one success erased all the failures.

When people ask me whom I've written for (and many times when they don't), I say, "I've written for Bob Hope, Phyllis Diller, Carol Burnett, Tim Conway . . . "Wouldn't it be silly to say, "I didn't write for Henny Youngman, Joe E. Lewis, and thousands of others?"

To get your comedy career progressing, you're going to have to do some research. You owe it to yourself and your craft to learn as much about your profession as possible. You're also going to have to expose yourself: your precious material is going to have to be evaluated and judged, and it won't always get good grades. But that shouldn't dissuade you from continuing. Everybody doesn't have to like your material. Just somebody who can write checks that don't bounce.

20 PRACTICING YOUR TRADE

A woman went into a butcher shop and asked how much the veal cutlets were. The proprietor said, "Eight dollars a pound." The woman was astounded. She said, "What? I can get them across the street for six dollars a pound." The proprietor asked, "Then why don't you get them across the street?" "They don't have any," the woman said. "Oh," the proprietor said. "When we don't have any, they're only five dollars a pound."

I've remembered that joke from about twenty-five years ago when Myron Cohen told it on the Ed Sullivan Show. His skillful dialects did it much more justice than the printed page ever could. Nevertheless, there's a moral here: you can't sell anything unless you've got it to sell. You can't market material unless you've got material to market.

That seems fairly obvious, but I've found through experience that it isn't. I've worked with beginning writers and have periodically been able to recommend them for assignments. "Send so-and-so some samples of your work," I'd tell them. "Well, I can't," they'd reply. "I don't have anything."

What have we been doing all this month? It happens time and time again. A writer shows promise. That potential will be confirmed. Then they sit home and wait for someone to hire them before they get around to writing again.

It won't happen that way. Anyone you query or anyone you are recommended to will want to see samples of your work.

Unfortunately, there is only one way to get samples of your material and that is to *write* material.

I've already said a few times that the best advice I could give a beginning comedy writer is to set a quota and stick to it. It needn't be a demanding quota, but it *should* be inflexible. In Chapter 3 we discussed the benefits of setting yourself a quota but let me repeat why it's an advantage from a marketing standpoint: by faithfully writing you'll build up enough material to assemble a showcase of your skills.

We writers would like to feel that everything that rolls out of our typewriters is brilliant but we know better. Some days it sparkles and other days it stinks. The percentage of sparkle to smell is what makes a good writer. Should anyone ask to see some of my work, I select some of the proven sketches from the Carol Burnett or Tim Conway shows and proudly exhibit them. No way am I going to show them all the work I did in the period of one month on those shows, though—there may be some bombs in the bunch. In there might a sketch I wrote that was so bad, Joe Hamilton (Carol Burnett's husband) came on stage in the middle of the taping and said, "Stop doing this." Carol Burnett was so pleased that she kissed him, turned to the audience, and said, "He has just saved our marriage."

The beginning writer must build up a backlog of material from which to select a representative portfolio. The best way to do that is to write, write, write.

Some of you may feel that this isn't a fair indication of your writing skills. Shouldn't the buyer be able to know how much you can write in a given period and how good that material is? Not really. The buyer wants to know how good you are. He wants to see your top material. He knows the facts of life—some days you'll be slow, some days you'll be bad. But if you show him good material he'll know that it'll be worth the wait.

Besides, the purchaser of comedy material can afford to be rather cold-blooded about your problems. He wants good, funny stuff. How long it takes you to turn that out and how much work it is for you are *your* problems.

Always present your best work and let the buyer beware. This lesson hit me just recently. A producer friend called with a problem. He had fallen behind on scripts and needed some shows immediately if not sooner. I went in and worked out a story with him, and got an assignment for a script. He pleaded with me to have it to him the next day. That was out of the question—we normally allow two weeks for a first draft to be written. However, I did promise that I would work on it over the weekend and have it delivered by Monday, a total of three days' work.

I wrote the script quickly, and delivered it by messenger on Monday morning. Later a mutual friend asked the producer how he liked my script. "It didn't knock me out," was his reply.

This isn't sour grapes, because I agree with the producer. The script wasn't a knockout. I did see the rewrite his staff did when the show aired and it was terrific. However, the story points out that none of us considers the time or effort spent on a project. We all just consider the results: Is it funny?

So any time you're exhibiting your wares, include only those you're most proud of.

This leads to the second marketing reason for setting an inflexible quota for your writing. You'll not only have more samples to select from, but your material will get better and better. You can't afford *not* to set a quota for yourself.

Do It Yourself

While we're speaking of improvement, let me once again advise the apprentice to deliver some of her own material. Sometimes this lesson can be extremely painful (when your material doesn't go over) but even then it is invaluable. There is no substitute for actual experience. Even those who have no ambition to stand at a podium and deliver funny lines should try it once or twice. It will make your comedy writing that much better.

That's because, regardless of how much we study or how expert we become on a subject, we never really know it until we experience it. Why? Because there are always surprises. I'm always amused at watching boxing matches on TV when one of the poor combatants is taking a beating. In the corner, his seconds are bombarding him with all sorts of valid advice. "Jab to his face and then follow up with a right. One good right and you can knock this bum out." That theory is sound and, diagrammed on paper, it's probably flawless. But the advisors don't have to get in the ring with the other fellow—who may be quicker, smarter, and stronger. Every time the guy throws a jab, his opponent counters with three or four stinging blows to his already aching nose. He's coming to the painful conclusion that theory don't cut it against this fighter.

Jack Benny once was the manager of the Hollywood Stars baseball team when they played an exhibition at Dodger Stadium. He told the first batter to hit a home run. The batter got out. Benny slammed his cap to the ground and left. He said, "If you're not going to follow orders, I quit."

This was the kind of fun that made the game a delight for the fans, but again there is a moral. It's easy to give advice—even correct advice—but it's not always easy to follow it. Since you're going to be the strategist, the writer, the brains behind the comic, it'll serve you well to know problems a comic faces.

To speak seriously about Benny's joke line, he might not have said, "Hit a home run" if he knew how difficult an assignment that was. I know I'm drawing conclusions from the absurd, but some writers do what Jack Benny did: they ask the comic to take their material and "hit a home run" with it when they really don't know how difficult a task that is. That's why it would be beneficial for them to step to the plate a few times.

There are certain practicalities that one can only learn from experience. Certain words are nearly impossble for a comic to say and maintain his rhythm. I've learned from experience that I can't get out the phrase "shoulder holster" without fumbling over it; other people have difficulties with other word combinations. If a comic says, "I can't say this joke as written," you have no right to quarrel with him unless you've actually stood in front of an audience with a great punchline and said, "Shoulder holder . . . holder shoulster . . . holster shoulster . . . ."

For "The Tim Conway Show" I had written a series of blackouts about an Indian and a cavalry officer making peace. Each time they went through the ceremony, Tim, as the Indian, would do something accidentally to start the war up again. In one gag, Tim was holding a long spear. In moving to break it over his knee, he accidentally tripped the cavalry officer and stabbed him.

As we were shooting this routine, Tim kept changing the joke. Finally, I asked him to do the gag as written because it was much funnier than the gags he was experimenting with. He handed me the spear and said, "Show me exactly what you mean." I took the long, heavy spear, stood in his place, tried to do what I had written—and discovered it was physically impossible. Naturally, I called the writing staff and got a new joke. I can't create when I'm embarrassed.

No one has had more experience with jokes and with audiences than Bob Hope. Several of us writers sat with him in the London Palladium rehearsing a monologue he would do at a command performance for the Queen. He came to one joke and took it out of the monologue. It was my joke.

I said, "Why are you taking that joke out?" He said, "I don't want to do that in front of the Queen." I objected, "There's nothing wrong with that joke. The Queen will love it." (I know all her likes and dislikes.) Bob Hope said, "Is that right?" I said, "Sure." He handed me the cue card and said, "Then you do it."

If you absolutely, positively refuse to or cannot get in front of an audience to speak, then at least work along with someone who will. It's not tough to do. Anyone who loves to speak will welcome humorous input.

At least you'll get some experience with audience reaction. But listen to your speaker. Your tendency will be to defend what you've written. Since you haven't stood before the crowd yourself, you may smugly blame the speaker for the wrong inflection, or fault the audience for not being receptive enough. Don't. Smother your pride in favor of the lessons to be learned. Let your speaker tell you why your stuff failed and learn from him. If you're intent on a writing career, you'll have plenty of times later on to defend your material.

Save Your Work

We've already agreed that to have material to show, you must first write it. You must also *save* it. Again, it seems that I'm belaboring the obvious, but many writers submit material for critique, read the notations, and then discard it. If you're serious about writing, you should preserve everything you write. There are other reasons besides having it to show prospective buyers.

It Will Show Your Improvement

Keeping all of the material that you compose will be positive reinforcement that your writing, as you continue, is becoming more professional. Sometimes our improvement is so gradual that we hardly notice it, and even believe it nonexistent. A look back at some of your earlier work can be vivid proof that you've learned quite a bit.

It Can Help You Over Today's Dry Spell

Reviewing some of the good material you've written can prove you can do it again. There are days when the blankness of the page can be overpowering. You don't feel funny. The topic isn't inspiring. You have better things to do than write foolish lines about silly things.

These are only three causes of writer's block. There are 8,452,327,261 other documented causes of it. Basically, it's fear that you can't do a good job on a project, so you subconsciously find ways of avoiding it. But rereading some of your brilliant past work may show your subconscious how foolish it's being. You'll do as professional a job on this assignment as you have done on others. Turn on the typewriter and destroy the whiteness of the page.

You Can Reuse Much of the Material

History does repeat itself. That's nice for the gagwriter, because many jokes still apply the second time around. I learned this lesson early in my career. I was working for Slappy White and wrote some jokes about the fight in which Sonny Liston knocked out Floyd Patterson in the first round. The one I wrote that I was proudest of was:

> *That fight was so short, when they raised Liston's arm I thought it was a deodorant commercial.*

During the show that night, Slappy did not only that joke, but a whole routine on the fight. He had lines like:

> *"I had a hundred-dollar seat for that fight and*
> *Patterson, he sat down before I did.*

> *"A guy asked me if I thought Patterson would*
> *ever fight again. I said, 'As much money as*
> *I lost on this fight, when he sees me he'll*
> *fight again.'*

> *"But I'd like to see Patterson come back . . .*
> *and finish that first round."*

I asked Slappy where he could get a whole routine that fast. He said, "Remember the Marciano-Wollcott fight?" I sure did. I watched that in my living room, went out to get a bottle of soda, came back, and the fight was over. (And that was before they had instant replay.) Slappy said, "Same jokes."

I've capitalized on history's repeating itself many times since. The jokes may have to be changed around a bit, but often only the names have to be changed to protect the topicality. Christine Keeler caused headlines years ago with a sex scandal in British politics; those same gags applied when Liz Ray shook up American politics. Some of them were still usable when Rita Jenrette confessed to naughtiness in the nation's capital. Next year or the year after, there will be a new name waiting to be typed into the blank spaces.

Your old material will also prove useful even when the same jokes can't be used. Chances are you'll be working on similar topics. Inflation causes a controversy periodically. The stock market declines every so often. We do a Bob Hope show about football once each season. Going back over old routines may not actually provide usable jokes in these cases, but they *will* give you an idea on different slants to take with the topic.

You put in a lot of effort to create humor: you should preserve it all for future reference and possibly for future use. Naturally, the material you save is of little use to you unless you can find it again, fairly quickly.

I have a system that has worked for me. It's simple and it's fast, requiring little maintenance or bother. I'm not recommending it over any other system, since I haven't really studied filing procedures, but because it has served me well I'll take a moment to pass it on to you.

It's simply a chronological listing of my writing with an accompanying index. First of all, I break the writing down into the different contracts that I have. If I'm writing for Joe Blow, Jackie Lenny, and Lenny Jackie, I have three different indexes going. Make that four, because I'd probably have one for "general" or "miscellaneous." Then each routine I do for each client is numbered from one to whatever. The first routine I write for Joe Blow is numbered JB # 1, the tenth routine for Jackie Lenny is JL # 10, and Lenny Jackie's fortieth routine is LJ # 40.

Then I keep a separate looseleaf book with an index for each client. As I write the routine, I list the number and what the material is about.

A typical listing for Joe Blow, who does topical material, might read something like this:

JB # 010 Valenzuela negotiations with Dodgers

JB # 011 Princess Di expecting

JB # 012 Soap opera popularity

JB # 013 Male stripper clubs

JB # 014 White House tablecloths

JB # 015 Maureen Reagan in politics

and so on.

I keep a copy of everything I write, either in a looseleaf book or in a file folder. If I want to research past material, I read through the index until I find the appropriate number, turn to that page in the looseleaf book, and there it is.

I follow the same procedure on most of the shows I work on. Each assignment is numbered and listed in an index, then filed accordingly.

It's a simple system because each routine is just noted and then filed as the next entry in a book. Once that's completed, it never has to be altered. It's there for when you want to find it.

I have a collection of over twenty volumes of monologue material containing almost 100,000 jokes. I also have material from twelve different seasons of television writing. I can retrieve any material from this collection in less than half an hour.

I can't retrieve individual jokes with this system: I can only find the topics and search through all the monologues until I happen across a particular joke. But I can retrieve a particular sketch from a show.

The benefit of the system to me is that it is simple and maintenance-free. The topic is written once in one place and the routine is filed once. It takes no more time than writing the title once in a book.

The important point is that your material should be saved and readily available to you. How you do that depends on your own ingenuity. I list mine as one example only.

The essential step, though, is to get that material out of your archives and into the marketplace. That's what we'll talk about next.

21 COMPLETING SPECULATIVE WORK

Since I've been critical of colleagues who fail to meet their writing quotas, I don't want you to think of me as an insensitive taskmaster. Assembling a collection of original material is demanding. I understand that. I remain unyielding, but I *do* understand it.

Writing requires not only creativity and skill, it also demands discipline. Perhaps the discipline is even more important than the expertise. Why? *Because a mediocre writer who is prolific will most likely be more successful than a brilliant writer who never gets anything typed.*

The question we ask in television is, "Can he put it on paper?" We may know people with brilliant comedic minds who are witty and inventive all the time. But can they put it on paper? Can they be witty and inventive when the deadline threatens? Do they have the discipline to put away the party comedy and turn out the material we need to plug a hole in the upcoming show? Let's return to Hugh Prather's quote, which opens Part Two: "If the desire to write is not accompanied by actual writing, then the desire is not to write."

Mr. Prather is harsher than I am on non-quota writers. These folks have a desire to write, but it isn't accompanied by actual writing. What goes wrong? All of us who have ever wrestled with a typewriter know that there are any number of excuses for not caressing the keys. There are pencils to be sharpened, desks to be straightened, drawers to be rearranged, and 1,532,653 other reasons to delay writing. But none of them is valid enough for us to abandon our efforts.

Yet some people do abandon their projects. Why? One of the reasons could be that the immensity of the assignment defeats them. This feeling is not unfamiliar to me because much of my work comes in spurts. I'll have nothing to do for some time and thoroughly enjoy it. Then I get a bunch of assignments at one time, each one with a demanding deadline. The inclination is to fret so much over the supposed impossibility of it that it really becomes impossible. But when I sit down and begin chipping away at it, it gets done.

There's a proverb that says something to the effect that the longest journey begins with the first small step.

My family loses patience with me because I'm a terrible traveler. Some of my childhood traits remain with me—notably the one that prompts me, when we begin a long journey, to ask, "Are we almost there?" On a long drive I'm constantly looking at the mileage indicator and figuring out how much further we have to go. I destroy the enjoyment of the journey because I'm overwhelmed by the enormity of it.

Writers can react the same way. Presumably, we all like to write. Why then do we all worry about how large an undertaking is? We should rejoice that it is almost interminable. That means we'll have that much more opportunity to write.

Following are a few hints that I've used to help me get through a formidable task.

Convince Yourself That You're Being Paid

Television performers sometimes use any device to get their lines changed. Writers don't like to change lines. It's an affront to our judgment and, more importantly, it means more work. So we have occasional conflicts. I remember one actor saying, "I don't understand my motivation for saying this line. I mean, I can't act unless I *feel* it. I have no reason to say this line. I mean, what's my motivation?" Our producer, bless his soul, said, "After you say it, you get a paycheck. That's your motivation."

A great incentive for getting work done is the money we're

paid for it. Look back at the jobs you've performed in whatever you do for a living. Try to visualize your work in some measurable and visual form. See all your paperwork bound into books, your handiwork assembled on a loading platform. The accumulated work that you've done is astounding.

Yet you got it all done because a paycheck was dangled before your wallet each Friday. If someone asked you to do that much work starting now, you'd probably say it was impossible. Yet you did do it—because you got paid for it.

So pay yourself for the speculative writing you're going to do. How? Steal it from somewhere else. Let some of the labor you get paid for subsidize your labor of love.

Let's suppose you work in a department store and earn $5 an hour. Assign that last hour of each workday as your salary for writing two hours a night. All of a sudden you're making $25 a week for writing. Not bad. If you want a raise, give yourself the last hour and a half of work. Bingo. You're earning $37.50.

We're making light of it, but it's not as silly as it sounds. It's the same thing people do when they put themselves through college. They work to get money to invest in themselves. In a sense, we all do it. We work not for money, but for the things that money can buy. If we want a color television, we buy it with the money we earn. If that set costs $500 and we make $5 an hour, we have in effect bought that TV with 100 hours of labor.

However, there's no need to defend the theory. Admittedly, it is a mind game. The important point is, if it works for you and helps you get your writing assignments completed, use it.

Select A Project That You'll Enjoy

Some of you may think that the preceding helpful hint is ridiculous. You're probably right, but if it's the first ridiculous suggestion I've made in this book, you've certainly gotten your money's worth. However silly it may be, it will work for some readers. If you're among those who feel cheated being paid with pretend money, then don't expect to be paid at all.

I'm assuming that all these projects we're discussing are speculative. Otherwise, you'd have to finish the task. No one is going to pay for incomplete work. Since no one is paying you for the projects, you have the right to choose what they are. Select something you enjoy. Then it becomes its own reward.

People don't expect to get paid for building model airplanes or doing crossword puzzles. They do them because they're relaxing and they enjoy them. Treat your project the same way. Do it because it's fun. Should it make money for you later, that's profit.

Prepare Your Project

I've already told you what an annoyance I am on long motor trips. I also have a terrible sense of direction. A moment of panic hits each time we leave for a new destination. I turn to my wife and say, "Did you remember to bring the directions?" She always smiles and produces a crumpled piece of paper covered with hieroglyphics that will magically get us where we're going. She smiles because she knows this always happens. It's her quaint little way of saying, "Only a fool would drive this far without knowing where he was going."

She's right. When I get on a plane, I assume the pilot knows where he's going. I'd be terribly annoyed if he came back while they were serving cocktails and said, "Does anybody know the way to Portland?" He should take care of details like that before he gets up in the air.

So should a writer who is tackling a large project. It's easy to get hopelessly lost in writing any work of any size. Even a short story can ramble aimlessly if it's not well outlined. As producers, my partner and I always wanted to see a detailed story outline before a freelancer could begin a half-hour script—not only because it gave us more control over the project, it also made the writer's work easier. The script would be completed much more quickly if the author knew from the start where the story was going and how it would end.

Begin by outlining your project in broad strokes. What form will it take? What will its point of view be? Conceive a generalized, overall vision of your venture.

Then allow yourself some time to gather information. Be more specific and more detailed in outlining your undertaking. If you're attempting a screenplay or teleplay, what is covered in each scene and what are the plotpoints? If you're doing a book, what are the chapter headings?

Be careful, though. Sometimes this planning can be used as an excuse to effectively scuttle the entire venture. It's easy to drag this stage of the project out for so long that the writing never happens. To prevent this, exercise even more discipline. Set a rigid time limit for this work and a daily or weekly quota to be met.

Once you've gathered all the preliminary information, arrange it into a logical and coherent form. Set your scenes in chronological order, or arrange your chapter headings in some workable progression.

Let me walk through the planning I did on a previous book of mine. It was a major undertaking for me, and, quite frankly, one that I feared. This was the first book I had tried to write. Until then most of my writing had been jokes—one or two sentences at a time. I had also done much dialogue writing. But the publisher wanted 60,000 words.

I was so terrified of the assignment that I faithfully followed all the rules I'm outlining here. (The book, incidentally, is entitled *Hit or Miss Management.*)

The first week was devoted to the broad strokes. Here I decided to write the book as if I were an expert on management procedures. The author would be a pompous, dogmatic, know-it-all, who in effect knew nothing. (Not unlike the author of *this* book.) I would generate a history of this man that would show at the start the book was tongue-in-cheek, and that nothing the author said was to be believed. It was also decided that this "authority" would base all his theories on observations from nature and from things his mother taught him.

From there we got down to details. I set aside three weeks during which time I would daily write down ten topics relating to office work or management. These would be random thoughts with no real rhyme or reason. One day's sampling looks like this:

- Embarrassing situations for managers and how to handle them
- Office decorations
- How to make decisions
- How to appear knowledgeable at meetings

- How to handle "give me a raise or else"
- Employees you want to avoid having in your office
- Conducting job interviews
- How to avoid graffiti in the men's room
- Delegating authority
- How to know when you're through (head-rolling time)

Arithmetic tells us that ten topics a day, five days a week (I still refuse to work weekends), for three weeks, generates 150 topics. That's a pretty solid foundation for a book of 60,000 words.

Then I allowed one week to review and rearrange these headings. Some of them on second inspection didn't seem to be worthwhile; they were dropped. Others might be grouped together under one heading.

The final topics I chose then seemed to fall into three categories: the manager relating to himself, the manager relating to his employees, and the manager relating to his superiors. I arranged the chapter headings logically under these three headings and was ready to move on to the next phase. Let's move on to that phase together.

Set Your Goals and Begin Your Work

Everything in the world is reduceable to bite-size chunks. Regardless of size, everything is the sum of its parts. So any large undertaking is able to be completed simply by completing its parts. In fact, it's impossible to do anything *except* by doing the parts. You can't give an hour speech. You can only say individual words that add up to sixty minutes total. You can't write a book. You write chapters. In fact, you write characters that add up to words that form sentences making paragraphs begetting chapters totaling a book.

Accepting that, then, you have to divide your project into those bite-size pieces. You have to break this enormous undertaking into workable sections. It's a mathematical exercise.

Now you divide what has to be done by the amount of time you have to do it in and that generates your quota. If you have a 30-page story to write and ten days in which to write it, you have to write three pages of text each day.

Sometimes you'll have a deadline that dictates this division, but on speculative work you'll be able to determine your own deadlines. In that case, be nice to yourself. Don't make the workload so demanding that you overburden yourself. Make it realistic enough to keep your interest up. I like to allow myself room for tiny rewards. For instance, if I have to write three pages a day, I might struggle and do six in one day and take the next day off. Again, we're playing mind games, but whatever works, works.

Now you've finally arrived at that magic moment when all that remains is to sit at the typewriter and crank out creativity. All your excuses have been exhausted. You know where you're going and you know how to get there.

Again, let me walk my project through this phase with you.

This also is pure mathematics, so have your calculator handy (unless you trust my figures). We finally settled on 26 chapters for the book and I had allowed myself three months for completion. That meant that I had to complete an average of two chapters each week. Each chapter had to be roughly 2,500 words in length, which meant about 13 of my typewritten pages. So for me to stay on schedule and complete the project, I had to generate approximately 26 pages of typing a week.

All these numbers sound like mumbo-jumbo, I'm sure, but something very important has happened here. I've just taken a complete book, 60,000 words, 315 typewritten pages—a task that scared me—and reduced it to five or six typewritten pages a day. That's manageable. It's completable. I did finish the book. My friends and relatives all have copies and a few people even bought it.

You can take the terror out of any project, reducing it to painless segments and enjoying each part of it on its way to completion.

To market your product, you have to *have* a product. These hints might help you get that product on paper.

22 MARKETING YOUR MATERIAL

While visiting a wealthy friend, I noticed a portrait of him in his office. In it, he had a stern expression and seemed to be sneering down at anyone looking up at him. When I kidded him about it he laughed and said, "I call that my 'I got mine—you get yours' portrait."

The same principle applies in marketing your wares: each person must find his way by means of his own ingenuity and creativity. Humor is a very personalized art form. I may not like a certain comic even though I admit his talent. Someone else may have few technical skills, but just be zany enough to get laughs from me. I may like some material I read and recommend it to other people who I think will like it equally as well. They may not. But other people who I suspect would dislike the material may fall in love with it.

All this makes standardized recommendations almost impossible. Your task is to write good material—humor that satisfies you. You have to know it's good, then you have to find some influential people who agree with you. That's not an easy task no matter how expert your writing is. Most people don't buy talent, they buy results. It's the old chicken-and-egg riddle and job-and-experience dilemma. You can't demonstrate results until you get a chance to show your skills, and no one will give you a chance to show your skills until you've shown some results.

Take heart. It's not an unsolvable problem—we do have chickens, and people get new jobs all the time.

More importantly, we have many talented new faces in comedy each year. However, there is no set formula for YOU. As we said earlier, a doctor follows steps one, two, and three to become a doctor. But becoming a humorist requires more resourcefulness.

I'll sketch out some broad suggestions, but you'll have to pick and choose. You'll have to try one and see if it works for you—at the same time investigating others. And you'll meet with many failures: that's inevitable using a hit-or-miss system.

Here's an example to encourage you. Direct mail advertisers admit up front that their campaigns might only produce about a 2 percent return; that means 98 percent of the recipients reject the sales pitch. Yet many people in the business say that direct mail is the most efficient form of advertising. That two percent pays for the entire undertaking.

You'll have to do the same as the direct-mail people. Concentrate on the positive and ignore the negative. In your mind you have to follow the advice of the old song and "accentuate the positive and eliminate the negative." Remember that one "yes" can erase thousands of "no's."

"All right, already," you're muttering to yourself. "How do I get started on this perilous journey?"

It's a Gift

One way to start *immediately* is to work for free. I love Samuel Johnson's statement that no one but a blockhead ever wrote except for money. It's not contradicting Johnson, though, to promote yourself so you can get around to *making* money. A real blockhead is someone who withholds his services until he gets paid—and winds up withholding his services for the rest of his life.

I was walking a picket line outside Universal Studios during one of our writers' strikes a few years back. A young man introduced himself as a student in a Writers Guild class—to encourage new writers, the Writers Guild of America, West, the union all TV writers belong to, offered free classes to beginning writers—and we struck up a conversation. He told me that he had written an outline for a screenplay that the teacher felt showed much promise. The boy received expert suggestions on his project and was told to rework it. I congratulated him. He said, "Yeah, but if they want me to do that much work, they're going to have to pay me something."

I went back to walking in circles holding a sign and knew that I could forget this lad's career.

Writing for free is a great educational tool. You can do it immediately and learn how the audience reacts. I say you can do it immediately because newspaper columnists will accept material from you if you let them know that you don't expect payment. A friend of mine, for instance, often puts humorous poems about local professional teams in sports journalists' columns. Local comics will gladly try out material for you—or at least read it over. The guy emceeing some shindig for the company or the lodge meeting will gladly take comedic input.

Aside from the educational aspect, you get promotional value. People will now know that you write humor. When someone wants to buy it, they'll remember where to get it.

My professional career actually started with giveaway material. A local TV personality wanted to write a column for the morning newspaper. I had sent him a query letter and some samples of my writing, which he liked, and I began writing purely on speculation. My letterheads were on his desk when a national comedian was a guest on his television show, and while they were in the office after the show, the comic read the material upside down, jotted down the phone number from the top of the page, and called me to write some material for his act.

That led to my first paying contract and I was with the man for six years earning a nice part-time income.

You needn't donate all your time to charity, though—there's no sense having you mad at me or Samuel Johnson mad at you. Just be a blockhead for a little while.

Working into Magazines

First, try selling some of your material to the easier markets—the many small magazines, periodicals, and newspapers that publish a lot of humor, although they pay relatively little. Your chances of acceptance are considerably better here.

But doesn't it make more sense, you ask, to start with the higher-paying, exclusive markets and then work your way down? The big ones just might accept the submissions. If they do, you make a lot of money. If they don't, you send it somewhere else.

Yeah, that makes sense, but there are some pitfalls. The rejection rate is tremendous and, despite your good intentions, that can become discouraging. You might surrender before getting to the markets that *will* buy your material. Also, if the stuff you're selling is topical, it won't last long enough to survive several rejections. I used to submit current material to Kiplinger's *Changing Times* magazine; if they didn't buy it that month, it was useless to me.

This isn't to discourage you from attacking high-paying markets. If you're good enough you deserve to be and eventually will be in them. But at the beginning, it's a big morale booster to make a sale. The amount isn't as important as the acceptance. So pursue the smaller markets. Explore the more prestigious ones, also, but not exclusively.

Finding the Comics

If you're writing monologue material, contact comics. Most of them depend on material to keep their careers alive. It's the life blood that keeps their acts vital. We all think, "Oh, they won't look at my stuff," but comics need material and it's not easy to come by. Most of them will look at your submissions: they may not *buy* them but they'll look at them.

That's a generalization, of course. Some comics do their own writing or are content with the writers they employ. They won't be bothered reading material. You and I don't know who they are, though. So there's no harm in a polite query and a few samples included. The comic may say "no," but let *him* do it. Don't do it for him.

Here again, you might try the shotgun approach. Try several different tacks simultaneously to see which brings the best results. Contact local comics. They may not make as much as the big names, but they want to be just as funny. Landing a contract with a weekend comic might be the steppingstone to the next level.

How do you contact such a comic? Spread the word among friends that you'd like to write for him; it's amazing how easy it is to find someone sooner or later who knows the guy. He may be listed in the phone book. He probably belongs to the American Guild of Variety Artists (AGVA) and the local office might be able to put you in touch with him. Keep an eye on the entertainment section of the newspaper, and send a letter to or call the club where he's appearing. Go see his act and send a message backstage that you're a comedy writer and would like to talk briefly. Always have material with you, and say so. Sometimes they may not want to see you, but might want to read over your stuff.

At the same time, don't be frightened away by the celebrities. The bigger the comic, the more material he needs and the better it has to be. It follows that it's the hardest to get.

Celebrities guard their privacy. It's sometimes hard to reach them, but with persistence and some ingenuity, it's possible. It's probably better to reach these people when they're on the road rather than find their agent's number or their home address. At home, they're bombarded with mail and it sort of overwhelms them. When they have a tantalizing collection to choose from, they naturally concentrate on the most important. A fledgling comedy writer, no matter how good, might not be in that category. But should you find out where they're appearing and send a letter to that club or hotel, it might be the only piece of mail they get there. It's hard to resist opening it.

The weekly *Variety* is a good way of finding out who's appearing where. *Variety* has an extensive listing of nightclub engagements, along with reviews of most of the acts.

I've used this listing to call clubs across the nation. I didn't always reach the celebrity, but I could explain to someone that I had material that I wanted so-and-so to see, and was given an address to send it to.

It's possible, too, to talk with people when they come to your home town. As a beginning writer in Philadelphia I had pleasant visits with many celebrities. A few of them even bought some material.

I discovered that most celebrities stayed at one of two or three favorite hotels. When I found out from the papers that they were in town, I'd call those hotels and ask for them. If they were there, I might be connected to the room; if they weren't, I'd be so advised. At least I knew where they weren't.

Politeness Above All

I fear as I type this that it might be misunderstood, that I might seem to be creating comedy-writing *papparazzi* who follow celebrities around and harass them by waving pages of typed one-liners in their faces. That's not the intent here at all; in fact, you'll do yourself only harm by becoming an annoyance. In your letters, phone calls, or whatever, be polite, considerate, and aboveboard. Tell the comics that you have material you'd like them to see and ask if that would be convenient. They can always refuse, but if you're tactful, they can't be offended by the request.

Approaching a Producer

Submitting material for television shows is fairly simple because you just mail it in care of the network to the producers who are credited either at the beginning or at the end of the show you want to write for.

Some producers require a release form with any unsolicited material. Some don't. Again, it's trial and error to find out who will and who won't. I feel that in this case a letter of inquiry sometimes is self-defeating. It's true that all producers need product, but it's also true that we're basically parochial and a bit lazy. We subconsciously feel that the only really good writers are in New York or Hollywood; we also want to find talent without having to read too much. Consequently, a query letter might be greeted with a polite reply that says "Thanks, but no thanks."

It might be advisable to simply send your script in and take your chances. If the producers read it, fine; if they return it unopened, you can follow with a letter requesting the proper release forms.

Television, as we discussed earlier, is a difficult medium to begin your career with. You should establish some sort of reputation in other areas of comedy writing before tackling it. However, I include these recommendations because there's no set pattern to attacking your career. You might be ingenious enough to impress a producer with your script.

One nice thing about being a writer is that your material does your selling for you. When you go out on a job interview you have to dress and behave properly; you could well be turned down because of something that has nothing to do with your qualifications. I've always felt sorry for actors who come in for auditions. They put themselves on the line, and when you reject them for a part, you're rejecting a person. But a writer can audition without ever being present; the typewritten page is his representative.

However, that page is important. It is representing *you*. A strange thing happens when a writer turns in a sketch to a head writer. The head writer will begin to read the script—and automatically reach for a pencil with his free hand. Subconsciously he's saying, "I know something is going to be wrong with this."

Editors are the same with newcomers even though they may be reluctant to admit it. They're looking for a quick reason to turn the manuscript down and not have to read it through. Your job is to slam the door on that avenue of escape. Avoid obvious errors.

The most obvious one is the form your document takes. Any manuscript that is typed out improperly screams "amateur," and is generally quickly abandoned. You must pay attention to format no matter what you write.

Magazines

There has been plenty of material printed on submitting to magazines, and most magazines will send a freelancer a copy of their guidelines on request. The only thing I might add is what will apply for all submissions: it should be neat, typewritten, with plenty of margin space allowed.

In sending filler material for magazines, I recommend sending each gag on a separate sheet of paper, preferably a 3x5 card. This makes the editor's job easier. If there are one or two worthwhile bits among your submissions, and she can separate them from the others quickly and easily, your chances for a sale are increased. Suppose there is a choice between yours and someone else's. The editor, being human, will select the one that makes her job easier—the one that's already separated from the others.

Include your name and address on each card, too. (Your name and return address should be on everything you submit.)

Monologues

Monologue submissions can take almost any form. Some buyers prefer all caps; others won't accept that. Some prefer single-spacing to double-spacing. Naturally, give your clients exactly what they demand, but until you find out, you can use your own standard form.

Begin with your name and return address at the beginning of the submission. Whatever form you decide on, separate the jokes by three or four lines of white space. It makes them a little easier to read and it forces the reader to stop and look for the joke.

Bob Hope says, "Wait for your laugh." Sometimes the audience completely misses a subtlety unless you let them know it's there. In the same way, readers can get going at such a rate of speed that they pass right by extremely clever gags. Separating the gags forces the reader out of curiosity to go back and find the humor in each joke.

Television Scripts

Scripts are generally in two basic forms: tape and film. I don't know why there's a difference, but there is. Dialogue in tape scripts is double-spaced; in film scripts it's single-spaced. I've included a few pages of a movie script at the end of this chapter to show you the form. For the tape script, refer to the sketches included in Chapter 16.

For reasons of economy, scripts in book form will sometimes be changed, so don't follow this style in submitting teleplays or screenplays:

DICK: See Spot run.
JANE: Yes, see Spot run fast.

Your Writing's Not All You're Selling

An important part of marketing your comedy material is marketing yourself. You have to let people know you're in the comedy-writing business.

Word of mouth can be a surprisingly effective promotion. Let people know that you're writing. Show them your material. Tell them whom you'd like to work for. It's astounding how quickly a network can form that can lead you to interesting people and assignments.

Local newspapers are interested in your success. There aren't a lot of humorists around and you might make good copy; good copy may lead to additional interesting assignments.

Document some of your experiences and sell them to magazines. It's great prestige to have your byline on a magazine article about comedy writing. Some of the things you learn along the way may be of interest to other people making the same journey. You might have some information that could be useful to writer's magazines like *Writer's Digest* or smaller publications like my own *Round Table*.

Believe in Yourself

One facet of marketing that should never be overlooked is your own confidence. You must believe that you can do it.

Now, understand that *believing* you can do it doesn't mean you *can* do it. (What'd he say?) I said, "*Believing* you can do it doesn't mean you *can* do it." Remember when you first learned to drive a car? You couldn't drive, but you had no doubt that you could learn, pass your test, and drive as well as anyone on the road. That's the kind of confidence you need to market your writing.

Right now maybe you can't do it yet, but belief in yourself will get you working hard enough to improve. You'll learn how to do it, the same way you learned how to drive.

Then you'll know you're good. When you know you're good the marketing will happen. You'll use some of the hints in this book and you'll find some avenues of your own. As you become a better and better writer, people will discover you.

There's an exciting adventure ahead of you. You're about to cut your own path to the writing success that you want. It won't be similar to anyone else's—no two have been the same yet. I hope this book has been some help, but the ultimate responsibility is yours. You have to set the goals. You have to define the disciplines. You have to write and write and improve and improve. You'll enjoy the rewards.

Comedy is an entertaining profession all along the way. I just hope you'll become successful enough to offer me a job soon.

Good luck—and have fun.

SAMPLE MOVIE SCRIPT

FADE IN:

EXT. CITY STREETS—MONTAGE—CREDIT SEQUENCE

The OPENING CREDITS ROLL OVER a MONTAGE of scenes showing FATHER BOB walking along the city streets of his parish.

We ESTABLISH that this is a Puerto Rican ghetto area. We can SEE from the storefronts and graffiti and the boarded-up houses that this is a poverty area also.

We ESTABLISH that Father Bob is conversant with most of the people and, as much as possible, that he is popular and respected by these people.

We END THE CREDITS, then FOLLOW Father Bob up the steps and into Our Lady of Guadalupe Rectory. He goes inside, and we STAY on the bronze plaque that identifies the building. Then we . . .

                                                      CUT TO:

INT. RECTORY FOYER—DAY

Father Bob goes to a table in the foyer and picks up a stack of mail. He goes through these and selects those that are for him, takes them with him and goes into the kitchen.

INT. RECTORY KITCHEN—DAY

Father Bob enters the kitchen where the housekeeper, JOSEPHINE PIN-TAVALE, is busy preparing the evening meal.

Father Bob takes out a jar of peanut butter and takes a knife from the drawer.

                    JOSEPHINE
        Father, don't eat anything now. I'm preparing a nice
        meal. Linguini, wth meatball sauce . . . some nice
        bracciola . . .

> BOB
> I'm gonna skip dinner tonight, Josephine. I just want
> to get a little snack and get a little rest.

He opens a cupboard door and searches for something. He doesn't find it, so he takes down a box of saltines.

As he spreads peanut butter on them and puts them on a plate:

> BOB
> (continuing)
> Josephine, I wish you would buy those little round
> crackers . . . you know, the Ritz . . . instead of
> these. I keep asking you, but you never buy them.

> JOSEPHINE
> Yes, Father.

Bob cleans out the peanut butter jar and goes over to throw it away. By the trash container he notices a large rock on the counter near the door to the schoolyard.

> BOB
> Josephine, what is this rock for?

> JOSEPHINE
> Father, there's a big dog that comes around here and
> always goes through our trash. He makes a mess. I'm
> gonna hit him with this rock.

> BOB
> Josephine, you can't hit a dog with a rock like that.
> You could do some serious harm. That poor dog is
> only doing what it is supposed to do. It is hungry and
> it's looking for food.

Bob pours himself a glass of milk.

                    JOSEPHINE
Why does he have to look for food in our trash?

                    BOB
Because you make the best food in the whole city.
Now, get rid of the rock, please.

                    JOSEPHINE
Yes, Father.

Bob takes his milk, his letters, and his plate of peanut butter crackers and
starts out.

                    BOB
I'm going up to rest awhile, Josephine, but if anyone
comes to see me, it's all right to disturb me, all
right?

                    JOSEPHINE
Yes, Father.

Bob exits.

INT. BOB'S APARTMENT—DAY

We SEE Father Bob, in his shorts, asleep on the couch. He is awakened by
SHOUTS from outside his room.

                    JOSEPHINE (O.S.)
You can't go up there. Father Cosgrove is resting.

                    HECTOR (O.S.)
Father Bob will see me.

                    JOSEPHINE (O.S.)
You go up there, I'll call the police.

                    HECTOR (O.S.)
Let go of me, you old bat.

Father Bob wakes up fully and goes and opens the door.

INT. RECTORY STAIRWAY—DAY

Father Bob comes to the head of the stairs, still in his shorts, while HEC-TOR and Josephine are fighting partway up the stairs. From Hector's appearance and manner, we see that he is not quite all there.

> JOSEPHINE
> I don't want you disturbing the Father.

> HECTOR
> Father Bob told me to come and see him, you stupid macaroni maker.

> BOB
> Josephine . . .

They both stop fighting and turn to look up. When Josephine sees it is a priest in his shorts, she is horrified.

QUESTIONS AND ANSWERS

APPENDIX

After each one of my lectures, I always allow time for a few questions and answers. "Ask me anything," I tell the audience, "Because if I don't know the answer, I'll give you one anyway."

I don't know why this book should be any different. Of course, you can't raise your hands and shout questions out to me, so I'll do that work for you: here are the questions I hear most often.

Question: How do I know if my stuff is funny or not?

Answer: Actually, you don't. The audience is the only true judge of that. If an audience consistently laughs at something you say or have written, it's funny. If they steadfastly refuse to chuckle, abandon the line.

I once had a client call and rave about a line I'd written. Naturally I was delighted, but also a bit confused—I had written the line about nine months earlier. I asked why she was calling now. She said, "I never thought the line was funny, so I didn't use it until last night." (I've had the opposite happen, too.)

The best way to learn what's funny and what isn't is to stand up in front of an audience and deliver your own material. You can control the timing, the voice inflections, and the positioning in the routine—everything but the audience response. You'll get a great education in comedy.

You really can only guess at what's funny and what isn't. But when most people ask this question they're really looking for acceptance. You know your material is funny when someone is willing to pay you for it. Cash in hand is the greatest confidence-builder. So look for that first sale.

Question: How do I protect my material?

Answer: Comedy writers are obsessed with this problem. They feel that any time they send material out, it's completely out of their hands—and that's largely true. I remember the terrible feeling I had when my family and I moved from Philadelphia to the West Coast. We watched some strangers load all our belongings onto a truck and then drive away. I said, "How do we know we'll ever see that stuff again?"

Of course, with comedy material you send out, you hope *not* to see it again. You'd prefer to see a check in its place. But most of it you can't really protect.

It's not worth a lot of concern, though. A writer's most valuable work isn't the material that's been written, but what is *going* to be written. Your real worth lies in being able to come up with more funny material.

A comic doesn't just want your funny jokes, but a constant supply of them—and he can't steal your ability to turn them out.

If you have a piece of material that has tremendous value and can't easily be reproduced, get a lawyer's help in protecting it. I have sometimes mailed material to myself via registered mail and then not opened the envelope; this assigns a date to the material.

Short humorous pieces or monologues I just send out unprotected. If they're stolen, I consider it a compliment to their quality.

Question: In studying comics, is it better to limit yourself to one or analyze many different styles?

Answer: Someone once advised me that no education will ever do you any harm. We should always be learning more and more about our trade.

However, I feel that in the beginning it might be best to concentrate on one style that you prefer and feel you can write best. The key to good comedy is the basic idea: a workable comedy idea can be slanted toward any style.

You want to get your style perfected and then with some adjustments it can accommodate most of your clients. Once you convince yourself that you can write funny, you can write funny for almost anyone.

Question: How do you write for television?

Answer: On a variety show such as "Laugh-in" or "The Carol Burnett Show," there is generally a staff of about ten writers, who work in teams.

Our first task is to get some premises for sketches. We might do this in a group session with all ten of us in there, or it might be just one team working along with the head writers.

At these sessions, we just throw ideas out for discussion until one of them seems to have some potential. That idea will then be discussed further and formed into a primitive outline, then assigned to one of the teams. "Assigned" sounds sort of dictatorial; the team has to like the basic idea because the head writer knows it is foolhardy to ask a team to write something they don't believe in.

That team will then write a first draft, which will be reviewed by the head writers, notes given, and a second draft written. The head writers may polish the second draft and include it in the script. After it gets into the script, it is rehearsed and changes are made in it even up to the day of shooting.

Situation comedies are written the same way, except the story and the first two drafts may be purchased from outside writers. Most variety shows are totally staff-written.

Question: How much does a comedy writer make? How do you get paid?

Answer: That depends. Freelancing in television isn't easy now because many shows depend on their staff to provide all scripts. A half-hour sitcom pays over $7500, so it depends on how many assignments you can get.

A staff writer will contract for so much per show and will work for so many weeks—you may agree, for example, to do 22 shows over a period of 40 weeks. Then you can elect to get paid either by the show or prorated on a weekly basis. Staff writers earn near six figures, since they draw a salary and still get paid in full for any scripts they write.

Writing special material or monologues depends on how many contracts you can land, and what fee you can demand.

Payment for special material can be designed many ways—so much money per minute, so much per joke, a standard salary—almost anything.

Question: Are friends and family good people to test comedy material on?

Answer: This is largely a matter of personal choice. It depends, too, on whether your family members are good laughers or not. When you investigate this, you'll find that by testing material on acquaintances, you're really looking for support; their approval doesn't mean that much. If they love a joke and the buyer hates it, you still have no sale. If they hate a joke and the buyer loves it, simply endorse the check and look around for something to spend it on.

There *is* a danger, however. Writing humor isn't the easiest chore in the world. It requires a creative atmosphere. A negative comment could cause you to lose enthusiasm for the project and abandon it before giving it all the effort it deserves. If your surrogate audience doesn't approve of the material, you might never send it to the potential buyer, thereby losing a sale. Or their negativism could alter your thinking about the project, changing it just enough to destroy it.

For those reasons, I don't recommend testing unfinished material on anyone. Keep it to yourself until all your enthusiasm has been transferred to the printed page; then their comments are only opinions and not as disruptive.

That's why I can hardly wait to finish this book, so I can let the family read it.

Question: How many times should you rewrite a gag? Is there such a thing as worrying them to death?

Answer: There is no strict rule on rewrites. Comedy is a personal art and being satisfied with a joke or a bit of humor is an intuitive feeling. If you're happy with a gag, why bother to rewrite it? But if you feel the joke just isn't right yet, allow it some more time and effort.

Your time schedule and deadline may dictate how much a

joke is rewritten. If your routine has to be done by evening, you can't devote all day to polishing and rewording. You either accept the joke as is or drop it totally.

Gags *can* be worried to death. I've seen it happen many times, especially in group sessions: they're very difficult because the material has to satisfy everyone in the room. Practically every person there has veto power.

Here's an example. We needed some lines showing Hollywood phoniness. One of the lines that was thrown out drew immediate, loud, honest laughs from everyone: "Did you know John Wayne sleeps with a night light?"

But after a beat or two, some of the writers questioned the line. "It's not clear," they argued. "If you mean John Wayne is afraid of the dark then you better tell the audience that." "John Wayne is so afraid of the dark that he sleeps with a night light." You can see that that takes all the surprise out of the punchline. We debated the line so much that we eventually dropped it.

Another example is a classic from that great editor of humor, Jack Benny. He had a gag in which he wanted to get invited to a prestigious Hollywood party, but nothing was working. Finally, he called his agent and tried to dump the problem on him: "What do you mean you can't get me invited to the party? Why am I paying you nine percent?"

It was a beautiful line to illustrate how cheap he was—even with his agent. The writers wanted to change the line to five percent, figuring the bigger cut would make the line that much funnier. Benny rightfully overruled them, saying that five percent would destroy the subtlety of the line.

Question: How do you feel about "blue" material?

Answer: "Blue" material, of course, means dirty material. This is as subjective as the humor itself. What is dirty to one person may be cute to someone else.

In nightclubs, a certain amount of blue material is accepted—certainly more than is allowed on television.

As a writer, you can always incorporate it because the comic is going to have the final say. If a line is too rough, the comic can cut it.

Blue material is interesting in that the same thing that makes it attractive to the writer is also the same thing that makes it dangerous: it's easy. It's shocking, so it gets that kind of laugh. It's generally a surefire laugh-getter even though some folks may later regret that they laughed at it. Sometimes, they don't even know *why* they laughed.

That's why it's dangerous for a writer. It's so easy that you come to depend on it. You immediately shoot for the "naughty" and forget the "funny."

Question: Is there a publishing market for humorous essays? How about books?

Answer: Humor is in constant demand in all fields. An interesting phenomenon about comedy is that when it's good, you have to like it. For example, there may be singers or musicians who you will readily admit are technically outstanding, yet you don't like their sound. That's reasonable. It's more difficult to do that with comedy: if you like the craftsmanship, you almost have to enjoy the humor. Good wit is enjoyed by more people than almost anything else.

In glancing through various types of magazines, like women's magazines and in-flight publications. I almost invariably see a humorous piece. Slick magazines like *Playboy* and *Penthouse* carry a good deal of humor. It's marketable. Editors are always crying for good humorous material, but they see a lot of "humor" that's not tailored to their readership, or that the editor just doesn't think is funny, or that's simply not very good. For these reasons, you shouldn't query an editor about a humorous piece—just submit it and let her decide.

When I see the way Erma Bombeck's books are stacked so high in the book stores, I have to conclude that it's a salable commodity in book publishing, too—as long as the author has established a following in one of the media.

Question: What do you do when you just can't think of anything to write?

Answer: Facing that blank page in the typewriter can sometimes induce a blank mind. I find different reasons for writer's block. There are times when a writer can't get started at all. Other times, the author will have written so much that he's just drained. Conceivably, it can be hard to generate anything if an assignment isn't thrilling; it doesn't inspire creativity.

I have different ways of combating each of these. When inspiration hits, the typewriter has a hard time keeping up with me. But when the whiteness of the pages seems unfillable, there is only one solution—write. Write anything, but *write*. I'll sometimes resort to doing some of the preparatory work: I write down different facets of the topic, or jot down what I expect to cover when I finally get around to writing the scene. Sometimes this triggers inspiration. If it doesn't, then I begin to write anyway. I figure even if what I write is terrible, it has to be better than the blank page. It can always be polished and rewritten later.

Other times, I may be writing well and just burn myself out on a given topic or style of writing. In this case, I take a total break. Concentration has limits and when these are exceeded, I have to get away from the work for a while. Regardless of the deadline that's facing me, I get away from the office. It might just be long enough for a walk. I might watch some TV. I might even go to a movie or play a few sets of tennis. I can always catch up on my assignment later when my mind is clear, and I can work faster and better.

If the topic I'm assigned doesn't excite me, I sometimes search for related topics to work on. For instance, suppose I'm writing about the royal wedding of Prince Charles and Lady Diana, and I can't think of a thing that's funny about it. I might cheat a bit by saying that Prince Charles was among our most eligible bachelors and could have married anyone he wanted. Now I can do jokes about Dolly Parton, Raquel Welch, Miss Piggy—practically anyone I want.

But don't just listen to me. Writer's block is a very personal phenomenon and different people have different ways of overcoming it. Experiment.

Writing is an emotional occupation and you can sometimes capitalize on that emotion to generate inspiration. I know writers who listen to tapes of famous comedians just to get their minds thinking funny. I sometimes walk around the office humming the theme song of my particular favorite. Even look-ing at still photos of your comic idol might stir you up enough to get your typewriter humming.

Question: Where do you draw the line on good taste and how do you know the material you write won't offend someone?

Answer: Actually, these are two different questions—very dif-ferent, in fact. You determine the good taste line yourself. In tel-evision, for example, we have censors, but most of the policing is done by the writers themselves. The networks don't want to offend anyone who can cost them money. The writers are a bit more idealistic: we really don't want to offend anyone. The two philosophies often don't coincide.

Humor is a powerful and beautiful force, but it can cause pain if misused. You simply have to be objective and learn that if a joke runs the risk of offending someone, you drop the joke rath-er than take the chance.

You can set your own standards for taste, but you can't really be assured that your material won't offend anyone. My col-leagues and I have written sketches we were proud of because they championed the cause of senior citizens—and then re-ceived angry letters berating us for making fun of old people.

One example I remember was a sketch showing problems Americans were all bothered by—smog, high taxes, poor work-manship, and so on—and we mentioned that you couldn't even eat eggs because they were so high in cholesterol. Well, we re-ceived an irate letter from some official egg council for claiming that eggs were an unhealthy food.

You just can't guarantee that you won't offend someone. The only answer is to be true to your own conscience and keep your material within your own standards of taste. Then, if people take offense, it's really their problem and not yours.

Question: Does it help to be a fairly decent writer in other media (newspapers, magazines, radio, etc.) to become a proficient comedy writer?

Answer: Surely it would help, because the disciplines re-quired to become proficient in any of these related areas assist you in becoming a good comedy writer. Not having that background, however, does not rule out becoming a competent humorist.

It probably requires fewer technical skills to write comedy than anything else with the possible exception of graffiti. What is required is a sense of what's funny. Sentence structure, grammar, syntax, and all those other techniques disappear in writing a good one-liner. The punchline becomes all-important. If bad grammar makes the joke funnier, use it.

A top executive once hired me to write some humor for his speeches. When I delivered the material, he spent several minutes going over it with a pencil changing every "gonna" to "going to." It's not that I couldn't spell—I just made "gonna" a part of my comedy vocabulary.

Each year I speak to the fifth graders at our local school because that's when they begin studying "creative writing." I get some raised eyebrows when I tell the youngsters not to worry about spelling, grammar, or punctuation. It's not important. "If you have a creative thought," I tell them, "get it down on paper so you can communicate it to someone else." Even poorly punctuated or misspelled, thought can be communicated—Muhammad Ali made more grammatical errors than he made comebacks, but listeners rarely misunderstood his point.

Later in the talk, I redeem myself with the teachers by explaining that you can more effectively communicate your thoughts if you know grammar, punctuation, and spelling. So, too, you might be a better humorist if you're skilled in other fields of writing. However, if you're funny, don't let the lack of technical skills hold you back.

Question: Are there any taboo areas—especially for TV—that a beginning comedy writer should avoid?

Answer: So many formerly taboo subjects have been opened up on TV that I can't really think of any. "All in the Family" did a rape show. "Maude" did one on abortion. "The Mary Tyler Moore Show" did a very sensitive and funny show about death. The only restriction is that they be handled tastefully, and as always, funny.

Of course, common sense dictates that some areas will always be taboo. Some material that a young writer trying out for a staff job submitted to me showed that he had a great sense of humor—however, it was so scatological that not one line showed us that he could write acceptable material for television. We passed, because his stuff labeled him as too much of a gamble.

Question: If you were to give a beginning comedy writer three bits of advice, what would they be?

Answer: First, set a quota and stick to it religiously. Second, get some audience feedback, ideally by speaking yourself. If you can't speak, then work with someone who can—and observe the audience reaction. Third, learn to accept rejection. Now let me go into each phase in more detail.

Set a Quota

By setting a reasonably demanding quota, *and then sticking to it,* you will force yourself to write. Only by writing can you teach yourself to write. Also, whatever mental processes that are employed in writing will become schooled and you'll find yourself writing faster and better. You'd be able to shortcut many of the preparatory processes in writing humor.

Get Audience Feedback

Without feedback, your writing can stagnate. You won't know where or how to improve. Worse yet, you may never *learn* that you have to improve.

The best way to get this feedback is to stand up there and deliver your lines yourself. The lessons will hit home harder then, because there is no avenue of escape. You can't blame a third party.

If you absolutely, positively, cannot stand before an audience, then work with someone who will. But don't cop out. If there is negative feedback, assume that it is your fault. Try to correct it, and observe again. It's invaluable training if you don't let your ego interfere.

Learn to Accept Rejection

It's not a pessimistic outlook for a beginning writer to presume rejection: it's a realistic one. Rejection will come. It's not always justified, but it's always a possibility.

It's important to be ready for it, because if you're not, it could destroy a promising career. Rejection can be so discouraging, especially in the beginning, that it can tempt you to quit. Once you admit the reality of rejection and can accept it, you defuse it, and you can struggle through to the acceptance that you have worked hard for and deserve.

INDEX

Other Writer's Digest Books

General Writing Books

  Writer's Market, $18.95

  Beginning Writer's Answer Book, edited by Polking, et al $9.95

  How to Get Started in Writing, by Peggy Teeters $10.95

  Law and the Writer, edited by Polking and Meranus (paper) $7.95

  Make Every Word Count, by Gary Provost (paper) $6.95

  Teach Yourself to Write, by Evelyn Stenbock $12.95

  Treasury of Tips for Writers, edited by Marvin Weisbord (paper) $6.95

Magazine/News Writing

  Craft of Interviewing, by John Brady $9.95

  Magazine Writing: The Inside Angle, by Art Spikol $12.95

  Magazine Writing Today, by Jerome E. Kelley $10.95

  Newsthinking: The Secret of Great Newswriting, by Bob Baker $11.95

  Stalking the Feature Story, by William Ruehlmann $9.95

  Write On Target, by Connie Emerson $12.95

  Writing and Selling Non-Fiction, by Hayes B. Jacobs $12.95

Fiction Writing

  Fiction Writer's Help Book, by Maxine Rock $12.95

  Fiction Writer's Market, edited by Fredette and Brady $16.95

  Creating Short Fiction, by Damon Knight $11.95

  Handbook of Short Story Writing, edited by Dickson and Smythe (paper) $6.95

  How to Write Best-Selling Fiction, by Dean R. Koontz $13.95

  How to Write Short Stories that Sell, by Louise Boggess $9.95

  One Way to Write Your Novel, by Dick Perry (paper) $6.95

  Secrets of Successful Fiction, by Robert Newton Peck $8.95

  Writing the Novel: From Plot to Print, by Lawrence Block $10.95

Special Interest Writing Books

  Children's Picture Book: How to Write It, How to Sell It, by Ellen E.M. Roberts $17.95

  Complete Book of Scriptwriting, by J. Michael Straczynski $14.95

  How to Write and Sell Your Personal Experiences, by Lois Duncan $10.95

  How to Write & Sell (Your Sense of) Humor, by Gene Perret $12.95

  How to Write "How-To" Books and Articles, by Raymond Hull (paper) $8.95

  Mystery Writer's Handbook, edited by Lawrence Treat (paper) $8.95

  The Poet and the Poem, Revised edition by Judson Jerome $13.95

  Poet's Handbook, by Judson Jerome $11.95

  TV Scriptwriter's Handbook, by Alfred Brenner $12.95

  Travel Writer's Handbook, by Louise Purwin Zobel $13.95

  Writing and Selling Science Fiction, Compiled by The Science Fiction Writers of America (paper) $7.95

  Writing for Children & Teenagers, by Wyndham/Madison $10.95

  Writing to Inspire, by Gentz, Roddy, et al $14.95

The Writing Business

  Complete Handbook for Freelance Writers, by Kay Cassill $14.95

  How to Be a Successful Housewife/Writer, by Elaine Fantle Shimberg $10.95

  How You Can Make $20,000 a Year Writing, by Nancy Edmonds Hanson (paper) $6.95

  Jobs for Writers, edited by Kirk Polking $11.95

  Profitable Part-time/Full-time Freelancing, by Clair Rees $10.95

  Writer's Survival Guide: How to Cope with Rejection, Success, and 99 Other Hang-Ups of the Writing Life, by Jean and Veryl Rosenbaum $12.95

To order directly from the publisher, include $1.50 postage and handling for 1 book and 50¢ for each additional book. Allow 30 days for delivery.

Writer's Digest Books, Department B

9933 Alliance Road, Cincinnati OH 45242

Prices subject to change without notice.

10/12